# The Andrew R. Cecil Lectures on

# Moral Values in a Free Society

established by

The University of Texas at Dallas

## Volume XIII

Previous Volumes of the Andrew R. Cecil Lectures
on Moral Values in a Free Society

# MORALITY AND EXPEDIENCY IN INTERNATIONAL AND CORPORATE RELATIONS

# Morality and Expediency in International and Corporate Relations

RICHARD SCHIFTER
ANDREW R. CECIL
JOHN NORTON MOORE
FREDERICK QUINN
NICOLAI N. PETRO
ALEXANDER J. GILLESPIE, JR.
JON V. HEIDER

*With an Introduction by*
ANDREW R. CECIL

*Edited by*
W. LAWSON TAITTE

The University of Texas at Dallas
1992

*Library of Congress Catalog Card Number 92-081688*
*International Standard Book Number 0-292-78125-3*


Distributed by the University of Texas Press,
Box 7819, Austin, Texas 78712

# FOREWORD

The University of Texas at Dallas established the Andrew R. Cecil Lectures on Moral Values in a Free Society in 1979 to provide a forum for the discussion of important issues that confront our society. Each year since, the University has invited to its campus scholars, businessmen and members of the professions, public officials, and other notable individuals so that they could share their ideas on these issues with the academic community and the general public. In the thirteen years of their existence the Cecil Lectures have become a valued tradition not only for U.T. Dallas but for the wider community as well. The distinguished authorities in many fields who have participated in the program have enriched the experience of all those who heard them or read the published proceedings of their lectures by enlarging their understanding of the system of moral values on which our country was founded and continues to rest. In offering the Lectures on Moral Values in a Free Society, the University is discharging an important obligation.

The University named this program for Dr. Andrew R. Cecil, its Distinguished Scholar in Residence. During his tenure as President of The Southwestern Legal Foundation, Dr. Cecil's innovative leadership brought that institution into the forefront of continuing legal education in the United States. When he retired from the Foundation as its Chancellor Emeritus, Dr. Cecil was asked by The University of Texas at Dallas to serve as its Distinguished Scholar in Residence, and the Cecil Lectures were instituted. In 1990, the Board of Regents of The University of

Texas System established the Andrew R. Cecil Chair of Applied Ethics. It is appropriate that the Lectures and the Chair honor a man who has been concerned throughout his career with the moral foundations of our society and has stressed his belief in the dignity and worth of every individual.

The thirteenth annual series of the Cecil Lectures was conducted on the University's campus on November 11 through 15, 1991. The theme of the 1991 Lectures was "Morality and Expediency in International and Corporate Relations." On behalf of U.T. Dallas, I would like to express our gratitude to Ambassador Schifter, to Professor John Norton Moore, to Mr. Frederick Quinn, to Professor Nicolai N. Petro, to Mr. Alexander J. Gillespie, Jr., to Mr. Jon V. Heider, and to Dr. Cecil for their willingness to share their ideas and for the outstanding lectures that are preserved in this volume of proceedings. We are also grateful to Mr. Michael Arietti of the U.S. State Department for presenting Ambassador Schifter's text at the University when the Ambassador was called away suddenly.

U.T. Dallas also wishes to express its appreciation to all those who have helped make this program an important part of the life of the University, especially the contributors to the Lectures. Through their support these donors enable us to continue this important project and to publish the proceedings of the series, thus assuring a wide and permanent audience for the ideas the books contain.

I am confident that everyone who reads *Morality and Expediency in International and Corporate Relations,* the Andrew R. Cecil Lectures on Moral Values in a Free Society Volume XIII, will be stimulated by the ideas presented in its seven essays.

*Robert H. Rutford*

ROBERT H. RUTFORD, President
The University of Texas at Dallas
March 1992

# CONTENTS

# INTRODUCTION

## by

## Andrew R. Cecil

Secretary of State James Baker, addressing the American-Israel Public Affairs Committee on May 22, 1989, revealed the contents of his conversation with Prime Minister Yitzhak Shamir of Israel at their very first meeting, held in Washington, D.C. Shamir said that Baker had been described to him by the media as an ever-flexible pragmatist, while he himself had been described as an inflexible man of ideological principle. Then the Prime Minister declared that the media were wrong in both cases. "Yes," he said, "I am a man of principle, but I am also a pragmatist who knows what political compromise means." Shamir stated that he was confident that Mr. Baker was also a man of principle and that principle would guide his foreign policy.

The principle of the theory of pragmatism accredited to C.S. Pierce (1873) and introduced into familiar use by William Jones (1898) is—in opposition to principles based on metaphysical assumptions—to seek truth as tested by accomplished, practical results. Because of the lack of a common understanding of the meaning of pragmatism, we did not use this term for the theme of the 1991 lectures. The divergence between definitions of this term is best illustrated by the fact that Arthur O. Lovejoy, who was a professor at Johns Hopkins University, in his book on the subject found thirteen meanings of pragmatism, with several of them contradicting one another. *(The Thirteen Pragmatisms*, The Johns Hopkins Press,

1963.) We have therefore used instead the term "expediency" to refer to a policy based on self-interest and the use of any available means of achieving a particular advantageous end.

As to morality, when again confronted with a great variety of definitions, often conflicting with one another, we decided to refer to the common understanding of the terms "morality" and "morals." According to this general understanding, these terms refer to the common sense of the community with regard to decency, propriety, and respect for established ideas and institutions, among other things. The moral standards of the community—in the legal context—were described by Benjamin Cardozo as the "norm or standard of behavior which struggles to make itself articulate in law." As a generic term, morality contains the sum total of moral traits, including honesty, fidelity, peacefulness, and respect for human rights.

Some observers detect a perennial conflict between the values of expediency and morality in public and business life, and it is this conflict that the participants in the 1991 Lectures on Moral Values in a Free Society seek to reexamine in this series on *Morality and Expediency in International and Corporate Relations*. But, as Prime Minister Shamir's remarks quoted above indicate, the boundaries between these two guiding principles are not always in conflict. Indeed, the more deeply we examine the relationship between actions guided by moral principles and their outcome, the more likely we are to conclude that there is no true dichotomy here, since only actions undertaken in the spirit of morality are truly expedient in the long run.

As the flames of the struggle for human freedom against the dark forces of oppression are becoming increasingly visible around the world, a concern for human rights is becoming a global preoccupation. In the last three decades, Republican and Democratic presidents alike have committed themselves to champion the cause of human rights. President Dwight D. Eisenhower, in his address to the American Bar Association on August 24, 1955, pointed out that there can be no true peace as long as "we find injustice to many nations, repressions of human beings on a gigantic scale . . . with constructive efforts paralyzed in many areas by fear." In his address on March 17, 1970, at the United Nations, President Jimmy Carter stressed that "the search for peace and justice means also respect for human dignity. . . . Thus, no member of the United Nations can claim the mistreatment of its citizens is solely its own business. . . . The basic thrust of human affairs points toward a more universal demand for fundamental human rights."

Our commitment to promote human rights has a rich tradition that goes back as far as the Massachusetts Body of Liberties of 1641. That document asserts:

> "No man's life shall be taken away, no man's honor or good name shall be stayned, no man's person shall be arrested . . . no man's goods or estate shall be taken away from him . . . unless it be by virtue or equitie of some expressed law of the country."

The United States has a historical birthright to be associated with the concern of our foreign policy with the human rights issue.

Ambassador Richard Schifter in his lecture "America's Commitment to Human Rights in Foreign Policy" describes the process through which this historical American concern about the human rights of peoples throughout the world became a part of the official foreign policy of the United States. Traditionally, the internal affairs of other nations were considered off limits for diplomatic discussion. However, after the major nations of the world signed the final document of the 1976 Conference on Security and Cooperation in Europe, held in Helsinki, it became acceptable for violations of human rights by a particular government to become an issue in diplomatic dealings with that government.

Ambassador Schifter believes that the great changes we have recently witnessed in Eastern Europe and throughout the rest of the world might not have happened if the United States had not fought for the human rights declaration in Helsinki and had not pursued such a determined course in pointing out and condemning such violations whenever and wherever they have occurred since then. This forceful introduction of moral values into the arena of practical foreign policy is almost unprecedented, and—as I point out in my own lecture in this series—our own government set most of those precedents that do exist. It has been the conscience of the American people that has insisted that moral concerns must be a part of our foreign policy. And these moral concerns have had a major practical effect in changing the shape of the world political order.

My lecture on "Morality and Expediency in World Politics," like the other lectures in this volume, was presented before the collapse of the Soviet Union and the resignation of President Mikhail Gorbachev. Therefore the other lecturers and I were writing from the perspective of conditions just before that collapse and do not mention the Commonwealth of Independent States. In my lecture, I quote a passage that appeared in *The Federalist*, the eighty-five essays written in 1787, principally by James Madison and Alexander Hamilton, and published under the pen name Publius. In the fifty-first paper we find the famous sentence, "If men were angels, no government would be necessary." To paraphrase, we could say that if men were angels there would be no problem in reconciling morality and expediency in world politics.

Foreign relations is a very complex area. The rule of morality, as Hamilton wrote, "is not precisely the same between nations as between individuals," because the responsibilities of the state differ from those of individuals. An action of the state can influence many millions of lives, even those of generations to come, while according to Hamilton, "the consequences of a private action of an individual ordinarily terminates with himself." George Washington observed that it was "a maxim founded on the universal experience of mankind that no nation is to be trusted further than it is bound by its interest."

In reviewing the history of the various applications of expediency and moral rectitude to world politics, I have tried to point out that as long as we have independent nation-states lacking effective means of collective security, the balance of power doctrine at least protects a country against wrongful interference and prevents the aggrandizement of one nation beyond a certain limit. The question still unanswered is how to determine the ingredients of the power the diplomats seek to balance. Should the main criterion be the size of the territories of the rival states, the size of their populations, or their economic strength? Or is the balance of power almost exclusively based on military might? Throughout the history of world politics, diplomats have failed to provide a completely persuasive answer. It is also true that balance of power alone has never brought permanent peace. Countries outside the centers of power demand, and will undoubtedly continue to demand, a fair measure of participation in the handling of global affairs.

Men are not angels. As long as the nations do not find effective means of substituting the rule of law for rule by force, the balance of power theory in the context of the existing world system is at least ethically neutral in reconciling morality and expediency. The moral element enters when states have had to choose among actions that would affect the balance. Mankind's only hope is that in making their choice the statesmen responsible for world order and peace will be guided in their decisions by the light of morality, the light that will outshine the often appealing but false beacon of mere expediency.

It is one of the melancholy facts of our time that continuing world conflicts create apprehension and distrust that make discussions about a new world order sound almost like a medieval theological debate. Yet, in spite of the turmoil and the tensions pressing us from all parts of the globe, one of the most significant developments of our time is the determined effort to establish morality, law, and justice as the essential and decisive substitutes for force.

Some believe that international order can be protected by a balance of power, as I discussed in my lecture. A parity between the military capabilities of the superpowers, however, will not secure the atmosphere of peace with freedom and justice that we refer to when we talk about a new world order.

The international situation is an issue of thoughtful and prayerful concern for citizens in all walks of life. Their quest for peace has had a significant impact on mutual disarmament, the peaceful use of atomic energy, and the prohibition of nuclear testing. The preservation of world peace that will lead to a new world order is one of the crucial tasks shared by the entire world. "For God who inspires is not a God of disorder but of peace." (I Cor. 14:35.)

In his lecture "Morality and the Rule of Law in the Foreign Policy of the Democracies," Professor John Norton Moore finds that the next step in creating a truly new world order, now that most nations in the world have thrown off the shackles of totalitarianism and are beginning to accord their citizens basic human rights, is to establish the rule of law both within individual nations and in international dealings among them. In many countries that have known only the arbitrary and frequently changing rules of dictatorship, the people have never experienced the rational order and stable liberty that come from being ruled by laws rather than by the whims of men.

Professor Moore believes that the liberal democracies, without imposing their own views on their newly free neighbors, can be of enormous assistance in helping others to achieve the rule of law within their own countries. Many of those responsible for creating the new structures within these rebuilding societies are strongly drawn to the principles of democracy as we know it—to mention only limited and divided government, review of laws by an independent and impartial judiciary, and

constitutional guarantees. We must find ways to assist
these other nations by sharing our knowledge and experience with them. (As an afterword to his lecture, Professor Moore presents an overview paper outlining the
major components of the rule of law. As Co-Chairman of
the American delegation to the 1990 Seminar on the
Rule of Law in Moscow and Leningrad, he prepared this
summary of the components of rule of law as the final
statement of the American position; this is the first time
it has been published in English.)

In seeking a new world order, we have to adapt ourselves to practical necessities, to deal with the possible
and not with the ideal. These necessities may place limits
on our ability to act according to moral judgments of
universal scope. This does not mean, however, that
leaders acting in the political field should not try to
be guided by the unifying force of international law and
by their own moral insights.

Frederick Quinn in his lecture "Rule of Law in a New
Century" discusses the recent epochal events and their
future implications from the point of view of a former
Foreign Service officer who understands both the moral
force of a desire to live under the rule of law and the
practical impediments necessity has often put in the
way. The United States has been a shining beacon for the
other countries of the world in lighting their way toward
freedom and the rule of law. The great documents that
underlie our political system, especially the Declaration
of Independence and the United States Constitution,
have inspired many people around the world in their
quest for a better way of life. Now it is time for us to give
more practical assistance and advice as new governments around the world try to find structures and pro-

cedures that will suit their own individual needs.

Mr. Quinn also sets out the components of rule of law and describes some of the problems and needs of other nations and cultures in coming to grips with each of them. Even societies very different from our own, however, can profit from our desires and attempts to share our experiences with them. The current world situation gives us many opportunities to influence and be of assistance to the new governments forming all over the world. But it will take a strong commitment on the part of the American people and government if we are to have as much impact in this process as we did in the process that brought these political changes about in the first place.

The most dramatic changes on the international scene during the last year were those taking place in the territories formerly known as the Soviet Union. Under Stalin's and his successors' dictatorship, the Soviet Union violated almost every agreement it made, and expanded its territories by war, treason, and subversion. Its leaders followed the teachings of Lenin, who declared, "We do not believe in eternal morality, and we expose the deceit of all legends about morality." The fall of communism in Eastern Europe and the Soviet Union has strengthened our faith in the principle that nothing established by violence and maintained by force in opposition to what is right can endure. These historical events have also raised hopes for the end of imperialistic aggression.

In his lecture "Readjusting Our Moral Compass: Opportunities for U.S.-Soviet Relations After Communism," Professor Nicolai Petro examines the history of our attitudes toward and assumptions about the Soviet Union during the seventy-four years of its existence and finds that too often our policies were based on a narrow and false idea of expediency when a more principled stand would in fact have obtained better results. All too often, American policymakers assumed that communism had the support of a majority of the people of the Soviet Union. We now know better.

Professor Petro points out the continuity of spirit between the Russian people before the communist revolution and the people who suffered under the communist yoke. That continuity is becoming all the more evident as the shackles of communism are being discarded. More than ever, our relationships with the newly independent states of Eastern Europe must be based on moral principles and on a mutual respect for ethical and moral traditions that may differ in certain respects from our own. (It should be noted that when Professor Petro speaks of Russia and the Russian people he is not referring to the newly independent country of that name as a specific legal entity but to the spirit of Russia that endured even throughout the existence of the Soviet Union.)

Our moral concerns in the international arena are not limited to political issues. Our practical concern for the economic welfare of our fellowman should have a fundamental influence on our international relations. The growing belief in the interdependence of all nations and in cooperation as a precondition of international order calls for efforts to improve areas of collaboration in the economic as well as the political sphere. We can thereby reduce the potential conflicts arising in the world community and alleviate its economic difficulties.

More than 100 years ago, Abraham Lincoln said that this country could not endure half slave and half free. In the present era, we are justified in saying that this world cannot survive in peace with one-third of its people relatively affluent and two-thirds in misery, with unfulfilled expectations. The demand for respect for human dignity and fundamental human rights throughout the world community is meaningless as long as millions of people cannot satisfy their needs for sufficient food and shelter.

The impoverishment of any single people in the world means challenge, if not danger, to the well-being of all other peoples. The success or failure of developing countries affects the economic health and security of the world. The vitality of the economy of each country is attuned to the soundness of the world economy. It is essential, therefore, that nations work together to find mutually beneficial solutions to global economic problems. One of these solutions is offered by foreign investment. Although the attitude toward foreign investment with a particular country may be affected by a growing nationalism, adjustments resulting from interdependence of the world community must be made.

The economic self-interest of the private capital invested in a foreign land should be combined with economic enlightenment in the country in which investments are made. The private investor has a duty to see that his relations with the states in which he invests are constructively serviceable to their people, with due regard to the ways in which their situations differ from those in his own country. By making his talents and capital available, he encourages the growth of other nations. This activity deserves the protection accorded by law to the investor's acquired rights.

In his lecture "Investment from Abroad—No Longer Just an Option," Alexander J. Gillespie, Jr., reminds us that Eastern Europe is not the only area of the world in which profound changes have taken place in the last decade. Though superficially less dramatic and certainly less publicized, the profound political—and especially economic—changes in many other countries throughout the globe have just as much promise for improving the lives of their citizens as well as for contributing to international peace and prosperity.

Mr. Gillespie examines the political and economic changes that have recently overtaken three Latin American countries to demonstrate how quickly economic advancement can come when a government realizes that global economic interdependence is a reality. If a nation wants to improve the life of its citizens and become an important part of the world economy, it must overcome its distrust of outside interference and open the doors to international investment and development. The countries of the Pacific Rim have pointed the way, and recently many other countries, including a number in Latin America, have set out in the same direction. The last decade has seen many dictatorships topple in all areas of the world, not just in Eastern Europe. The nations of Eastern Europe can benefit enormously from the economic lessons provided by other newly free countries around the globe.

This same concern for the welfare of our fellowman has had a great impact on economic policies and behavior in our own country as well as abroad. In the Middle Ages, the social teaching of the church looked at commerce as a dangerous activity and at trade as an occupation that serves, according to Aquinas, "the lust of gain." Only with the rise of the secular state did signs of a divorce of economic realities from religious doctrines become evident. This divorce became a reality during the seventeenth and eighteenth centuries, the era of progress in economic thought, of growth in trade (described by a member of the British Parliament as the "fairest mistress in the world"), and of the recognition of economics as a subject for scientific study.

The expansion of trade, the accumulation of wealth, and an irrepressible desire for economic gain were no longer sins denounced by saints and sages but became virtues leading to the conquest of the world. What had been considered the deadly sin of avarice, committed when a man sought more wealth than was necessary for a livelihood in his state of life, now emerged as a virtue of social power and economic opulence.

The rise of purely economic criteria to evaluate human behavior led to an outburst of economic enterprise and of economic progress, but the new materialistic civilization was indifferent to the need for a just social order. This indifference led to exploitation and recurrent revolts against the social order.

To avoid such economic action in the absence of social convictions, we have to keep in mind that, although economic expediency is indispensable for the success of the businessman, such success cannot endure when it is divorced from moral considerations and when the businessman's activities violate the rights of his fellowman to self-respect and dignity.

To succeed economically, the businessman has to accept social responsibility. His efforts to succeed economically must be combined with the responsibility for promoting the well-being of the society in which he lives. No economic action can be sound without an accepted system of moral values. Moral principles must be trans-

lated into practice and cannot be sacrificed to purely
selfish desires to realize material gains.

Jon V. Heider in his lecture "Ethics, Morality, Legality in Corporate Relations: Sometimes It's Not Easy"
demonstrates the difficulties in creating a legal system
that puts such moral concerns into practice without also
creating undesirable side effects. Mr. Heider believes
that many American business executives truly do have
the public welfare, as well as the success of their own
companies, at heart. He also believes that those executives who deliberately set out to act wrongly should be
punished. But a corporation is a large and intricate
structure, and although legally it is a single entity, it is
in reality composed of many individuals, each of whom
is constantly making moral and ethical choices, for
better or for worse.

Mr. Heider examines the issue of how best to make
laws to monitor these moral and ethical choices. When
should a corporation as a whole be punished, and when
should top executives be held responsible for the actions
of their employees? Mr. Heider believes that the top
management of a company should be held accountable
for the general direction of that company and its policies.
But too many recent laws and regulations have imposed
a standard of accountability that is irrational and impossible for any individual to live up to—no one can
personally supervise the actions of all the individuals
of a large corporation. In our desire to have our laws
reflect our moral concerns, we must exercise common
sense to determine what is just and what is unjust, and
what is unreasonable and what is reasonable enough to
be carried out.

In the 1991 Lectures on Moral Values in a Free Society, the theme is repeatedly stressed that—in the perspective of history—immoral expediency is short-lived and that no action can be expedient without being morally right. The proceedings of the 1991 Lectures also explain the enormous moral force of freedom that emerges in all its strength as a powerfully expedient force as well. Undergirded by this desire for freedom, the inner conscience of a person can survive all kinds of oppression and follow the guiding light of truth. Together with all the other moral values, freedom will always remain the most important formative influence on man's relations with his fellowman as well as in business and international relations.

# AMERICA'S COMMITMENT TO HUMAN RIGHTS IN FOREIGN POLICY

by

Richard Schifter

# Richard Schifter

*Since November 1, 1985, Richard Schifter has been the Assistant Secretary of State for Human Rights and Humanitarian Affairs. He is also a member of the Board of Directors of the United States Institute of Peace and serves as a State Department representative on the Commission for Security and Cooperation in Europe.*

*During 1984–1985 Mr. Schifter served as Deputy United States Representative in the Security Council of the United Nations, with the rank of Ambassador. From 1983 to 1986, he also held the position of United States member of the United Nations Human Rights Commission.*

*A lawyer by profession, Mr. Schifter practiced law in Washington, D.C., from 1951 until his entry into full-time government service.*

*Mr. Schifter participated for many years in the educational affairs of his home state of Maryland as a citizen member of various boards and commissions. His service encompassed twenty years of membership on the Maryland State Board of Education, including eight years as the Board's Vice President and four years as its President. He also served on the Executive Committee of the Board of Visitors of the Maryland School for the Deaf, as Chairman of the Governor's Commission for the Funding of the Education of Handicapped Children, and as Chairman of the Maryland Values Education Commission.*

*Mr. Schifter was born in Vienna, Austria, in 1923, and came to the United States in 1938. He graduated summa cum laude from the College of the City of New York in 1943 and received his LL.B. from Yale Law School in 1951. Mr. Schifter served in the United States Army from 1943 to 1946.*

# AMERICA'S COMMITMENT TO HUMAN RIGHTS IN FOREIGN POLICY

by

Richard Schifter

Around the beginning of this century, Henry Adams observed that the conduct of foreign affairs involved the most aristocratic branch of American government and that it was the least susceptible to popular pressures. In those years and for many years following, our diplomatic service sought to emulate the West European diplomatic services. Foreign policy, as our diplomats viewed it, should be conducted in the interest of the nation by an educated elite, trained in international statecraft and uniquely able to chart a course that would indeed serve the national interest.

About six years ago, more than eighty years after Henry Adams had spoken so glowingly of a foreign service divorced from popular pressures, I heard a different description of American diplomacy. I served at the time as head of the United States delegation to a human rights meeting held in Ottawa under the sponsorship of the Conference on Security and Cooperation in Europe, also known as the Helsinki Process. From time to time I would meet with heads of friendly delegations at dinner to discuss the formulation of a common strategy. As the meeting was drawing to an end, the issue before us was whether to try to come up with a joint statement on which all the participants in the conference, including the Soviet Union and its East European allies, could agree.

31

Mikhail Gorbachev had come to power a few months earlier, but *glasnost* and *perestroika* were still in the future. Andrey Gromyko was Foreign Minister of the Soviet Union, and the policy of the time, which later came to be known as the period of stagnation, defined the behavior of the Soviet delegation. Given the continued violations by the Soviet Union and its allies of the basic human rights precepts contained in the Helsinki Final Act, the United States took the position that we should not strive for a joint statement at the conclusion of the meeting if that meant papering over our concern about violations of fundamental freedoms in Communist Europe. Some of our friends disagreed. They wanted us to search for some words and phrases to produce a final document that all of us could sign. Our delegation argued that such a statement would serve no useful purpose but would, on the contrary, tend only to demoralize the men and women behind the Iron Curtain who had stood up for the cause of freedom.

Every action taken by a meeting under the Helsinki Process requires unanimity. The mere fact that we would withhold our consent to a joint statement would mean that there would be no such statement. At our last dinner with our colleagues from friendly countries, I made it clear that we believed that our individual statements and those of other Western democracies throughout the session had eloquently stated the case for the cause of freedom and that a concluding joint statement would significantly detract from the effectiveness of the message that we had sent.

I still recall the reaction of one colleague who had strongly favored an effort at a joint statement. He was on most occasions affable and courteous, but as the evening progressed, as did the consumption of liquid refreshments, he revealed his true feelings. Facing me directly, he intoned, "European diplomats plan their action with thought and care. We know where we want to go and lay out the road to get there. As we progress, we set milestone after milestone." And then came his telling point: "You Americans, on the other hand, are driven only by politics. Your burning issues have a half-life of three days. Today it is Mrs. Sharansky who influences your actions. Tomorrow it will be someone else coming off the streets."

At the time of this meeting, Natan Sharansky was in his eighth year in prison. His wife had been to Ottawa but had not met with me. The position that the United States had taken was not determined by the protests of Mrs. Sharansky but did indeed reflect concern about the fate of her husband and of hundreds of other prisoners in the Gulag. Seven months later, Sharansky was free, with the rest of the prisoners following him within a few years, in significant part because of the strong position taken on this issue by the United States in Ottawa and wherever else we had a chance to confront the Soviets on human rights matters.

Would we have taken that strong position on Soviet human rights violations if in 1985 we had adhered to the ideas on the management of foreign policy that Henry Adams had articulated in 1904? The answer is, undoubtedly, no. George Kennan, who, in retirement, is still one of our country's most respected traditional diplomats, has consistently criticized U.S. foreign policy decisions based on human rights grounds. These human rights concerns were infused into our foreign policy, as my colleague at the Ottawa meeting grudgingly pointed out, because international human rights issues matter to a great many Americans.

In my years as Assistant Secretary of State for Human Rights and Humanitarian Affairs, it has often been my responsibility to explain our human rights policy to the officials of governments that we deemed responsible for human rights violations. In doing so, I have contended that this was not a matter of our government "interfering" in the affairs of another government. After all, we were not *compelling* the foreign government in question to change its behavior. I explained that what was involved was a matter of United States domestic policy. How we relate to another government, to whom we grant assistance, how we vote in international lending agencies, what our tariff policy might be are matters of *our* concern.

Under our democratic system of government, the decisions taken by the government ultimately reflect the will of the general public. And the general public, in turn, has friendly feelings toward peoples elsewhere in the world, is concerned by reports that some citizens are deprived of basic freedoms by their own governments, and then insists that the United States Government factor this feeling of concern into decisions that may have economic consequences for the countries in question.

This formulation, which I have found much more productive than sermonizing, also has the advantage of truthfully reflecting the circumstances that frequently bring me face to face with representatives of governments accused of human rights violations. Our human rights laws, including the law that established my position, are indeed a response to popular demand. What I would now like to discuss are the two distinct factors that have produced this policy: (1) the concern of the American general public with the cause of international human rights and (2) the ability of American voters to translate this concern into governmental policy.

As Alexis de Tocqueville observed more than 150 years ago, the new republic in North America was a state in many ways different from its European counterparts. One of these differences, I submit, was the outlook of its citizens on issues of foreign policy. This difference in outlook stemmed in large measure from our unique geography. Following the War of 1812, concerns about our relations with European powers and about our northern border diminished significantly. Following the Treaty of Guadalupe Hidalgo, the same was true regarding relations with Mexico and our southern border. As our country felt increasingly secure against foreign encroachment, most citizens concerned with public policy focused on domestic issues. Foreign policy was indeed left to a professional elite.

While Americans of different ethnic strains joined in building a new country, developing a new culture, and creating a new national identity, Europe, from which so many of them stemmed, remained the scene of continuing disputes based on nationality differences. A great many nationality groups looked with suspicion, often with hostility, at their neighbors. Territorial disputes were commonplace. There was continuing fear of one nationality group being overrun by another, a fear that often became reality. Though foreign policy matters in Europe, as in the United States, were in the hands of professional elites, the European citizenry was most assuredly concerned with and involved in certain narrow, specific foreign policy issues, principally involving relationships with next-door neighbors. The concern of these citizens covered the very same field that constituted the subjects of interest to diplomats, namely, national security, the resolution of border disputes, and commercial relations.

These topics were not of great continuing interest to the general American public. To be sure, once the age of intercontinental ballistic missiles arrived and we had to be concerned, for the first time in more than 140 years, with the possibility of devastating military attack on our country's heartland by a major power, we did indeed pay attention to that issue. But our concern over Soviet power was brought into focus by what we viewed as the evil character of the Communist system, the oppressive measures taken by Communist governments against their own people and their immediate neighbors.

This concern over the relationship between foreign governments and the peoples over which they rule has indeed been the hallmark of foreign policy interests of the general American public. The fact that a country wanted to be friendly with us, as was the case with apartheid South Africa and Pinochet's Chile, was not of interest to us. Racial discrimination and political oppression, respectively, defined the American public's outlook on those two countries. The fact that India adopted a relatively unfriendly attitude toward us was equally irrelevant. After all, wasn't it the world's largest democracy?

Moral judgments have invariably played a key role in the formulation of American public opinion on issues of war and peace and on support of presidential decisions to commit military forces. Looking at the conflicts in which we participated during the current century, we can note that our entry into World War I received public support because Germany's unrestricted submarine warfare in the North Atlantic was deemed morally wrong and because President Woodrow Wilson emphasized that this would be a war to make the world safe for democracy. Our assistance to Britain prior to entering World War II after Pearl Harbor won public support because we viewed the Nazi regime as immoral, both in its domestic and its foreign policy. Our role in the Korean War and in Vietnam won support, initially, because it was part of our international struggle to contain Communist totalitarianism. An important element in the ultimate decline of support of the war in Vietnam was the general acceptance of the allegations that the government of South Vietnam was corrupt and undemocratic and, for that reason, not worth defending. Finally, while our concern over control over the region that produces most of the world's oil was our national interest reason for mounting the military effort against Iraq, the fact that the public recognized Saddam Hussein as a thoroughly evil person played a significant role in the public's decision to support that war.

Decisions on war and peace are, of course, made by the country's elected political leadership, the President and the Congress, but only after taking popular sentiment carefully into account. Our foreign policy professionals in the State Department simply take orders. There are other major issues, short of war, when the President, as head of the executive branch, makes the basic decision irrespective of, or perhaps even contrary to, State Department advice. One such case, in which the President's judgment of what was *right* was squarely opposed to the State Department's idea of what was in the national interest, was the decision in May 1948 to give de facto recognition to the new state of Israel.

The technical issue, in 1948, of de facto recognition was of interest and concern only to specialists, but the general American public understood the broad outlines of the issue, the idea of creating a Jewish state in the British Mandate of Palestine. There was overwhelming support for that idea. President Truman was similarly sympathetic. The State Department, on the other hand, was deeply concerned that recognition of the Jewish state would not be in the national interest, given the larger number of Arabs whom recognition would offend. The State Department had, in fact, come up with the proposal that after the British withdrew from Palestine, the United Nations should assume the role of trustee for the area of the mandate, thereby reversing an earlier United Nations decision to split the country between a Jewish and an Arab state. The General Assembly of the United Nations was, in fact, in session, debating the trusteeship resolution, with State Department representatives lobbying heavily in favor of it, when word reached the assembly hall that the White House had announced the de facto recognition of the new state of Israel, thereby pulling the rug out from under the trusteeship resolution. There is probably no other case in which the general public's idea of what was morally right had triumphed so obviously over the professionals' notion of what was in the national interest.

I have, so far, referred only to major issues of foreign policy concern in which the public's view of the morality of a particular act turned out to be of critical importance. In each such instance it was ultimately the President who saw to it that policy was executed by the executive branch in keeping with popular sentiment. But these were individual instances involving major policy issues. There remained the problem of how a broad policy approach, that of factoring a country's human rights record into our dealings with that country, could be instilled in a diplomatic service that had long adhered to the principle that what another sovereign government does regarding its own citizens is the business of that sovereign government and none other. Just how that was done, step by step, since the end of World War II is what I shall now try to present for your consideration.

When representatives of the victors in World War II gathered in San Francisco in April 1945 to write the United Nations Charter, at least some of the delegations present wanted to take into account the frightful lessons that the war had taught. These delegations, with the United States usually in the lead, advanced the proposition that the Charter should deal with the issue of human rights. They succeeded. They saw to it that the Charter would provide that one of the purposes of the United Nations would be the protection and preservation of human rights. Thus, for the first time in the close to 250 years in which our civilization had come to recognize and respect the concept of human rights, was that concept identified as one of international concern.

The concept of human rights, as defined by John Locke and the writers and thinkers who followed him, was based on two essential propositions, namely, (1) that a government, to be legitimate, must govern with the consent of the people and (2) that individual citizens were endowed with fundamental rights and freedoms of which no government may deprive them. As the idea of human rights first evolved, however, it was viewed exclusively as a matter between a sovereign and his or her subjects. Our own Declaration of Independence expounded on this concept with utmost clarity. In 1945, another player was brought in: The international community, as represented in the United Nations, was to preserve and protect human rights.

It was relatively easy to get the words written into the Charter. It was much more difficult to have these words take on real meaning. After all, once the Charter was written, the task of carrying out its provisions was to be left to diplomats, to professionals who had been carefully trained to distinguish between those issues properly the subject of discussion among nations and those that were to be considered of purely domestic concern. The cheerful approval of the Charter by Joseph Stalin's Soviet Union demonstrated that at least one member of the new organization did not believe that the commitment to human rights would be taken seriously.

Stalin and other cynics had underestimated the determination of human rights advocates such as Eleanor Roosevelt and France's Rene'Cassin. In 1946 the United Nations Human Rights Commission was created under Mrs. Roosevelt's chairmanship. Her drive and leadership produced in 1948 the Universal Declaration of Human Rights, which was adopted by the United Nations General Assembly on December 10, 1948. By this time the countries espousing Leninism had woken up to the possibility that United Nations activity in the area of human rights might ultimately haunt them. When the Universal Declaration of Human Rights was put to a vote, eight members of the United Nations abstained. They included the six votes from Communist countries that then belonged to the international organization, namely, three votes cast by the USSR (including votes for Ukraine and Byelorussia, in addition to the USSR proper), and those of Czechoslovakia, Poland, and Yugoslavia. The other two countries abstaining on this vote were Saudi Arabia and South Africa.

South Africa was by then on notice as to what United Nations activity in the field of human rights might mean to it. Beginning in 1946, resolutions had been presented in United Nations forums regarding South Africa's policy of discrimination based on a person's ethnicity. Clearly reflecting the concern of a great many diplomats that the United Nations not overstep its jurisdiction, the resolutions focused exclusively on the treatment of persons of Indian or Pakistani origin and noted that South Africa's treatment of these minorities burdened relationships among members of the United Nations. The resolutions did invoke the human rights provisions of the Charter as well but did so only secondarily. It took another few years, until 1952, before the United Nations was prepared to approve a resolution that dealt squarely with the issue of human rights by focusing on discrimination against blacks in South Africa. This was viewed as a sufficiently sharp departure from traditional diplomacy to create a division of opinion within the U.S. State Department as to how to deal with the issue. The matter had to be referred to the Secretary of State, Dean Acheson, for decision. The final result was that the United States would vote for the resolution but not speak in support of it.

South Africa, a relatively easy target, has remained on the United Nations agenda ever since. Given the fact that the Nazi practices of discrimination and ultimately mass murder based on ethnicity had given rise to the human rights provisions of the Charter, it was indeed logical to make South Africa's race-based discriminatory policies the initial test case for invoking the Charter's human rights provisions. But there were other, glaring examples of serious violations of human rights by members of the United Nations, above all by Stalin and his imitators throughout the Soviet bloc, which the United Nations carefully avoided. South Africa was not a strong power in its own right and was not the member of a bloc that could shield it against United Nations criticism. That indeed made it an easy target for such criticism.

It took more than twenty years before South Africa was joined by another similarly small, friendless, and blocless country, Pinochet's Chile, to be followed by Somoza's Nicaragua. Until 1982, when the United Nations Human Rights Commission criticized Poland for its repression of the Solidarity Movement, no formal action was taken by the United Nations against human rights violators from the Soviet bloc. Even then, United Nations actions in this field against members of significant voting blocs remained cautious, hesitant, and carefully circumscribed.

Though the United Nations record of action regarding human rights violations has been inconsistent and of only marginal effectiveness, the fact that it broke the diplomatic taboo against the consideration of human rights questions at the international level was, in itself, of major significance. After all, we could not argue that Zhivkov's Bulgaria denied its citizens First Amendment rights. Nor could we easily get into disputes over what protections the Bulgarian constitution might provide. But we could contend that *internationally recognized* human rights now existed and could call attention to the fact that some countries acted in contravention of internationally recognized standard-setting documents.

Though we could indeed do so, for many years we rarely did. Many professional diplomats continued to consider it inappropriate to use the United Nations forums to criticize the behavior of the governments of member nations toward their own citizens. Only on some occasions, when heads of United States delegations to the United Nations Human Rights Commission, who would not be professional diplomats, insisted on speaking out on the subject of human rights violations, would the United States go on record on that subject.

The climate was, however, right for the United States to do more than speechmaking. The Kennedy and Johnson administrations, responding to United Nations sanctions resolutions, acted promptly to enforce an effective arms supply cutoff against South Africa.

A few years later, in 1974, the United States Congress went one step further: Deviating from the international pattern, it took on a country that was then untouchable in the United Nations system: the Soviet Union. As the Soviet Union had increasingly followed an anti-Israel policy internationally, the country's traditional anti-Semitism had come to the fore, reflected in discrimination in the fields of education and employment. Under these circumstances, more and more Soviet Jews became interested in leaving the Soviet Union. But emigration was at best difficult, at worst impossible. Many applicants were not only turned down but lost their jobs and other benefits.

Responding to this Soviet violation of international human rights standards, which did specify that anyone should be allowed to leave any country, including his own, Senator Henry Jackson decided to add teeth to our appeals to the Soviet Union to allow those who wished to leave the country to do so. As the Congress was in 1974 considering a new trade act, Senator Jackson proposed that Communist countries would be eligible for Most Favored Nation (MFN) status only if they made significant moves toward freedom of emigration. This statutory provision, which became know as the Jackson-Vanik Amendment, was enacted into law over the strong opposition of the State Department. It sent a message to the countries subject to this restriction on MFN status, making them understand very clearly that their emigration policy mattered to the United States. It played a key role in causing the Soviet Union to change its long-standing anti-emigration policy.

Following the Jackson-Vanik Amendment, the Congress enacted a number of laws that mandated economic measures against countries that engage in "a consistent pattern of gross violations of internationally recognized human rights." Such countries would not be eligible for U.S. economic assistance. Moreover, the United States would oppose development loans to such countries from international financial institutions.

In this time frame, the middle seventies, Congress enacted another law that initially appeared to be merely a reporting requirement but had a profound impact on U.S. diplomacy. It was the law requiring the State Department to furnish the Congress annually with a country-by-country report on human rights conditions worldwide. I believe that the authors of this law did not, at the time of enactment, know how profound an impact this new statutory requirement would have on the executive branch of the United States Government.

After the reporting requirement had become law, the State Department had to decide how to discharge this new responsibility. It concluded that the embassies in the countries in question would prepare the initial drafts of the country reports on human rights. As a result, the chief of mission of every United States diplomatic post abroad would appoint a human rights officer, whose task it would be to prepare the initial draft of the annual human rights report. Though the drafting exercise would take place once a year, the officer to whom the task was assigned would necessarily have to keep track of human rights problems throughout the year, observing developments relating to human rights as they occurred and noting them down. In countries in which information about human rights violations did not appear in the official media, the human rights officer of the embassy had to reach out to opposition elements as well as look for and read clandestine publications. United States embassies thus began to deviate from normal diplomatic custom in that prominent dissidents would visit these embassies or would regularly receive American diplomats as visitors. Our embassies would as a result be the best informed about human rights conditions in countries in which opposition elements were repressed.

Diplomats are used to reporting promptly on developments in the areas of their responsibility, and human rights officers were not exceptions to this general rule. Thus, once embassies had been staffed with human rights officers, a flow of messages started notifying Washington of human rights conditions in problem countries. These messages began, in the first instance, to inform the State Department of human rights problems. But they did

more. The prevailing sentiment in our American culture
is that where there is a problem there must also be a
solution. Thus, once Washington became aware of the
details of human rights violations, we began to think of
ways of dealing with those issues. Congress had mandated certain economic sanctions if the violations were
particularly serious. Even if they were not serious
enough to require the imposition of sanctions, the question being considered was whether our embassy should
be asked to make appropriate representations to the
government in question or whether the United States
Government should make a public statement expressing
its concern. It was in that manner that human rights
factors were gradually infused into United States foreign policy formulation.

Not long after enacting the requirement to produce
annual reports, Congress took another step with significant bureaucratic implications. In 1977 it established
the position of Assistant Secretary of State for Human
Rights and Humanitarian Affairs. Responsibility to
recommend appropriate action in the human rights area
was thus given to an officer of the State Department with
a rank sufficiently high to make it possible for human
rights issues to be presented directly to the top leadership of the State Department.

I need to explain what this means in practical terms.
When the State Department prepares a policy paper
dealing with a particular country, the so-called regional
bureau dealing with the country in question normally
writes the paper, which is signed by the Assistant Secretary who heads that bureau. But if the policy recommendation has implications involving a subject for
which a so-called functional bureau is responsible, the

Assistant Secretary for that functional bureau must sign off on the memorandum. Thus, if the issue concerns economic affairs, the memorandum will be co-signed by the Assistant Secretary for Economic and Business Affairs. If it involves military matters, it will be co-signed by the Assistant Secretary for Politico-Military Affairs. And if the issue posed has human rights implications, it was now to be co-signed by the Assistant Secretary for Human Rights and Humanitarian Affairs. The result of this grant of authority is that the bureau that initiates the recommendation must either get the agreement of the bureaus that must be consulted for co-signature or present the Secretary of State with alternative recommendations.

The process just described may appear to be little more than one of bureaucratic routine. To be sure, it does involve such routine, but the process is of the utmost importance in policy formulation. It does not guarantee that human rights will at all times be the dominant factor when a policy decision is made, but it assures that the human rights perspective will be presented and considered.

It took time for this fundamental reorientation of United States foreign policy to take hold. Congress would on occasion push for more stringent action than the administration was prepared to espouse, but more often than not the two branches of government were in agreement about the policy line to be adopted. What was increasingly recognized was that mere pronouncements on human rights concerns, though emotionally satisfying, would advance the human rights cause only if they were part of a thought-through strategy designed to achieve results. Our goal, we have had to keep in mind, is

to improve the lot of those who have been the victims of
human rights violations, not just to make ourselves feel
good about having denounced the violators. This requires in each instance a careful analysis of the problem,
a determination of who is responsible and what that
person's or group's motivation might be, and the development of a strategy to deal with the problem. In some
cases a public pronouncement might fit into the strategy. In other instances quiet diplomacy is more likely to
achieve the desired goal.

At roughly the same time that human rights concerns
began to be systematically injected into the making of
American foreign policy, an extraordinarily important
development in the content and coverage of human rights
standards began unfolding through the Helsinki Process.

In the early 1970s, most European countries as well as
the United States and Canada came together in what became known as the Conference on Security and Cooperation in Europe (CSCE). The Soviets under Leonid Brezhnev
considered the Conference a useful tool of detente. In the
absence of a post-World War II peace treaty, they looked
to the Conference to ratify the status quo regarding
Europe's borders. As the discussions in this Conference
proceeded, the West Europeans came up with the idea of
adding human rights principles to the document that
was to be signed. With security cooperation known as the
first basket and economic cooperation as the second
basket, human rights concerns came to be identified as
the third basket. The United States, with Henry Kissinger
serving as Secretary of State, was initially reluctant
about the injection of human rights into the agenda but
went along. The Soviet bloc, well aware of the fact that
it had not been adversely affected by the human rights

provisions contained in the Universal Declaration on Human Rights or by its ratification of the Covenant on Civil and Political Rights, had no problem agreeing to the inclusion of human rights provisions in the document. Therefore, on August 1, 1975, Gerald Ford, Leonid Brezhnev, Helmut Schmidt of the Federal Republic of Germany, Marshal Tito of Yugoslavia, Prime Minister Olof Palme of Sweden, and thirty other heads of state or government signed the Helsinki Final Act.

This document was well publicized in many participating countries, including the Soviet Union, where it was reproduced in full in the official press. Publication there had a totally unintended and unexpected result, namely that some Soviet citizens took the document seriously. They had noted that by signing the Helsinki Final Act the Soviet Union had agreed to abide by the Universal Declaration of Human Rights, which, after all, provided for free speech, a free press, and freedom of assembly, of association, and of religion. These people decided to form the Helsinki Monitoring Committees, groups of courageous men and women who set themselves the task of publicizing Soviet transgressions against the commitments entered into at Helsinki.

As I noted earlier, the Helsinki Final Act was signed on August 1, 1975. The Helsinki Monitoring Committees began to organize themselves in early 1976. The response of the Brezhnev regime was not instantaneous. It took about a year for the apparatus of repression to move into action; but when it did, it came down hard. Beginning in early 1977, Helsinki monitors were arrested. They were then charged with anti-Soviet agitation and propaganda and were invariably convicted and sentenced to seven years of confinement and five years of internal exile. Let us keep in mind that in the Soviet Union there was no provision for time off for good behavior, only add-ons for what was deemed bad behavior.

In spite of the arrest of their leaders, the Helsinki Monitoring Committees continued their work, encouraged and, in fact, inspired by the man who had sacrificed his status of privilege in the Soviet Union for the cause of freedom, Andrey Sakharov.

The KGB was relentless: There were more arrests, more convictions, and an increasing stream of prisoners going off to the Gulag. In 1980, Sakharov and his wife, Yelena Bonner, were forcibly exiled from Moscow to Gorkiy. By then the Helsinki movement in the Soviet Union had been crushed.

The Soviet Union's Helsinki Monitoring Committees had their counterpart in Czechoslovakia in the Charter 77 Movement. Czechoslovakia's secret police responded as the KGB had done, with arrests, but Czechoslovak prison sentences were for lesser periods, four years being the maximum. Charter 77 just kept going.

What did the other signatories of the Helsinki Final Act think about these violations of commitments solemnly entered into by the Soviet Union and other Communist countries? That answer came soon after the initial arrests in the Soviet Union had begun, but it was by no means a clear response. The Helsinki Final Act had provided that the participating states would meet from time to time to review the implementation of the Accords signed at Helsinki. The first such follow-up meeting convened in Belgrade in 1977. To head the United States delegation, President Jimmy Carter had reached outside the State Department and designated a former

Justice of the United States Supreme Court and former Ambassador to the United Nations, Arthur Goldberg.

We were still in the period of detente and were trying to negotiate arms control agreements with the Soviet Union. The prevailing wisdom in the State Department was that while it was all right for the Assistant Secretary of State for Human Rights and Humanitarian Affairs to go after Latin American dictators, it was unwise to pursue East European dictators with equal fervor. It is to the everlasting credit of Justice Goldberg that he did not take kindly to that approach. He insisted that the United States would have to raise the Soviet Union's serious human rights violations at the Belgrade meeting and he prevailed. And so, for the first time ever, the Soviet Union found itself in Belgrade at the receiving end of a continuing barrage of pointed criticism of its human rights record.

That record was indeed fully exposed by the United States delegation. But the United States found itself alone. Its criticism of Soviet actions had shocked not only the delegations from Eastern Europe but those from Western Europe as well. By the time the meeting adjourned, the Soviet Union certainly understood that the United States had committed itself to the principle that its representatives would vigorously discuss human rights violations at the Helsinki Process meetings. There was no indication that anyone else would join.

The next follow-up meeting convened in Madrid three years later, in the fall of 1980. In the intervening period an event had occurred that had made a good many observers understand Soviet policies much better than they had before. It was the invasion of Afghanistan in December 1979. With detente a thing of the past, the

State Department fully supported vigorous discussion of Soviet human rights performance in the Helsinki Process. The head of the United States delegation, Max Kampelman, deliberately and systematically went about the task of encouraging our allies to join in these discussions. He was successful. So, for a period of three years—for the Madrid meeting lasted that long—the human rights violations for which the Soviet Union and the other East European Communist dictatorships were responsible were discussed over and over again, in substantial detail.

This was a totally unprecedented and unexpected development. The Soviet Union had signed the Helsinki Accords in the belief that the agreement would confirm its geopolitical position and strengthen its efforts to weaken the West's military preparedness. It had agreed to the human rights provisions as a sop to the West, not thinking that they had any bite in them. Yet bite they did. Over a period of three years, West Europe's media reported on the Madrid meeting and, thus, on Soviet and other East European human rights violations. Unanimous consent was required before the meeting could be adjourned, thus allowing the West to keep the meeting going as long as that was found desirable. The Soviets realized that little would be accomplished by simply walking out on a particular session.

A few months after the end of the Bulgarian Communist dictatorship, I had occasion to discuss the Madrid meeting with a high-ranking official of the Bulgarian Foreign Ministry who had been a member of his country's delegation at Madrid. He told me that the experience had been an eye-opener for him. He had listened to the statements by both the Western and the Eastern

European delegations. It had become increasingly clear to him, he explained to me, that the Western statements accurately reflected conditions and that the Eastern statements were simply lies. Many of his colleagues, he said, held similar views. They had to be cautious, he emphasized, but when they got back home they did share their new knowledge with their friends.

The education of East European diplomats participating in the Madrid meeting was not its only consequence. As I noted, over a period of three years, European media reported regularly and systematically on Madrid. The Voice of America, Radio Liberty, Radio Free Europe, BBC, Deutsche Welle, and other West European news broadcasts carried the message to Eastern Europe. Though there is no doubt that many factors played a role in bringing about the end of East European Communism in the period 1989 to 1991, there is also no doubt that the Madrid meeting was one of these factors. Madrid played the role that it did because the United States Government had committed itself to a policy of using an opportunity such as that presented in Madrid to speak clearly, thoughtfully, and effectively on the subject of human rights. Credit for the Madrid success finally belongs to the head of the United States delegation, Ambassador Max Kampelman, who not only eloquently presented the case of freedom at the meeting but did a truly masterful job orchestrating a unified Western position on fundamental principles of democracy and human rights.

As we look back over the years since human rights considerations were deliberately and systematically injected into our foreign policy, what can we say has been accomplished? I submit to you that we played an extremely important role in bringing Communism to an end in the Soviet Union and Eastern Europe. After having been bombarded by Communist propaganda in clever campaigns over a period of more than sixty years, democracy finally went from the defensive to the propaganda offensive, and it succeeded.

Now, following the collapse of Leninism in East Europe, we have granted technical help to governments that want to respect human rights but do not yet have institutions in place that can effectively protect those rights. Helping them build such institutions, particularly an independent court system, can be a most effective way to ensure the observance of basic rights.

As it is, the disillusionment of so many East Europeans with Communism does not mean that Eastern Europe is now solidly in the democratic camp. Throughout that region there is now a strong undercurrent in support of nationalism and authoritarianism and in opposition to political and economic reforms. Only the continuing engagement of the world's democracies with Eastern Europe can over time lay a solid foundation for democratic development in that region of the world.

The human rights provisions of the Helsinki Final Act and their effective utilization by the Western democracies resulted in the most spectacular success for the cause of human freedom worldwide. We should not, however, ignore that democracy has also been on the march in other parts of the world. From 1980 onward, thus preceding the Communist collapse in Eastern Europe, Latin America's military dictatorships fell one by one and were succeeded by democratically elected governments. Today Cuba's Fidel Castro stands alone as the only Latin American head of government lacking an electoral mandate from the people.

In Latin America, too, we are dealing with rather fragile democratic structures and the need for continuing support. Yet, as the years pass, as new elections take place, in many instances elections in which the incumbent party is defeated, quite a number of Latin American countries are now experiencing longer periods of democratic rule than they have ever before in their history. It is important for the world's established democracies to render the help necessary to continue that trend.

Then there is Africa. After the spectacular failure of Tanzania's experiment in socialism, many African leaders recognized that collectivism was not the answer to the region's economic problems. Following the changes in Eastern Europe, democratic ferment also became evident in Africa. Governments that had espoused Marxism-Leninism, such as those of Benin and Congo, have given way to multiparty democracy. Authoritarian governments are surrendering power to democratic institutions elsewhere on the continent. There is a good chance that democracy will now, at long last, take root in most parts of sub-Saharan Africa. But here, too, we must be aware of the fact that a great deal of outside assistance will be needed before democratic institutions can achieve a solid footing. Above all, the new governments will need to follow policies that will improve economic conditions.

In Asia democracy has come to such remote countries as Mongolia and Nepal. Yet we have also had the serious setback of Tiananmen Square.

I have, of course, not spoken of all parts of the world. Human rights are still repressed in many places, for example in China, the country that contains one-fifth of humanity. The progress worldwide of the last decade or so, however, has been truly spectacular.

Freedom has come to so many parts of the world in recent years because the people of the countries in question, including the brave men and women who faced the tanks in front of the Russian Federation Building in Moscow last August and then talked the soldiers out of attacking, wanted it and strove for it. These heroes of the democratic cause deserve our applause. Without in any way minimizing their key role, let me add that it is not unreasonable to assume that our own commitment, our determination to hold high the flag of freedom and democracy, has served as an inspiration to advocates of that cause worldwide.

# MORALITY AND EXPEDIENCY
# IN WORLD POLITICS

## by

## Andrew R. Cecil

## Andrew R. Cecil

*Andrew R. Cecil is Distinguished Scholar in Residence at The University of Texas at Dallas. In February 1979 the University established in his honor the Andrew R. Cecil Lectures on Moral Values in a Free Society and invited Dr. Cecil to deliver the first series of lectures in November 1979. The first annual proceedings were published as Dr. Cecil's book* The Third Way: Enlightened Capitalism and the Search for a New Social Order, *which received an enthusiastic response. He has also lectured in each subsequent series. A new book,* The Foundations of a Free Society, *was published in 1983.* Three Sources of National Strength *appeared in 1986, and* Equality, Tolerance, and Loyalty *in 1990. In 1976 the University named for Dr. Cecil the Andrew R. Cecil Auditorium, and in 1990 it established the Andrew R. Cecil Endowed Chair in Applied Ethics.*

*Educated in Europe and well launched on a career as a professor and practitioner in the fields of law and economics, Dr. Cecil resumed his academic career after World War II in Lima, Peru, at the University of San Marcos. After 1949, he was associated with the Methodist church-affiliated colleges and universities in the United States until he joined The Southwestern Legal Foundation. Associated with the Foundation since 1958, Dr. Cecil helped guide its development of five educational centers that offer nationally and internationally recognized programs in advanced continuing education. Since his retirement as President of the Foundation, he serves as Chancellor Emeritus and Honorary Trustee.*

*Dr. Cecil is author of fifteen books on the subjects of law, economics, and religion and of more than seventy articles on these subjects and on the philosophy of religion published in periodicals and anthologies. A member of the American Society of International Law, of the American Branch of the International Law Association, and of the American Judicature Society, Dr. Cecil has served on numerous commissions for the Methodist Church and is a member of the Board of Trustees of the National Methodist Foundation for Christian Higher Education. In 1981 he was named an Honorary Rotarian.*

# MORALITY AND EXPEDIENCY
## IN WORLD POLITICS

by

Andrew R. Cecil

Morality, like truth, belongs to a group of terms—such as religion, justice, beauty, and conscience—that have a great impact on human life. In searching for the substance of the qualities that those terms represent, we are confronted with a large variety of definitions often conflicting with one another, because some of them are too narrow and others too exhaustive. In this search, we also find that the focus of moral codes and of traditional moral values may differ in various geographical areas, cultures, and historical periods.

In trying to assess the morality of nations and national policies, furthermore, we should recognize that, even in the same geographical area and historical period, states differ. Not all are on the same moral level. A state that was founded on moral principles and is honest in trying, however imperfectly, to live up to them is a very different institution from a state governed by a totalitarian dictator.

## Conflicting Concepts

The concept of morality has preoccupied the minds of thinkers since the ancient philosophers of Greece and Rome, the Hebrew prophets, and the disciples and followers of Jesus of Nazareth. We find, however, discrepancies among various philosophers' concepts of morality, even

within the same generation. Such contrasting concepts
of morality are embodied in the philosophies of two giants
in the history of ethics, Plato and Aristotle, although
they lived in the same period and represented the same
tradition in ancient Greece.

## A. *Plato*

Plato's thought was characterized by the transcenden-
tal and mystical "Forms" or ideas, among which the idea
of the Good is the guide to morality. Like the other Forms,
the idea of the Good is the object of genuine knowledge,
as opposed to material objects, whose ontological status
is next to nonbeing. In his quest for knowledge and absolute and eternal values, Plato in the *Theaetetus* defines
God as "perfect" and states that man can perfect himself
only by imitating God. The intrinsic aim of man is to
become as similar as possible to God. The moral "norm"
of conduct is the one that leads to an effective harmony of
the whole, to the common order and welfare of the society, as well as of any other association. In *The Republic*,
Plato asks artists and writers to express only the image
of the good in their works.

The contrasting position that extols power and expediency is expressed by the Sophists as portrayed in the first
book of Plato's *Republic* by Glaucon and Thrasymachus,
who argue that "all men believe in their hearts that injustice is far more profitable to the individual than justice" (*The Republic and Other Works*, trans. by Benjamin
Jowett, Anchor Books, 1973, p. 44) and that "the just is
always a loser in comparison with the unjust." (*Id.*, p. 27.)
They believe that injustice applied on a large scale is
particularly rewarding, since "injustice, when on a suf-

ficient scale, has more strength and freedom and mastery than justice." (*Id.*, p. 28.)

Again in the dialogue *Gorgias*, the Sophist Callicles denounces morality as the weapon of the weak, who because of their inferiority praise justice in order to enslave the strong. He makes a distinction between slave morality and hero morality. The suffering of injustice, according to Callicles, "is not a part of a man but of a slave," since "when he is wronged and trampled upon, he is unable to help himself; or any other about whom he cares." The Sophist continues:

> "The reason, as I conceive, is that the makers of laws are the majority who are weak; and they make laws and distribute praises and censures with a view to themselves and to their own interest; . . . and they say that dishonesty is shameful and unjust; meaning by the word injustice, the desire of man to have more than his neighbors; for knowing their own inferiority, I suspect that they are too glad of equality. . . . But if there were a man who had sufficient force, he would shake off and break through, and escape from all this; he would trample under foot all our formulas and spells and charms, and all our laws which are against nature." (*The Dialogues of Plato*, Liveright Publishing Corp., pp. 483, 484.)

A straight line leads from this argument to the power politics of tyrants and dictators (which we will describe in more detail later). The history of such leaders who have sought expediency in evil, however, gives ample evidence that their "injustice" in the long run has not been rewarding.

## B. *Aristotle*

Aristotle, in the *Politics*, agrees with Plato that men imagine "not only the forms of the Gods, but their ways of life to be like their own." (*The Basic Works of Aristotle*, ed. by Richard McKean, Random House, 1941, p. 1129.) But while Plato is absorbed in the mental abstraction of morality as "the Form of the Good," Aristotle is a realist concerned with the external presence of reality. Human behavior, Aristotle states, cannot be judged by the Platonic universal moral law since ethics is a practical science that deals with particular persons or groups involved in particular times and places.

Aristotle rejects Plato's theory of the Forms and insists that the basic moral principle is inherent in our activities. That principle can be discovered through studying these activities, although opinion about the nature of the moral principle may differ. The "good" we are seeking is different, for instance, in medicine, in military strategy, in architecture, and in other realms of human endeavor. In medicine, the good is health; in military strategy, victory; in architecture, a building both useful and beautiful. Even the same man identifies "the good" with different things: with health, for instance, when he is ill, or with wealth when he is poor.

In the *Poetics*, Aristotle sees two kinds of poetry, which reflect the differences in character between individual poets: One represents noble actions and noble personages, the other produces invectives and the actions of the ignoble. Like Plato, Aristotle relates art to morality as well as to the benefits it provides to mankind by pointing out that "to be learning something is the greatest of pleasures not only to the philosopher but also to the rest of mankind, however small their capacity for it; the reason of the delight in seeing the picture is that one is at the same time learning—gathering the meaning of things." (*Id.*, p. 1457.)

In his *Nichomachean Ethics*, the first systematic treatise of Western moral philosophy, Aristotle reaches the conclusion that in a "morally strong man" his soul "accepts the leadership of reason, and is perhaps more obedient in a self-controlled and courageous man, since in him everything is in harmony with the voice of reason." (*Nichomachean Ethics*, 1102b [25], trans. by Martin Ostwald, The Library of Liberal Arts, 1962, p. 31.)

Aristotle makes a distinction between practical and theoretical reason. Ethics deals with varying behaviors of individuals; therefore, the theoretical or universal concept of reason cannot be applied to individual human behavior, which in some measure is guided by expediency. This does not mean that the individual should not seek perfection. Man, according to Aristotle, can achieve moral goodness and perfection through contemplation, through the exercise of the distinctively human faculty of reason. Thus the life of contemplation, the life of the intellect, is the best, the most godlike. It leads to the imitation of God, since the activity of God that "surpasses all others in bliss must be a contemplative activity, and the human activity which is most closely akin to it is, therefore, most conducive to happiness." (*Id.*, 1178b [20], p. 293.) Of all animals, man alone possesses reason, which gives him the capacity to attain something resembling the divine activity of contemplation—the chief good, the source of the blessedness and happiness enjoyed by the gods. Within the ascending scale of goods, all other, lesser goods serve as a means toward the attainment of this end.

Plato and Aristotle had a large impact on philosophers of the seventeenth and eighteenth centuries who followed the idea of aiming art toward the inculcation of virtue and traditional values. Among those influenced by Plato, we need mention only Anthony Shaftesbury (1671–1713), the English statesman and philosopher who originated the term "moral sense" (by which he meant man's natural sense of right and wrong in a universe that he found essentially harmonious, even though it might appear discordant); Johann Winckelman (1717–1768), the German classical archaeologist and historian of ancient art; and Denis Diderot (1713–1784), the French encyclopedist and historian of art and literature.

Not only the philosophy but also the literature of ancient Greece reflects the conflict between morality and expediency. The story of Agamemnon and his daughter Iphigenia is part of the background of two of the greatest works of Greek literature, Homer's *Iliad* and Aeschylus' *Oresteia* trilogy, and is the subject of one of Euripides' most famous dramas, *Iphigenia in Aulis*, which has been much translated and imitated. Seeking to revenge the theft of his brother's wife, Agamemnon had set sail from Hellas as the head of the Greek armies. Harbored in the port of Aulis, the entire fleet found itself unable to sail because of unfavorable winds brought about through the action of gods whom Agamemnon had offended. When the great king inquired of his priests what course their oracles recommended, he was told that he was required to sacrifice his daughter Iphigenia. In spite of the protests of his wife, Clytemnestra (as well as those of Iphigenia's suitor Achilles in Euripides' version of the story),

Agamemnon follows this advice. This expedient sacrifice achieved its immediate end—it enabled Agamemnon to embark his armies to Troy. But this immoral act in the long run forged a chain of hatred and revenge that ended in Agamemnon's murder by his wife and her murder by two of their other children.

## C. Cicero

Aristotle's view that the exercise of reason leads to man's perfection was taken up and emphasized by the Roman Stoics, who saw the purpose of life as living in accordance with nature, which is governed by a universal reason they called the *logos*. For them, only actions for which reasons can be given can be considered moral. They distrust the emotions, which they claim tend to disturb the balance of the soul.

It was the Roman statesman and philosopher Cicero who, following his studies in Greece, brought the treasures of Greek thought within the reach of the Roman public. In his *De Officiis*, Cicero sees moral goodness, in the true and proper sense of the term, as the exclusive possession of the wise; it "can never be separated from virtue." (Trans. by Walter Miller, Harvard University Press, 1961, p. 281.) Cicero praises the wise man, who is guided by reason that "has proved that moral worth is the sole good." The wise man is "rightly the one and only free man, a subject to no man's authority." No bondage can enchain his soul. (*Finibus Bonorum et Malorum*, trans. by H. Rackham, Harvard University Press, 1971, p. 295.)

Cicero discusses in detail the conflict between expediency and moral rectitude and reaches the conclusion that "there never can be such a thing as a conflict between expediency and moral rectitude." (*De Officiis*, p. 277.) He sees no reason for introducing the counterbalancing of right and expediency or weighing the moral right against expedience, since expediency and moral rectitude are for him identical. "No more pernicious doctrine" could be introduced into human life than the separation of moral rectitude from expediency. (*Id.*, p. 177.) The usage of the word "expediency," according to Cicero, has been "corrupted and perverted" since a thing cannot be morally right without being expedient, and nothing can be expedient without being morally right. "[No] greater curse," wrote Cicero, "has ever assailed human life than the doctrine of those who have separated" the two conceptions of morality and expediency. (*Id.*, p. 201.)

Cicero simply denies that anything that is morally wrong can ever be expedient. For him, the good, the morally correct, action is the only action worth considering: "[I]t necessarily follows that the morally right is either the sole good or the supreme good. Now, that which is good is certainly expedient; consequently, that which is morally right is also expedient." (*Id.*, p. 303.) To neglect this truth, for Cicero, is to open the door to assassination and murder, to theft, forgery, and embezzlement, to lust for excessive wealth and for despotic power.

It is only in situations where "knavery wears the mask of wisdom" that the expedient seems to conflict with the good. The only way to prevent such conflicts, according to Cicero, is to apply a single standard in which expediency and moral rectitude can be judged. For Cicero, there is no advantage, whether a material gain or a political success—not even a victory in war—that is worth having at the sacrifice of a person's reputation and good conscience. "What is there that your so-called expediency can bring to you that will compensate for what it can take away, if it steals for you the name of a 'good man' and causes you to lose your sense of honor and justice?" (*Id.*, p. 355.)

Cicero's well-reasoned defense of morality against the spurious claims of expediency appears to break down when he examines the issue of conflicting loyalties to the state and to the family. Even in matters of serious moral transgression, Cicero seems to be saying, family loyalty overrides other moral claims. Even if a father were "robbing temples or making underground passages to the treasury," a son should not report his father to the authorities but should, rather, defend his father if he is indicted. (*De Officiis*, p. 365.)

But Cicero's defense of loyalty to the family founders on the issue of crimes against the state itself. In the case of treason, or in the case of the usurpation of power that would abolish the Republic and erect a monarchy, Cicero asserts that it is the duty of a son first to plead with his father not to do the wrong, then to chide and even threaten him. But in the end, if the father will not be dissuaded, the son must "sacrifice his father to the safety of the country." (*Id.*, p. 367.) Cicero would deny that this is a case of expediency. He would argue that the state simply has a higher moral claim on the individual than family unity does.

On a similar note in *De Amicitia,* in discussing the laws of friendship—with loyalty as one of its distinguishing qualities—Cicero maintains that loyalty cannot go so far as to cause a person to commit a crime against the republic. The first law of friendship is to do for a friend only what is honorable. This law forbids one to ask a friend to perform dishonorable acts or to do them oneself if asked. It is dishonorable for anyone to plead loyalty as a mitigating circumstance in defense of sins against the state committed for "the sake of a friend." No one, according to Cicero, can argue that it is permissable to follow a friend "when waging war against his country." (*De Amicitia*, trans. by William Armstead Falcon, Harvard University Press, 1971, pp. 151–158. For an additional discussion of Cicero's treatment of the topic of loyalty, see my book *Equality, Tolerance, and Loyalty*, The University of Texas at Dallas, 1990, pp. 64–66.)

The Roman historian Tacitus concurs with Cicero that the claims of the state outweigh other claims; he praises a violation of moral claims in the interest of the state in terms that leave no doubt that expediency has overtaken morality. Tacitus reports a debate in the Roman Senate over a case in which some of the Senators want to dispense with an ancient law requiring all slaves in a household to be executed when one of them rebels and harms a master.

The senator Gaius Cassius argues that the ancient law should be upheld; in fact, it has in his view become even more important because so many of the slaves are being imported from less civilized corners of the empire: "You will never coerce such a medley of humanity except by terror." He is willing to stand against the outcry that thus innocent lives must be lost and compares the situation with the slaves to that of the practice of decimation of a routed army, when the lot of death may fall on the brave as well: "All great examples carry with them something of injustice—injustice compensated, as against individual suffering, by the advantage of the community." (Tacitus, *Annals*, Book IV, xliv. Trans. by John Jackson, Harvard University Press, 1937, p. 179.)

This is another classic statement stressing that moral justice must be sacrificed on the altar of expediency for the sake of "public welfare." Cicero's idea of the "safety of the country" or Tacitus' of the "advantage of the community" were forerunners of Machiavellianism, which carries the implication that the root of political effectiveness and success is force, unrestricted by considerations of generally accepted moral values. (We shall return to Machiavelli's ideas later in our discussion.) Cicero and Tacitus, both honorable men, undoubtedly based their views on the premise of a state worthy of loyalty and respect, founded on the old Roman principle *salus populi suprema lex*. A claim of moral obligation to a state dominated by totalitarian dictators would be a vicious error, however, since such a claim would exonerate terror, which uses such means as the encouragement of family members to denounce one another. We have seen the heartbreaking results of this practice in Stalin's mass arrests and in his awarding medals to sons who denounced their parents, and more recently in the case of the Chinese massacre in Tiananmen Square and the subsequent reward of a mother who had denounced her son and of a sister who had denounced her brother.

## D. *The Old Testament*

The ancient Hebrews did not use the tools of philosophy to discover a code of right and wrong. Their God was their lawgiver, and their code was a matter of supernatural revelation, first given at Sinai and later elaborated on and intensified by the prophets. Knowledge of what constituted good and evil was taught by parents to children (Proverbs 1:8), passed on by the instruction of the wise (Proverbs 13:14), and acquired by a life of holiness and "fear of the Lord."

Did the Hebrews and their leaders follow these commandments that their God had given them? Not at all. The historical account of the eras of the Judges and the Kings in the Old Testament sets forth three centuries of wars, intrigues, religious conflicts, barbaric assassinations, treason, and fratricidal murder.

The width of the gulf between the sublime morality that marked Hebrew belief and the stark reality of its practice can be seen in the lives of the two greatest Old Testament political leaders, David and his son Solomon. David received God's favor at an early age, was credited with a deep spirituality that attributed most of the Psalms to his authorship, and was the prototype and ancestor of the promised Messiah. Yet his life was marked by grave transgressions. His most famous wrongdoing, which provoked him to write the penitential Psalm 51, was the seduction of Bathsheba and the order that her husband, Uriah, should be sent to his death in battle. For his sin against Uriah, David was severely rebuked by the prophet Nathan.

Even on his deathbed, David's conduct was far from forgiveness and gratitude. The dying king instructed his son by Bathsheba, Solomon, to kill Joab, the general in chief of his army, despite Joab's great contribution to the creation of David's empire. Joab's loyalty to David can be seen from the fact that it was he whom David had relied on to see that Uriah would die. Nevertheless, at the end of David's reign, Joab was slain "in the tent of the Lord"—even while he was claiming sanctuary by holding onto the horns of Jehovah's altar—for his part in the plot to make Adonijah, rather than Solomon, David's successor to the throne. Before his death, David also sought revenge on old enemies. He ordered his successor to bring the head of his foe Shimei "down to the grave." Shimei, a Benjamite of the clan of Saul, had cursed and thrown stones at David when he came to the village of Bahurim while fleeing from Absalom. The vow David had made at that time not to punish Shimei was obviously not binding on Solomon, who gave orders for Shimei to be killed when he violated an order not to leave Jerusalem.

Solomon's reign became emblematic in later Jewish history for a period of magnificence and tranquility. But there was a sad irony in the contrast between the reputation of Solomon as the wisest of the wise and his behavior. The tales of Solomon's atrocities include the murder of his elder brother Adonijah and the "levy of forced labor" that numbered 30,000 men sent in relays of 10,000 a month to cut cedar wood in Lebanon to build a palace for the king and a temple for Jehovah. Solomon's religious loyalty also was compromised by his sacrifices to the national deities of his numerous wives.

Purges and assassinations of rivals or potential opponents may seem to be expedient in the short run, but in the long run nothing established by vindictiveness, violence, coercion, and oppression can endure. Without adherence to a moral code and to the commandments conveyed by the prophets, the kingdom of the Hebrews was destined to deteriorate. With the end of Solomon's reign, the northern half of his kingdom, oppressed by high taxation, broke off from Jerusalem to become the kingdom of Israel, while Jerusalem remained the capital of the tribe of Judah, which was encircled by enemies.

Surrounded by Egypt, Syria, Assyria, and Phoenicia, the Hebrews sought alliances with their neighbors, to mention only the friendly relations of David and Solomon with Hiram, the king of Tyre; the marriage of Solomon to a daughter of Pharaoh; and the exchange of diplomatic letters between King Hezekiah and the king of Babylon. The prophets continually not only warned against trusting in such alliances but also foretold that disaster would occur unless the kings and the people repented from their evil ways and again fulfilled the commandments.

The varying alliances—first with one and then with another against the first—ended when Israel fell into captivity by Assyria (721 B.C.) and when Judah, after becoming an Egyptian tributary, fell before Nebuchadnezzar II of Babylon (604 B.C.). The four centuries of the Hebrew kingdom thus came to an end when a great part of the Jewish nation "that had escaped from the sword" was carried away to captivity in Babylon. The conqueror also "burnt the house of God, and burned down the wall of Jerusalem and burnt all the palaces thereof with fire, and destroyed all the godly vessels thereof." (II Chronicles 36:18–20.) According to the interpretation of the prophets, this evil had come upon the people because they had forsaken the ways of goodness that their God had revealed to them.

## Christianity: The Authority of the Church

The prophets offered comfort to the exiled Jews in two ways. They prophesied that the people would eventually

return to the land of Israel, that the glory of their kingdom would be restored. This promise was, in addition,
extended to a reassurance that the Jews were the chosen
people of God, even though dispersed through other
lands, and that God would send them a Messiah who
would realize the promises made to Abraham and
through the prophets. The followers of Jesus of Nazareth
found in Him the Messiah described by the prophet
Isaiah:

> "He was despised and rejected by men. A man of
> sorrows and acquainted with grief, he was wounded
> for our transgressions and bruised for our iniquities,
> upon him was the chastisement which makes us
> whole, by his stripes we are healed...."(Isaiah 5:3-7.)

The rapid spread of Christian teaching extended into
Asia Minor and throughout the Mediterranean basin. In
337 A.D., Constantine the Great, emperor of Rome, was
baptized a Christian on his deathbed, and Christianity
became the official religion of the Roman empire.

The Christian morality expressed in the teaching of
Jesus about the Kingdom of Heaven stressed God's universal fatherhood, the brotherhood of all mankind, and a
new birth of the human soul in the kingdom of love. His
teaching removed all barriers between man and God.
Forbearance and renunciation, He taught, must be cul-
tivated in order for a person to enter the spiritual kingdom of heaven. Loyalty to God rests on three virtues that
converge in Christ—faith, hope, and love—and should
emanate from integrity of heart.

The Christian concern with otherworldly salvation
as the unifying and rewarding good and with eternal
damnation as a moral sanction was combined with, and

perhaps contradicted by, a reliance on expediency and political ambitions on the part of some Christians to turn the world into a "spiritual society," with the church as the ruler over all the nations. Thus loyalty to God became entangled with the problems of loyalty to the church as an institution that wanted to change this world into a theological kingdom of heaven.

Although the prophetic teaching of Jesus called for a purity of heart that would establish the kingdom of God in the hearts of men, the church abandoned His teaching by becoming a political body patterned after the traditions of the Roman empire. The pope took the title of *pontifex maximus* (which the emperors had held) and, in his capacity as the only lawgiver of Christendom, demanded supremacy over the kings who ruled terrestrial states. The autocratic church thus became involved in violent controversies and political struggles.

In the Sermon on the Mount, Jesus taught, "Blessed are the peacemakers." The history of the church in the eleventh through the thirteenth centuries is one of constant struggle between heads of state and the popes. The church demanded that all earthly monarchs must be in subjection to the church, since the monarchs ruled the body while the church, as the ecclesiastical ruler of the world, held dominion over the spirit. The principle of investiture (the issue of who had the power to select and install bishops) was the cause of warfare between Pope Gregory VII and Holy Roman Emperor Henry IV. Pope Innocent III, to cite another example, was constantly active in the political affairs of the empire and assumed the role of self-appointed arbiter of all the world's conflicts.

Although the teaching of Jesus transcended all social, political, and economic circumstances, the morality of the New Testament discriminates in favor of the poor, beginning with Mary's Magnificat: "He has torn imperial powers from their thrones, but the humble have been lifted high. The hungry he has satisfied with good things, the rich sent empty away." The church, for the sake of expediency and in contradiction to the spirit of the One whose name it bore, sought power as well as riches. Acting like a state within a state, it had its own law courts with a jurisdiction not limited to matters of faith, maintained prisons, levied taxes upon its subjects, and accumulated enormous wealth by acquiring vast properties and income from fees.

Jesus, who passionately praised poverty as an ideal that leads to purity of heart, came riding into the Holy City on the back of an ass, a beast of burden, a symbol of humility. The popes preferred to live in royal luxury to assert with vanity and pride their own omnipotence. They strove to affirm that the papal power with its arbitrary authority should prevail over the power of secular rulers. This struggle for power is well illustrated by the conflict, mentioned above, that took place in the eleventh century between Pope Gregory VII and Emperor Henry IV. When Gregory excommunicated Henry, the German emperor went to Canossa to appear as a humble suppliant before the pope. For three days in midwinter he waited as a barefoot pilgrim to beg the pope's pardon. Figuratively speaking, "going to Canossa" has become a standing symbol for humiliating submission.

Jesus taught, "Blessed are the merciful" and "Love your enemies." The church that bore his name found a more expedient way of dealing with its enemies. The intolerance that the church exhibited over the centuries was abominable. Those who dared to dissent were executed—burned to death or hanged or subjected to yet worse torture. The twelfth-century monk Arnold de Brescia, who advocated the idea that the church had no right to hold property, was tried and executed by the Roman Curia. The Italian Dominican friar Savonarola, who preached against corruption and predicted an ensuing punishment of the church and its subsequent regeneration, was hanged by the Florentine government after it had forced him to confess that he was not a prophet.

John Wycliff, an outspoken critic of the corruption of the church and a scholar whose translation of the Bible was an important landmark in the history of English literature, was condemned twice as a heretic for spreading the doctrine that the scriptures are the supreme authority of the faith. The pope ordered Wycliff's book to be burned. By a decree of the Council of Constance (1415) and at the command of Pope Martin V, his remains were dug up from his grave and burned. Jan Huss, the Bohemian reformer and leading opponent of the condemnation of Wycliff's writings, presented himself at the Council of Constance under the protection of Emperor Sigismund's safe-conduct, only to be imprisoned, tried, and burned at the stake as a heretic.

Even in matters of salvation, the church used vicious expedients to justify persecution for the sake of religious conformity. The leaders of the church argued that Christ's commandment to "go out on the highway and hedgerows and make them come in" (Luke 14:23) justified forced conversion. When torture was used as a means of conversion, the leaders of the church maintained, the pain used to coerce agreement was nothing compared to that which "heretics" and "schismatics" would suffer in hell, where those who remain outside the faith are condemned to burn forever. If a person died in the process of torture, at least he was rewarded with eternal life.

Expediency divorced from morality satisfied the exalted immediate worldly ambitions of the church, but it brought the church to its lowest point spiritually. Ecclesiastic offices and honors were bought and sold for money and power. By the purchase of indulgences, the buyer's soul was protected from suffering in purgatory. For payments of money, the church set aside its binding laws and provided dispensations.

After the Reformation, the early Protestants, like the Catholics, believed that any opposition to their religious practices implied evil and had to be eradicated. If someone remained outside their faith, he was condemned to burn forever in hell. Therefore, it was reasoned, he should be compelled by force, even by torture if necessary, to change his beliefs. Michael Servetus, the Spanish physician and theologian (1511–1553), was condemned by John Calvin for his antitrinitarian writings, seized in Geneva by Calvin's order, and after a long trial burned at the stake on October 27, 1553.

Hugo Grotius, a Dutch humanist and jurist (1583–1645), the "miracle of Holland" who at the age of eleven was admitted to the University of Leiden and who later received recognition in the academic world as the "father of international law" and the "father of natural law," was sentenced to life imprisonment and forfeiture of all property for endorsing the Arminian faction in its controversy with the Gomarist faction of the Protestants in the

Netherlands. The Arminians challenged the doctrine of unconditional predestination, a challenge that contradicted the conservative Calvinism that was strong among the Netherlands Protestants. After his conviction for treason and imprisonment in 1619, Grotius in 1621 escaped into France, where he published his famous masterpiece, *De Jure Belli ac Pacis*. The leader of the Arminians, Orden Oldenbarneveldt, was less fortunate; he was tried and beheaded.

### The Renaissance: Machiavelli

In the secular world, the Renaissance—which is generally identified as stretching from the fourteenth century through the seventeenth century—was the age both of a weakening of the Catholic church's hold on the consciences of people and of the concentration of power in the hands of the European monarchs, such as the Holy Roman Emperor Charles V (who held sway over more territory than any other European ruler), King Francis I of France, and King Henry VIII of England.

The art of governing, suitable for rulers who seek power, was expounded by Italian political theorists, especially Niccolo Machiavelli (1469-1527). By divorcing the study of effective politics from the study of ethics, Machiavelli completely dissevered himself from the traditional concepts of the power that conscience should wield over individuals. In his writings, which became the blueprint for efforts of dictators and absolute monarchs, he stressed that the root of political expediency and success is force, unrestricted by considerations of generally accepted moral values.

A ruler, according to Machiavelli, "must not mind incurring the charge of cruelty for the purpose of keeping the subjects united and faithful." (*The Prince*, The New Library, 1952, p. 89.) Since it is difficult for a ruler to be both loved and feared, "it is much safer for a ruler to be feared than loved." (*Id.*, p. 90.) He should not hesitate "to act against faith, against charity, against humanity, and against religion" in order "to maintain the state." (*Id.*, p. 93.)

In order to achieve political ends, Machiavelli argued, a ruler may lie, deceive, intrigue, conspire, or use any kind of crooked means. In foreign policy, "a prince should therefore have no other aims or thought, nor take up any other thing for his study, but war and its organization and discipline, for that is the only art necessary to one who commands." (*Id.*, pp. 46–47.) It seems that *The Prince* continued to serve as a handbook for aggressors such as Mussolini, Hitler, Stalin, and his successors, who in accordance with maxims prescribed by Machiavelli sought through aggression increased power and a solution to their economic and political problems.

In the seventeenth and eighteenth centuries, with the recognized authority of the monarchies, such as the English and the French, and of the right to succession, the main political problems were: What are the remedies of subjects when fundamental human rights are violated? and How is peace to be preserved among nations? The principles of natural law made a great appeal to those interested in solving these problems. While on the domestic front the natural, fundamental human rights gained importance in shaping modern democracies, on the international stage a new concept of natural law had to be developed.

It was Hugo Grotius who sought to elaborate the natural law tradition in its application to international affairs in order to mold a coherent idea of world order. Among the leaders of nations, the theory of a balance of power gained popularity as the only hope for creating an international stage—combining political, legal, and moral considerations—and as the only hope for stability in the world arena where the struggle for power meant the struggle for survival.

## The Balance of Power

To begin our consideration of the balance of power idea with the most recent events, we may observe that since World War II the United States and its allies have tried to maintain a balance of power among the states in the Persian Gulf region, which is rich in oil reserves. In this three-sided region there are two ambitious, militarily strong but economically weak nations—Iraq and Iran—and a defenseless collection of rich monarchies—Saudi Arabia, Kuwait, and the Gulf emirates. In its desire to prevent a hostile power from gaining control over a source of energy deemed indispensable to the free world, the United States supported the Shah of Iran against the Muslim fundamentalists and later, after the fall of the Shah, was inclined to favor Iraq during its war with the Ayatollah Khomeini's Iran. After Iraq's aggression against Kuwait, to preserve a balance of power in the Gulf region as well as to remove the threat of Iraqi nuclear weapons, the United States and its allies sent their young men and women to war against Iraq.

Even while military strikes against Iraqi troops were taking place and soldiers were dying on the battlefield, world leaders, claiming farsightedness, remained concerned about weakening the balance of power in the Middle East. Although the immediate reason for going to war was to reverse Iraq's "naked aggression" against Kuwait, the essential strategy—derived from Gulf strategy in the past—was to keep a balance of power among the Gulf states.

With President George Bush's call for "a new world order" came the assurance that the purpose of the war was not to destroy or dismember Iraq. In balance of power terms it was not in the interest of the United States and its allies to tear apart Iraq. A greatly weakened Iraq could bring a dangerous instability to the region by enhancing the power of Iran and Syria, which, as experience shows, are as great a threat to the Free World's interests in this region as is Iraq. As paradoxical as it sounds, assurances were voiced that the purpose of the war was not to break up Iraq, but to maintain its territorial integrity and military power, which will enable it to serve as a counterweight to other powers in the Gulf region.

In international relations, according to the balance of power principle, the maintenance of peace depends upon the prevention of any nation's becoming powerful enough to endanger the independence of any other. Although the principles of the balance of power have been associated mainly with modern diplomacy, they can be traced to the political arrangements of the Greek city-states in the fifth and fourth centuries B.C. that preserved their independence by protecting them from a dominant hegemony of one of the states.

In the Middle Ages, the balance of power policy guided the city-states in Italy that gained their independence, as did other free towns in Europe, by revolt against their feudal lords. The rivalry of these independent towns was intense. The application of the balance of power mechanism assured the survivability of these city-states, which were prosperous but racked by frequent revolutions and bloodshed.

According to the balance of power theory, a country should, to preserve its own independence, intervene in a conflict outside its borders on the side of the weaker state, which would otherwise lose the war and thus disturb the military and political balance of a world divided into a number of viable political entities. Shufflings of alliances based on the balance of power principle have dominated European politics since the sixteenth century.

King Henry VIII of England (1509–1547) supported Emperor Charles V of Germany when Francis I of France was winning the conflict between them, then abandoned Charles when Francis had been defeated. The French prelate Cardinal Richelieu (1585-1642), prime minister under Louis XIII, joined the Thirty Years' War (1618-1648), a destructive religious conflict, on the side of the Protestant Swedes and North Germans in order to gain territory from Catholic Spain. The Treaty of Utrecht (1713), which concluded the War of the Spanish Succession between the Bourbons and the Hapsburgs by dividing a number of territories generously between them, contained a clause by which the signatories accepted the obligation to maintain the balance of power that the treaty established. The so-called balance of power thus became a principle of international order to be sought by diplomats in their negotiations, rather than a mere political cliche without real substance.

For reasons of expediency rather than morality, the balance of power doctrine caused alliances to shift frequently. In the middle of the eighteenth century, Great Britain and Austria were aligned against France and Prussia in the War of the Austrian Succession (1740-1748). Eight years later, Britain and Prussia were allied against France and Austria in the Seven Years War (1756-1763). In the nineteenth century, the Quadruple Alliance of Russia, Prussia, Great Britain, and Austria opposed French ambitions in Egypt in 1840. In 1879, the Dual Alliance between Germany and Austria was aimed at Russia and France. This alliance became known as another Quadruple Alliance when Italy in 1882 and Rumania in 1883 came into the Bismarckian system.

It was because of the threat of a French hegemony in Europe that Great Britain—which for a long time favored a multinational balance of power in Europe (on land but not on the seas, where it claimed preponderance)—tolerated the success of Bismarck's army in the Prussian wars with Denmark (1864), Austria (1866), and France (1870). Did the balance of power doctrine satisfy the demands of traditional moral values as well as the claims of expediency?

Jean Fenelon, a French theologian and author (1651-1715), gave an affirmative answer when he praised the balance of power idea in the early eighteenth century:

"Each nation is accordingly obliged to take care to prevent the excessive aggrandizement of each neighbor, for its own security. To prevent the neighbor from becoming too powerful is not to do wrong; it is to protect oneself from slavery and to protect one's other neighbors from it; in a word, it is to work for liberty, for tranquility, for the public safety: because the aggrandizement of one nation beyond a certain limit changes the general system of all the nations which have relation to it." (Quoted in Edward Vos Gulick, *Europe's Classical Balance of Power*, Cornell University Press, 1955, p. 50.)

John Stuart Mill, the famous nineteenth-century liberal, took a similar position. According to him, the balance of power is valuable to the freedom of the world and the interests of every civilized people. It safeguarded the liberties of the peoples of the Continent who were struggling against foreign aggression and tyranny. In a letter to James Beal, Mill wrote:

"Every civilized country is entitled to settle its internal affairs in its own way, and no other country ought to interfere with its discretion, because one country, even with the best intentions, has no chance of properly understanding the internal affairs of another, but when this indefeasible liberty of an independent country has already been interfered with; when it is kept in subjection to foreign power, either directly, or by assistance given to its native tyrants, I hold that any nation whatever may rightfully interfere to protect the country against this wrongful interference." (John Stuart Mill, *Collected Works*, Vol. 16, *The Later Letters of John Stuart Mill, 1849-1873*, ed. by Francis E. Mineka and Dwight N. Lindley, University of Toronto Press, 1972, p. 1033. Letter 799. To James Beal, from Avignon, April 17, 1865.)

Mill favored the interference of France in 1859 to free Italy from the "Austrian yoke" and the use of armed force in defense of the liberties of the peoples of the Continent who were struggling against tyranny.

## Moral and the Balance of Power

In examining the question of whether the balance of power doctrine combines moral values with its claims to expediency, we are reminded of a passage that appeared in *The Federalist*, the eighty-five essays written in 1787 by James Madison, Alexander Hamilton, and John Jay under the joint pen name Publius. In *The Federalist* 51 we find the famous sentence, "If men were angels, no government would be necessary." To paraphrase the assertions linked with this sentence, we could say that "if men were angels" there would be no problem in reconciling morality and expediency in world politics.

The idea of the balance of power grew in a world of independent nation-states, and as long as we have such independent states lacking effective means of collective security, the balance of power doctrine at least protects a country against aggression or wrongful interference. Throughout the centuries, concepts of morality have come into play when states have had to choose among actions that would affect the balance of power. Moral choices in the international sphere, however, are seldom self-evident. They depend on prudent choices between uncertain outcomes. One must appreciate the difficulty, even for the most upright and honorable statesmen, in choosing the best course for a nation. In the realm of international affairs, where so many imponderables can occur, often a course that seems wisest at the time it was taken may be seen as a wrong moral choice in the perspective of history. The central things are that the light by which leaders navigate should be morality and that moral considerations should outshine the false beacon of expediency in their hearts.

### The Holy Alliance: Talleyrand and Metternich

After the fall of the Napoleonic empire, the monarchs of Austria, Prussia, and Russia banded together at the Congress of Vienna in 1815 to create the Holy Alliance. The Alliance and the Concert of Europe that grew out of it sought to preserve the peace through a federation of great sovereigns. In the Holy Alliance, religious zeal was added to the moral aspects of political stability. The document establishing the Alliance opens, "In the name of the most Holy and Indivisible Trinity." In it, the participating monarchs agreed to protect true religion, acknowledged Christ as the real King of all Christian peoples, and committed themselves to act in consonance with Christian principles. In this pious ecstasy, Czar Alexander I managed to annex a great part of Poland, with smaller pieces being ceded to Austria and Prussia. Great Britain did not sign the document, rejecting it as "a piece of pious mystification."

The two leading spirits behind the machinations of the Congress of Vienna were Charles Maurice de Talleyrand-Perigord (1754–1838) and Prince Clemens Metternich (1773–1859). Talleyrand was a French statesman and diplomat whose name the history of diplomacy identifies with expediency. His insensitivity to principles of morality or loyalty was unique in that he managed to wield authority under four successive and mutually incompatible governments of France: the *ancien regime* of the Bourbons, the Revolutionary government, Napoleon's empire, and the restoration of the Bourbons. Trained for the priesthood and then ordained, he became a bishop and thus a member of the Estates General, where he identified himself with the ideas of the French Revolution by proposing the confiscation of the estates of the church. Denounced as a suspect during the revolutionary purges, Talleyrand was forced to flee. He returned to France after the fall of Robespierre to serve the Directory and the Consulate. Shifting allegiance with each new change in the wind, he became active, after Napoleon's defeat, in the restoration of the Bourbons and offered his diplomatic talents to Louis XVIII, who made him minister of foreign affairs.

The success at the Congress of Vienna of Talleyrand's arguments of "legitimacy"—which called for a restoration of the boundaries and of the reigning families of European countries as they were before the French Revolution—should be attributed to his powers of persuasion. This principle of legitimacy seemed to introduce a moral element into the diplomatic negotiations. Thanks to this ploy, Talleyrand achieved a new footing for France as a member of the Holy Alliance in place of his nation's former status as a conquered, powerless bystander.

Another prominent statesman instrumental in forming the so-called Holy Alliance was Prince Metternich, the Austrian minister of foreign affairs, who constantly sought to strengthen Austria's diplomatic position in international conferences. During the Napoleonic War, he succeeded in arranging the marriage of the Archduchess Marie Louise to Napoleon in 1810 and in arranging a temporary alliance of Austria with France in 1812.

In his desire to replace French supremacy with Austrian, he masterminded the Quadruple Alliance of 1814 (Austria, England, Prussia, and Russia), which sought to secure the overthrow of Napoleon and to restrict French territorial claims. The war of this coalition against France ended with allied victory at Leipzig in 1814.

With French domination checked, Metternich—who believed in the existence of general laws governing the relations between nations—tried to prevent a strengthening of Prussia and Russia that might upset the balance of power. Alarmed at the advances of liberalism and nationalism, he injected into the Holy Alliance the function of ideological surveillance. The power of his influence is evidenced by the fact that the period 1815–1848 has been called "the age of Metternich." In his contempt for liberalism, which he regarded as incompatible with the principle of the balance of power, he directed a repressive system based on espionage and political and religious censorship. Because he had suppressed the liberal movement, the Revolution of 1848 forced him to seek refuge in England. (He returned to Austria in 1851.)

The Holy Alliance and the Concert of Europe drew a map that was to last for nearly forty years on the face of the war-exhausted continent. Since the congresses and conferences that succeeded the Concert did not provide rules for settling vital international questions, the process of shifting alliances and alignments was resumed with zest by the great powers around mid-century. An example of the result of the clashing designs of Russia, France, and Great Britain for the Balkans was the Crimean War. In 1821 the insurrection of the Greeks against the Turks had taken place. Through a joint action of Britain, France, and Russia, Greece had become free. Russia invaded Turkey, and the French and English fleets destroyed the Turkish fleet. But when Russia sought a protectorate over the Christians in the Balkans and occupied the Danubian principalities in 1853, France and Great Britain cemented their insecure friendship in an alliance to side with Turkey against Russia. The defeat of Russia in the ensuing Crimean War prevented Russia from having a powerful influence in the Balkans.

## The Erosion of the Balance of Power: Bismarck's Realpolitik

Napoleon had attempted to overthrow the system of the balance of power, and the Congress of Vienna tried to restore it by injecting the new ideal of the Concert of Europe. According to some historians, the Congress served as a dividing mark between the old order and the modern order of Europe. The Congress, however, did not have the same impact as some other international treaties, to mention only the Peace of Westphalia of 1648 that ended the Thirty Years War. That treaty marked the beginning of the modern state system by acknowledging the existence of independent, sovereign states whose princes enjoyed the status of equality with emperor and pope. Under the Treaty of Westphalia, Christianity had ceased to be a relevant factor in international relations. Most of the monarchs participating in the Congress of Vienna considered the commitment they made to reconcile practical political pursuits with the dictates of Christian conscience as merely a pious gesture.

One of the great weaknesses of the balance of power theory was the difficulty in determining the ingredients of power. The question that has continually posed itself to diplomats has been whether the size of the territories of participating states, their economic strength, or the size of their populations should serve as an equalizer among states. The Holy Alliance did not provide an answer to this question since it did not quantify the concept of power. Its main purpose was to restore the conditions that existed before the French Revolution and the defeat of Napoleon. The new boundaries drawn in Vienna in disregard of ethnic considerations and language differences, along with the growing resentment toward the traditions of oppression established by the great monarchs, did not provide a climate suitable to a secure peace.

Furthermore, the balance of power implies a maintenance of the status quo, while change, as history teaches us, is inevitable. Change is the law of life. The advantages of mass military mobilization exploited by Napoleon and expanded by other European regimes, combined with the industrial revolution, with its technological developments that provided armies with rapid steam transport on land and sea, caused the destabilization of the peace and the erosion of the balance of power theory. It was presumed that victory would be achieved by whichever army could be mobilized quickly enough to strike first.

In the game of international diplomacy during the second half of the nineteenth century, attention shifted to a new Germany that had been formed by adding a number of smaller German-speaking states to Prussia. (It did not incorporate all of Europe's speakers of that language, since Austria maintained its own empire encompassing culturally and linguistically diverse nationalities.) The man who consolidated Germany under the Prussian

Hohenzollerns was Otto von Bismarck (1815–1898). After the defeat of France in the Franco-Prussian War of 1870–71, he created the German empire and became its chancellor.

For a number of years, Bismarck adhered to the balance of power reasoning by forming the Three Emperors League (composed of Germany, Russia, and Austria) in 1872, strengthened by formal treaties in 1881 and 1884, and the Dual Alliance with Austria in 1879, which became the Quadruple Alliance after Italy and Rumania came into the Bismarckian system in 1882. His systems of alignments and alliances can be attributed to a desire to achieve the inhibiting effect of a balance of power policy, but for many of his contemporaries Bismarck epitomized realpolitik, the science of politics guided by expediency and divorced from any moral consideration.

In his last novel, entitled *Endymion*, the English Prime Minister Benjamin Disraeli (who also wrote fiction in his spare time) is said to have based a character named the Count of Ferroll on Bismarck. Here is Disraeli's description of his phantom Bismarck:

> "He is a man neither to love nor to detest. He has himself an intelligence superior to all passion, I might say all feeling; and if, in dealing with such a person, we ourselves have either, we might give him an advantage." (Quoted in W.N. Medlicott, *Bismarck and Modern Germany*, Harper & Row, 1965, p. 190.)

For Bismarck, politics was "the art of the possible," the use of any advantage in order to coerce others to adopt policies favorable to Germany. For him international political life became a game played upon a gi-

gantic worldwide chessboard and in which he prepared
magnificent strategies for victory. Bismarck wrote, "To
be sure, one can bring individual matters to a conclusion,
but even then there is no way of knowing what the consequences will be. . . . In politics there is no such thing
as complete certainty and results," and "Politics is not
in itself an exact and logical science, but it is the capacity
to choose in each fleeting moment of the situation that
which is least harmful or most opportune." (Quoted in
Otto Pflanze, *Bismarck and the Development of Germany*, Princeton University Press, 1963, pp. 88, 89.)

The developments mentioned above—the idea of realpolitik combined with the new military technology developed after the industrial revolution, new mobilization
systems, and the rising wave of nationalism—disturbed
the stable equilibrium that had been offered by the balance of power peace. Expediency with the taste of swift
victory to be achieved by a first-strike offensive, along
with the animosities among the powers engaged in colonial expansion, led to World War I, in which the United
States intervened when disruption of commerce due to
submarine warfare and the stalemated war endangered
its economic well-being.

### Neutrality

From the beginning of its history, even before the
adoption of the Monroe Doctrine in December 1823, the
United States has tried to safeguard its hegemonic position in the Western Hemisphere; more recently it has
sought to maintain the balance of power in Europe. In
his famous "doctrine," President James Monroe declared
that, on one hand, the American continents "are hence-

forth not to be considered as subjects for future coloni-
zation by any European powers," and on the other hand,
the United States would not interfere in European affairs that did not concern the safety and interests of
America.

This major national policy with its firm, unambiguous
political warning, uttered well in advance, blocked Russian designs to extend Alaska southward, was applied
against Napoleon III and Maximilian when the presence
of the French army in Mexico constituted a radical in-
fraction of the Monroe Doctrine, and kept this country at
peace with external powers for almost 100 years. The re-
fusal of the United States to enter the League of Nations
may fairly be explained in part as a decision to adhere
to the policy laid down by the Monroe Doctrine.

Since the security of the United States and its pre-
dominance in this hemisphere could be challenged by
Europe, the only effective restraint upon the European
nations from seeking expansion beyond the ocean was
the maintenance of the balance of power in Europe. This
balance was indispensable for successful implementation of the Monroe Doctrine. The first century and a half
of our history as a nation is marked by a determination
not to involve ourselves in European power politics. Only
when the balance of power was disturbed by aggression
and the outbreak of two world wars threatened the peace
of the Western Hemisphere did we convert our potential
power into firing power.

*A. George Washington*

In the history of our nation, Monroe's principles of foreign policy were not new. The Treaty of 1778 between

France and the United States bound each to become the ally of the other in case of war. When during the French Revolution war was declared between France and England, Washington, in defiance of the treaty, issued the Proclamation of Neutrality (1793). (It should be mentioned that the treaty referred only to defensive wars, while France was waging an offensive war. Furthermore, the treaty had been made with the French king who had since been guillotined.)

What are the moral aspects of neutrality? Washington's proclamation of neutrality was met with bitter attacks against his character. His popularity suffered because the French Revolution found enthusiastic support in the United States. Jefferson, referring to the Revolution, wrote, "Rather than it should have failed, I would have seen half the earth desolated; were there but an Adam and Eve left in every country, and left free, it would be better than it is now." (The Federalists, called the "English party," deplored the lawlessness and the violence of the Revolution, while the followers of Jefferson became known as the "French party.")

Washington's staunch adherence to the principle of neutrality and his courage to stand against the participation of the young nation in the political adventures and wars of Europe can be explained by his determination to start a new nation with a new purpose and not to rehabilitate the old society that the settlers of the United States had left behind them. The society they founded had a radically different purpose from those existing societies in Europe.

This purpose was so firmly wedded to peace that in his Farewell Address Washington reiterated his position on neutrality: "The great rule of conduct for us, in regard

to foreign Nations, is, in extending our commercial relations, to have with them as little Political connection
as possible." (*The Washington Papers*, ed. by Saul K.
Padover, Harper & Brothers, 1955, pp. 321–322.) He had
no intention of accepting the principles of European nations as a pattern for the new American society and felt
that this hemisphere should be free of involvement in the
political and military struggles of Europe by refraining
from all direct or indirect participation in European
wars and by maintaining an impartial attitude toward
each belligerent.

## B. President Woodrow Wilson

By the time of President Woodrow Wilson, more than a
century after Washington, the place of the United States
among the nations of the world had greatly changed. At
the beginning of his presidency, however, Wilson believed, as Washington had before him, that it was better
for the United States to stay out of European conflicts.
Fundamentally a moralist, Wilson, the deeply religious
son of a Presbyterian minister, believed with a mission-
ary zeal that the role of this nation is to live and act on
moral principles of service to humanity and not to act on
dictates of immediate expediency. He was convinced
that the guiding principle for the United States in world
politics should be to serve not as a master among nations
but as a friend, with the moral responsibility to place its
power at the service of mankind.

In his faith in the supremacy of spiritual force, Wilson
tried to find a basis for peace through mediation rather
than by participation in the growing holocaust of World
War I in Europe. At the outbreak of the war, Wilson, by

presidential proclamation, dated August 4, 1914, declared the neutrality of the United States. Two weeks later he made an appeal to the Senate to help preserve the nation's disinterested position. "Every man who really loves America," he stated, "will act and speak in the true spirit of neutrality which is the spirit of impartiality and fairness and friendliness to all concerned." (*The Public Papers of Woodrow Wilson: The New Democracy*, Vol. I, ed. by Ray Stannard Baker and William E. Dodd, Harper & Brothers, 1926, p. 157.)

In the realization that this country was teeming with people drawn from many nations, chiefly from the nations at war, people who were divided into hostile camps of conflicting opinions, Wilson warned against such divisions that "would be fatal to our peace of mind and might seriously stand in the way of the proper performance of our duty as the one great nation at peace, the one people holding itself ready to *play a part of impartial mediation and speak the counsel of peace and accommodation, not as partisan, but as a friend.*" (*Ibid.* Emphasis added.)

Again on May 10, 1915, in an address delivered in Philadelphia, President Wilson made his famous "Too Proud to Fight" speech, in which he declared, "There is such a thing as a man being too proud to fight. There is such a thing as a nation being so right that it does not need to convince others by force that it is right." (Arthur S. Link, *Wilson: The Struggle for Neutrality, 1914-1915*, Princeton University Press, 1960, p. 382.) Some attribute Wilson's reelection in 1916 to his position on neutrality. (His popular election slogan was, "He kept us out of war.")

On January 22, 1917, Wilson outlined in his "Peace Without Victory" speech his new world policy, proposing that "no nation should seek to extend its polity over any other nation or people, but that every people should be left free to determine its own polity, its own way of development, unhindered, unthreatened, unafraid, the little along with the great and powerful." (Link, *Wilson: Campaign for Progressivism and Peace, 1916-1917,* Princeton University Press, 1965, p. 266.) He believed that the adaptation of the Monroe Doctrine to encompass the whole world would guarantee a permanent peace.

When Wilson in his "Peace Without Victory" proposals tried to give the world another chance to end the war on a basis of enduring peace, he was not aware of Germany's decision to conduct an unrestricted submarine warfare that made neutral ships subject to deliberate destruction. Germany's note dated February 1, 1917, announced this decision; it was followed by the torpedoing of three United States ships (the *Vigilancia,* the *Illinois,* and the *City of Memphis*). On April 2, 1917, the President addressed a joint session of the two houses of Congress and asked for a resolution declaring a state of war with Germany. "Property can be paid for," he declared, but "the lives of peaceful and innocent people cannot be. The present German submarine warfare against commerce is a warfare against mankind." (*The Public Papers of Woodrow Wilson: War and Peace,* Vol. I, ed. by Baker and Dodd, Harper & Brothers, 1927, pp. 7-8.)

The Congress declared war not for territorial gains but, as President Wilson pointed out in this speech, "for democracy, for the right of those who submit to authority to have voice in their own Governments, for the rights and liberties of small nations, for a universal dominion of right by such a concert of free peoples as shall bring peace and safety to all nations and make the world itself free." The United States went to war "to make the world safe for democracy." (*Id.*, p. 14.) In his idealism, Wilson had changed his mind about the moral implications of entering into the European sphere of politics and indeed into a European war.

Woodrow Wilson insisted that morality must go hand in hand with public policy, but political idealism does not always gain popular support. In ancient Greece, Aristides, the classic example of probity in public life, was ostracized by the Athenians in 483 B.C. because they became tired of hearing him called "the Just." Wilson was determined not to compromise or to deviate from what seemed to him an appointed path of service to mankind. After the fighting had concluded, he put his entire strength into trying to create a new world order based on the moral principle of self-determination. Eventually his health collapsed as a result of the intensity of his fight over the ratification of the League of Nations Covenant. From his sickbed he said, "Better a thousand times to go down than to dip your colors to dishonorable compromise." (Edith [Bolling] Wilson [Mrs. Woodrow Wilson], *My Memoirs*, The Bobbs Merrill Company, 1939, p. 297.)

### C. President Franklin D. Roosevelt

Similar to President Wilson's diplomacy of neutrality at the beginning of World War I was the policy of President Franklin D. Roosevelt in the years preceding and following the outbreak of World War II. In the years 1937-1939, when dangerous clouds appeared on the horizon of Europe, and in the two years following the outbreak of the war (1939–1941), Roosevelt on several occasions stressed his commitment to the policy of not intervening with arms to prevent acts of aggression. In a radio address on September 3, 1939, he stressed his hope that "the United States will keep out of this war." (*The Public Papers and Addresses of Franklin D. Roosevelt, Vol. 8, War and Neutrality*, The Macmillan Company, 1941, p. 463.) As late as October 1940, when the victorious German troops marched through Europe, Roosevelt declared, "I have said this before, but I shall say it again and again: Your boys are not going to be sent into any foreign wars." (*Vol. 9, War and Aid to Democracies*, 1941, p. 517.)

In the technical terms of international politics, neutrality may be either benevolent or hostile. These terms respectively imply sympathy or antagonism to one of the belligerents in a dispute. Under the Neutrality Act of 1937, the United States placed an embargo on the shipment of implements of war to all belligerent powers. The Neutrality Act that passed on November 4, 1939, changed that stance by permitting the Allies to purchase war materials in the United States. Furthermore, the Act authorized the President to forbid American citizens and ships to enter combat areas in war zones (to prevent the sinking of American ships in actions similar to those that brought the United States into World War I in 1917).

Faced with spectacular Axis military victories, President Roosevelt in a radio address of December 29, 1940, made the American people aware that such victories would mean "a new and terrible era in which the whole world, our hemisphere included, would be run by threats of brute force." (*Id.*, p. 635.) To prevent control of the seaways by hostile powers, the Congress passed the Lend-Lease Bill, which became law on March 11, 1941. It empowered the President to make available any defense article to "the government of any country whose defense the President deems vital to the defense of the United States."

Roosevelt's neutrality, like that of Wilson at the beginning of World War I, was of a benevolent character since the United States had taken the side of the Allies by sending them guns and supplies and by making loans. We nevertheless continued to refuse to assist them by using our military force.

The moral premise that neutrality would be an avenue to peace faded away in the light of the experiences of the two world wars. The torpedoing of American ships in 1917 and the bombing of Pearl Harbor in 1941 awakened America to the dangers of neutrality. The cause of peace in freedom makes neutrality impossible. There is no morality in sitting out hostilities and allowing one's friends to shed their blood as victims of aggression. Neutrality divorced from morality changes neutrality into selfishness, if not indeed into a cowardice that encourages new aggressions.

When a nation attempts to depend on itself alone, it turns into a captive state forced into unwelcome dominance by others. In 1914 and in 1939, we sought peace in neutrality only to learn that it is an obsolete concept that cannot save mankind from the scourge of wars. Only collective action, collective mutual security on a universal basis, combined with a policy of making clear in advance our intention of using armed force for the protection of friends facing hostile aggression, can prevent wars.

The two years before our entering the Second World War (1939–41) were years of hoping that our Neutrality Act would insulate us from this world conflict. A warning on our part, uttered well in advance, that we were ready to go to war for the sake of general peace in the wide world arena might have served as a deterrent to aggression. (It is only fair to point out that isolationist sentiment in the United States in the 1930s was so strong that it made such a warning impossible. Roosevelt went as far as he politically could; no one else could have done more.) Winston Churchill spoke of World War II as an "unnecessary war." It could have been prevented.

If all the nations that united to fight our common enemy in 1941 had been equally united when Japan first started aggression against Manchuria in 1931 and when Italy began it against Ethiopia in 1935, the return of the Saar to Germany in 1935, the remilitarization of the Rhineland in 1936, the annexation of Austria, and the subsequent German seizure of Czechoslovakia in 1938 would have been prevented and the war of 1939-1945 would not have taken place. The late Clare Boothe Luce, former Ambassador to Italy, once stated, "I never knew an Italian who did not insist that if the United States had given Mussolini a firm warning that the U.S. would, sooner or later, stand against Hitler, Italy would have stayed out of the war."

At the Nuremberg Trials, Colonel Eger, representing Czechoslovakia, asked Marshal Keitel, Hitler's chief of staff, "Would the Reich have attacked Czechoslovakia in 1938 if the Western Powers had stood by Prague?" Marshal Keitel answered, "Certainly not. We were not strong enough militarily. The object of Munich [that is, reaching an agreement at Munich] was to get Russia out of Europe, to gain time, and to complete the German armaments." (Quoted from Winston S. Churchill, *The Second World War: Volume II, The Gathering Storm,* Bantam Books, 1960, p. 319.)

Following a policy of timidity and retreat, the democratic leaders of Great Britain and France on September 30, 1938, capitulated to Hitler's demands at Munich and sold out Czechoslovakia, a small and threatened nation, to mass murderers. Prime Minister Neville Chamberlain returned to London and from the windows of Number 10 Downing Street he assured the cheering crowds, "I believe it is peace in our time." During the parliamentary debate on the agreement, widespread admiration for Chamberlain's efforts to maintain peace were expressed.

It was Churchill who had the courage in the course of his speech on the Munich agreement to evaluate it as "a total and unmitigated defeat." Events quickly proved him right. The "peace in our time" lasted less than one year. In September 1939, Hitler invaded Poland, which in 1938 had tried to grasp a share of the pillage and ruin of Czechoslovakia by annexing the frontier district of Teschen.

The immoral capitulation at Munich seemed to some of Europe's leaders to be expedient in securing peace. This "expediency" consumed the 50 million people who died in World War II. This experience should be contrasted to an American response to a crisis some years later. In 1955, when China aggressively threatened to invade Taiwan, Congress made our intentions clear in advance by authorizing the President to use the armed forces of the United States for the defense of our ally and our vital interests in that area. This action prevented aggression and contributed greatly to the preservation of peace. It would seem that the United States had learned something from the painful experience of the first half of this century.

### Containment and the Cold War

After World War II the United States emerged as the first atomic power, determined to hold the atomic weapon as a sacred trust. As President Truman expressed it, "the thoughtful people of the world know . . . that [trust] will not be violated." In spite of being the world's leading military power, however, we remained a passive observer of Russian aggression, which brought one-third of the world into its orbit as obedient satellites.

Our attitude in this era known as the "cold war" reminded us of President Theodore Roosevelt's warning: "In diplomacy, the worst possible thing is to shake first the fist, and then the finger." The Soviet Union succeeded in destroying the independence of the nations of Eastern Europe and in maintaining the Iron Curtain around them because of its confidence that our yearning for peace was so strong that we were incapable of resorting to force and of using the advantages that our monopoly of power for a brief period after World War II gave us.

The atomic monopoly of the United States shortly thereafter disappeared and was replaced by an atomic stalemate that Churchill characterized as a "balance of terror." Under this new, modern form of balance of power, the Soviet Union in an all-out nuclear war would be able to destroy the United States, and the United States would be able to destroy the Soviet Union. Nuclear war would bring catastrophe for both sides.

We scrapped the military establishment following World War I and again after World War II, only to learn when the Korean War came that unilateral disarmament does not produce peace. It required two world wars—followed by the frightening fact that eleven nations of Eastern Europe found themselves in the grip of the ruthless power of Soviet Russia, plus the expanding influence of Communism among the Asian nations exposed to an unceasing barrage of anti-American propaganda—for us to remember Lenin's blueprint for world domination: "First we will take Eastern Europe, then the masses of Asia. Then we will surround America, the last citadel of capitalism. We shall not have to attack. She will fall into our lap like an over-ripe fruit."

It required two world wars and untold suffering to realize that our own self-interest, combined with our responsibilities to the past and to the future, demands our involvement in world affairs. It required a great deal of blood to be spilled in those two world wars for us to realize that our own freedom is in danger when we insulate ourselves from the conflicts of the world by remaining indifferent to the destruction of freedom in nations conquered or infiltrated by imperialist aggression.

In order to save Greece, we adopted in 1947 what came to be known as the "policy of containment," which brought about radical changes in U.S. foreign policy. The frontiers of the United States were drawn wherever there was a danger of violence that could disrupt the world balance of power. This newfound active involvement of the United States in world affairs was expressed by the Truman Doctrine and put into practice with the Marshall Plan, the landmarks of a radical transformation of our foreign policy that combines morality with expedience, our moral responsibility toward the world with our safety and well-being.

By stationing American troops around the perimeter of the Soviet empire, we gave advance notice to the Soviet Union that any attempt to expand beyond the line of military demarcation established in 1945 between Russia and the West would mean war with the United States. Furthermore, we accepted responsibility for alleviating the problems faced by the international economic system by extending our assistance to nations threatened with economic disaster. The purpose of this radical transformation in our foreign policy was to express clearly our intentions to defend the cause of freedom and to discourage adventures caused by miscalculation or underestimation of our determination to serve this cause by accepting the risk of war. Those who seek world domination should be reminded that on the American national as well as presidential coats of arms, the American eagle holds an olive branch in its right talon and a bundle of arrows in its left. Both deserve the equal attention of countries with imperialistic ambitions.

## Exclusive Ideological Systems

The existence of ideological systems that are mutually exclusive obstruct the establishment of an international order on a worldwide scale. In our generation we have witnessed the fall of fascism in Italy, of Nazism in Germany, and of communism in Eastern Europe and the Soviet Union. These historical events raised hopes for global order since they strengthened our faith in the principle that nothing established by violence and maintained by force—in opposition to what is right—can endure. Their fall demonstrated that anything based on a contempt for human personality, which degrades humanity, cannot endure. Their fall demonstrated that—in the perspective of history—immoral expediency is short-lived.

At the same time, hopes for the establishment of a global international order have not materialized. After World War II, many states in Europe that had possessed traditions of liberty and freedom disappeared behind the Iron Curtain. In the language of the imperialistic Soviet Union and its puppets, peace meant deception and conformity to a pattern of conduct imposed by Moscow. The communist ideologues used the technique of Humpty Dumpty, who in *Through the Looking Glass* said, "When I use a word it means just what I choose it to mean." The words "socialism" or "democracy" meant despotism and dictatorship of the communist party, which received its instructions from the Kremlin.

The communist rulers offered the subjugated peoples of the captive states tyranny instead of democracy, injustice instead of justice, equality in general poverty instead of prosperity, and hypocritical slogans to conceal despair and the spiritual darkness of oppression. Communist rulers embarked on a worldwide, organized campaign of subversion against freely elected governments by using military pressure, deceit, propaganda, and terror.

Stalin's foreign policy was marked by bluster and brute force. His respect for force is well illustrated by his comments in reply to a suggestion that he should make a propitiatory gesture toward the Vatican: "The Pope, how many divisions has he?" The morality, or rather immorality, of Stalin's concept of appropriate methods of dealing with other nations was demonstrated by his statement, "A diplomat's words must have no relation to actions—otherwise what kind of diplomacy is it? Words are one thing, actions another. Good words are a mask for the concealment of bad deeds. Sincere diplomacy is no more possible than dry water or iron wood." The application of this doctrine was demonstrated by broken treaties and the subjugation of nations in Eastern and Central Europe along the periphery of the Soviet Union.

Machiavelli might have had the communist leaders in mind when he wrote of a ruler who "never preaches anything but peace and good faith, and to both he is most hostile, and either, if he kept it, would have deprived him of reputation and kingdom many a time." The crimes of Stalin—a madman whose paranoia took innocent people to the fringes of hell—were committed for the sake of "expediency." In 1990 the Soviet Union for the first time admitted the slaying of several thousand Polish army officers in the Katyn forest during World War II. This massacre—another outrage of the Stalinist era—was also carried out in the name of expediency in order to eliminate the cream of the Polish nation who might at some future time have become "counter-revolutionaries."

Faced with communist ambitions for world domination, the United States—realizing that we are a part of a worldwide human community—responded by carrying out its moral commitments to the objective of collective security and by sharing our abundance to relieve hunger and help economic growth in all parts of the world. The postwar recovery of Western Europe should largely be attributed to the Europeans' own ingenuity and industriousness, but a significant part of it was the result of the Marshall Plan, which prevented the eclipse of Europe and another Dark Age. (In 1948, Czechoslovakia indicated that it would accept the free economic assistance that the United States offered under the Marshall Plan—but instantly withdrew its acceptance upon instructions from Moscow.)

To aid the peoples struggling to break the bonds of mass misery, the United States not only offered material help but also mobilized the services of all those with the desire and capability to help foreign lands meet their needs for trained personnel. The formation of a national Peace Corps and the establishment of world food reserves were some of the endeavors aimed at the improvement of world order. We acted in accordance with Thomas Jefferson's advice to "act not for ourselves alone but for the whole human race" when we extended our assistance aimed at the preservation of the human spirit, which survives only when freedom, human dignity, fair play, and equal justice under law exist.

Those responsible for our foreign policy disliked the term "foreign aid," preferring "mutual security." They reminded us of the duties President Theodore Roosevelt outlined: "Our first duty as citizens of the nation is owed to the United States, but if we are true to our principles we must also think of serving the interests of mankind at large." This principle combines morality with expediency.

The impoverishment of any single people in the world means challenge, if not danger, to the well-being of all other peoples. Hunger and exploitation, misery and discrimination, were the best allies of the communist aggressors. President Truman, indicating the danger of "stomach communism," made pleas for the Point Four Program: "Less than one-third of the expenditures for the cost of World War II would have created the development necessary to feed the whole world, and thus prevent 'stomach communism' . . . . Unless we fight the battle and win it, we cannot win the cold war, or a hot one either."

Our desire for other countries to become self-supporting and attain a decent standard of living was not prompted only by the struggle with imperialism or by a fear of allowing any of these nations to slip behind the Iron Curtain. The guiding spirit of our concern for countries suffering social and economic injustice was our commitment to share our fellowman's destiny as well as the realization that as long as freedom and justice are in danger anywhere our own are not safe. Poverty, illiteracy, or disease anywhere is a real threat to our security. The sharing of our resources to alleviate the difficulties other countries faced was an investment in our own security since it reduced the potential conflicts arising in the world community.

## The Restructuring of the Political Universe

History, "the mother of all studies" *(Historia mater studiorum est),* has demonstrated again and again that despotism and dictatorship are more vulnerable than they appear. As Churchill put it, "The grand lesson of history is that tyrannism cannot last except among the servile races." Under the slogans of *perestroika, glasnost,* and democratization, the changes now occurring in the Soviet Union are the most dramatic since the Bolshevik Revolution in 1917. The rush of events that are following in Eastern Europe and in the Soviet Union is restructuring the major aspects of our political universe.

What prompted these changes? The overt defiance of communist oppression by an unknown Chinese man facing a column of tanks will be long remembered as an epochal event in China's dark hours. The despair of peoples suffering from the brutality of Marxist regimes was expressed by this resolute man when he shouted: "You have done nothing but create misery." The Soviet Union by mass violence colonized nations of different cultures and civilizations and offered them "nothing but misery." This union, doomed from the very beginning, had been soaked in the blood of innocent victims of oppression, ethnic strife, and economic decay.

Lenin once described the Russian empire under the czars as a "prison of nations." When these captive nations were reconquered by the Red Army, they were also reforged into a larger "prison." The Soviet Union brought fifteen diverse republics, spreading almost 7,000 miles from the borders of Poland to the Sea of Japan, under the Kremlin's monolithic rule. After World War II this rule was extended to satellite countries in Eastern Europe.

Without a tradition of democracy, President Mikhail Gorbachev has offered the communist world a plan of reformation that inadvertently is having an impact on not only the domestic policy of the Soviet Union and its relationship with its former satellite states but also on its relations with the rest of the world. Since the Bolshevik revolution, the ideas of the communist leaders have had an impact far beyond the borders of the Soviet Union. They have called on their followers everywhere to overthrow the capitalist system and to shape the world into a Marxist millennium, guided, of course, by the Kremlin. In the light of the near collapse of the economic and political system within the Soviet Union, it has become impossible for those in other countries to take such calls to revolution seriously.

Having embarked upon the road of radical reforms, Gorbachev has insisted that it is wrong to assume that they mean the collapse of socialism. Upon returning from his Crimean captivity, Gorbachev still asserted emphatically that he was "an adherent of socialism" and that implementation of socialist ideas leads to greater justice and liberty. Only after a series of consultations with his advisers did he resign as General Secretary of the Communist Party, recommend dissolving the Central Committee, and authorize local elected councils to take control of the party's extensive assets. Before the August 1991 coup, he attributed to Stalinism the tragic suffering of the Soviet Union and of its satellites that had vegetated under a totalitarian system.

The leaders of the dissident movement, to mention only Andrey Sakharov and Aleksandr Solzhenitsyn, have not believed that the blame for the atrocities should be put solely on Stalin. The early Soviet times, the "Lenin times," were also marked by terror, with thousands of people seized and shot, and by secret disappearances, frame-up trials, and "revolutionary tribunals" that executed people for belonging to the "wrong class." The doctrinaire Bolshevik dictatorship, guided by narrow class hatred, continued the tradition of the czarist police, only widening the orbit of persecution. Lenin's era had plenty of police but neither plenty of food on the table nor other material necessities.

During Gorbachev's momentous meeting with Pope John Paul II (he was the first Soviet communist party boss to set foot on Vatican soil), the Soviet president declared, "We need spiritual values, we need a revolution of the mind. This is the only way toward a new culture and new politics that can meet the challenge of our time." Is it possible for the "legacy of Lenin" to meet this challenge?

It is a myth that Leninism could offer spiritual values. Although doctrinaire communists pursued their ends with religious fervor, Marxism by definition is a materialist philosophy, denying even the existence of spiritual realities. This philosophy was borne out in inhuman policies. Under Lenin, from the earliest days of Bolshevism, the party controlled the life of the individual. Lenin saw in the communist party the only source of truth and authority. For the sake of expediency, the party as the "vanguard of the toilers" became the custodian of absolute power, and for over seven decades it preserved its unchallenged position.

Can socialism be humane? The young ex-Marxist Bernard-Henry Levy answered this question in his book *Barbarism with a Human Face*, in which he pointed out that the classless society offered by socialism is another name for terror, that it is the very real outcome of the unparalleled destruction of human beings. "The Gulag," he wrote,

> "is not a blunder or an accident, not a simple wound or after-effect of Stalinism; but the necessary corollary of a socialism which can only actualize homogeneity back to its fringes, which can aim for the universal only by confining its rebels, its irreducible individualists, in the outer darkness of a nonsociety. . . . No socialism without camps, no classless society without its terrorist truth." (Levy, *Barbarism With a Human Face*, tr. George Holoch, Harper & Row, New York, 1979, p. 158.)

The measures Gorbachev has taken to remedy the inherent weaknesses of communism are far from giving evidence of success. Earlier Soviet reform attempts failed, and no historical background exists for the drastic changes taking place after the so-called Second Russian Revolution. The unanswered question, therefore, remains, Which course will the Soviet Union follow?

The pace at which changes are occurring is unprecedented. The frenetic and still growing speed of political liberalization is illustrated by the fact that, as *Time* magazine pointed out, what took ten years in Poland took ten months in Hungary, ten weeks in East Germany, ten days in Czechoslovakia, and ten hours in Rumania. In 1917 the communists seized power in Russia through a coup. When the Russian people were on the verge of overthrowing their yoke after seventy-four years of communist dictatorship, those who had been in power for so long tried to restore their hegemony by means of another coup. But they failed. The paralyzing despair of the suffering people under the communist yoke was converted into the courage to oust, and to prevent the return of, the oppressive governments.

## Moral Principles and Practical Necessities

There are some who believe that the source of these events that are changing the human face of the world is a desire to turn toward our form of capitalism. This judgment sees the reform movements in the wrong perspective. Socialism has failed in Europe, but there is no certainty that Europe will choose our kind of capitalism. Although the United States maintains its position as the largest economic entity in the world, it shows signs of weakness that warrant real concern.

The flaws in our economy include the constant budget deficits, trade deficits, volatile exchange rates, failing banks and savings and loan institutions, a growing wave of business bankruptcies, stock scandals caused by the corruption of highly placed traders and industry officials, consumer credit dangerously outgrowing the rate of savings, giant takeovers, mergers and acquisitions, and mammoth leveraged buyouts financed through "junk bonds" paying very high interest rates reflecting their high risk (which have caused an explosion of corporate debt and become a hot political issue). Because of these flaws, our economic system does not offer a cohesive system of values to which the reform movement of Eastern Europe could be attributed.

What kind of moral principles should we apply to the existing order of the world? The logical answer would seem to be Christian ethics, since this system of values has survived the fall of empires and national monarchies. It was never identified with the mundane dogmas of political parties, social systems, or established regimes. Yet Christianity, which for more than 1,500 years was predominant in Europe, failed to stop wars. It would be naive to expect that all people will become as self-renouncing and sacrificing as a St. Francis and to assert that all the world's immediate problems are to be solved by following Christ's teachings.

As we asserted above, men are not angels. No one expects that "offering the other cheek" will prevent us from becoming an easy prey for an enemy seeking world domination and offering annihilation and slavery. History teaches us that a constructive policy of legitimate defense, since it deters an enemy from initiating a war, serves the cause of peace better than does appeasement.

The Sermon on the Mount embodies the main principles of Christian ethics. Referring to this passage in the Gospel of St. Matthew, Churchill stated that national leaders cannot always follow these principles in discharging their responsibilities. The safety of the state and the lives and freedom of its citizens (to whom such leaders owe their positions)

> "make it right and imperative in the last resort . . . that the use of force should not be excluded. And if this be so, so it should be used under the conditions which are most favorable. There is no merit in putting off a war for a year if, when it comes, it is a far worse war or one much harder to win." (*Op. cit.*, p. 320.)

It was a concept well-known even to the Founding Fathers of this nation that the rule of morality, as Alexander Hamilton wrote, "is not precisely the same between nations as between individuals," because the responsibilities of the state differ from those of individuals. An action of the state can influence many millions of lives, even those of generations to come, while according to Hamilton, "the consequences of a private action of an individual ordinarily terminate with himself." George Washington observed that it was "a maxim founded on the universal experience of mankind that no nation is to be trusted farther than it is bound by its interests."

The moral principle of peace and the practical necessity of self-preservation demand a steadfast commitment to collective security through military strength.

The best way to preserve peace without sacrificing freedom is to have an effective retaliatory deterrent. The sage advice *Si vis pacem, para bellum* ("If you desire peace, be prepared for war") is not an idle refrain. After the "Second Russian Revolution," the Red army, 4 million strong (against only 2 million in the United States armed forces), is still not disbanding or demobilizing. The Soviet strategic nuclear forces are still intact and are even being dramatically modernized to the state of highest capacity. There is no way of knowing whether or when the Soviet Union will join the free world's democratic community.

The Soviet economy continues to deteriorate, and the establishment of a market economy is proceeding very slowly. Yet more than half of all industrial production is aimed at military purposes—the Soviet defense budget rose from 26 percent of the total budget in 1990 to 36 percent in 1991 and takes between 20 and 25 percent of the Soviet gross national product. Alexis de Tocqueville warned that "the most perilous moment for a bad government is one when it seeks to mend its ways." (*The Old Regime and the French Revolution*, tr. by Stuart Gilbert, Doubleday, 1955, p. 177.) Even though we rejoice with the Free World in the hope of a non-nuclear world that may result from the reduction in nuclear weapons initiated by President Bush, we should not overlook the lesson of the Gorbachev era that our foreign policy should never rely exclusively on the goodwill of a single individual—we must be prepared if the fast-moving changes in the Soviet Union should swerve in unforeseeable and undesirable directions.

We cannot afford to forget that the Soviet empire survived only through aggression. Milovan Djilas, a close associate of the late Yugoslavian dictator Marshal Tito, after a long experience with communism in the Soviet Union and Yugoslavia, wrote, "Soviet communism . . . is a military empire. It was transformed into a military empire in Stalin's time. Internally, such structures usually rot; . . . but to avoid internal problems, they may go for expansion . . . if it is stopped, the process of rotting will go faster." (Djilas was a member of the Yugoslavian Politburo from 1935 to 1954 and was vice president of Yugoslavia when he suddenly left the communist party in 1954.)

Unilateral disarmament may encourage aggression on the part of an enemy seeking world domination. It can turn peaceful nations into the prey of war and of other forms of violence not less terrifying than war—namely, colonialism, oppression, and deprivation of freedom and identity. There is a basic right to counter force by the use of force. There is a basic responsibility to strengthen the world's democratic foundations in order to prevent the multiplication of dictatorships, whether in this hemisphere or in other parts of the world. This can be accomplished by military strength able to deter aggressors who try to impose their will by force.

A compelling need for the strategic deterrent of the United States and its allies, which has kept the peace in Europe for over forty years and contained Soviet expansion, continues to exist. Our deterrent force cannot be dismantled as long as we must remain on guard in this unstable world. In spite of reductions of its armed forces and their restructuring, the Soviet Union is still able to blow up the United States, if not the entire world, many times over. Soviet weapons (including 70,000 pieces of armor and artillery) have been transferred to sanctuaries east of the Urals and can easily return to Eastern and Central Europe. With memories of World War II still vivid in our minds, we should be reminded that in spite of reductions in armaments the Soviet military force, with its 27,000 nuclear weapons, is more powerful than the Wehrmacht was in 1939 when Hitler deployed its power to plunge the world into that war.

"Peace through strength" is not just a slogan. It is practical necessity, a proven strategy, crowned with success. Moral principles and practical necessities are parts of the same reality. Among the practical necessities is the need for unity among the nations opposing aggression and adhering to principles of peace.

A lack of unity among principled nations, resulting in complacence in the face of growing imperialism, militarism, and secret diplomacy, led to World War I. A lack of unity in reacting to the many acts of aggression in the 1930s, discussed above, and to the Nazi-Soviet pact dividing Europe into spheres of influence, as well as the policy of compromise at Munich, were in large measure responsible for the outbreak of World War II.

No nation, acting alone, can assure world peace. The future of each nation depends on a community of nations pulled together by a common resolve to meet the challenge of defending their freedom from aggressions and wars.

We have seen the truth of these propositions in the recent Gulf crisis. The worldwide United Nations economic sanctions against Iraq, the international boycott of its and Kuwait's oil, the freezing of those nations' assets, the participation of Arab military forces in the war against Iraq—another Arab nation—mean that the world has passed the test of international unity against an aggressor with ambitions to become the dominant ruler of the Arab world. Saddam Hussein's renegade ambitions brought about an unprecedented cooperation of major world powers and of Arab nations prepared to fight shoulder to shoulder with American and European forces against their Arab "brothers." This unanimity of purpose may define the future of the post-cold war world.

The "moral rectitude" of faith in the essential worth and dignity of each individual, when applied to international relations, demands a preparedness to put forth all resources and energies in order to maintain a union of self-respecting free nations and to protect their freedom and dignity against oppression.

The international tensions we witnessed after World War II could have been prevented if the leaders of the Free World had not abandoned—in Tehran, Yalta, and the other conferences following that war of brutal aggression—the peace aims President Wilson outlined: "No special or separate interest of any single nation or any group of nations can be made the basis of any part of the settlement which is not consistent with the common interest of all." (The "Five Particulars" of September 27, 1918, *Public Papers: War and Peace*, Vol. I, p. 257.) "Every territorial settlement . . . must be made in the interest of and for the benefit of the populations concerned, and not as a part of any mere adjustment or compromise of claims among rival states." (The "Four Principles" of February 11, 1918, *id.*, p. 183.)

The changes taking place in Eastern Europe and the Soviet Union demonstrate vividly that the peoples of Bulgaria, Czechoslovakia, Estonia, Hungary, Latvia,

Lithuania, Poland, Rumania, and the other "captive" nations within the Soviet empire were never reconciled with the idea of having their destinies sacrificed on the altar of a "compromise of claims among rival states," disregarding the "benefit of the populations concerned."

After 74 years of oppression, the citizens of the Soviet Union rebelled against the communist institutions imposed on them by the totalitarian state. After 52 years of enslavement, the Baltic states of Estonia, Latvia, and Lithuania—annexed by the Soviet Union under the shameful secret agreement between Hitler and Stalin—regained their independence. After 400 years of Russian colonialism, the republics that became a part of the Soviet Union are seeking independence, since none of them voluntarily joined the Russian empire.

It will undoubtedly take years before Eastern European living standards can rebound from the damage caused by long-term communist rule. Recent events have shown, however, that the tyranny that wrought such economic havoc could not despoil the spirit of the people. What has transformed the human face of Eastern Europe and of the Soviet Union is the enormous moral force of freedom, which can temporarily be suppressed by tyrants but never ceases to undergird human aspirations. In reaction to human humiliation, freedom emerges in all its strength as an enormous expedient force. Together with the other moral values, it will always remain the most important formative influence on human behavior.

Traditional moral values, such as freedom, justice, prudence, love, fidelity, honesty—which were recognized by Plato, Aristotle, and Moses and by Christ's teaching as the virtues that develop the whole person—

remain unchangeable. On August 10, 1787, in a letter to his nephew Peter Carr, Jefferson wrote:

> "Man was destined for society. His morality therefore was to be formed to this object. He was endowed with a sense of right and wrong merely relative to this. This sense is as much a part of his nature as the sense of hearing, seeing, feeling. . . . The moral sense, or conscience, is as much part of man as his leg or arm."

The developments in Soviet Russia and Eastern Europe show the extent to which the inner conscience of man is able to endure and to overcome and survive all kinds of oppression and atrocities. As Czechoslovakia's President Vaclav Havel expressed it, human conscience remains "the interpreter or mediator between us and this higher authority." This "higher authority" calls for responsibility to something higher than the country, the company, the family, or the individual's own success. This responsibility, according to Havel, is "responsibility to the order of Being, where all our actions are indelibly recorded and where, and only where, they will be properly judged." (Address delivered to the Joint Session of Congress, February 21, 1990.)

Characteristically, both Havel and the chairman of Solidarnosc, the Polish leader Lech Walesa, who in 1990 became president of Poland, have pointed out that our Declaration of Independence, our Bill of Rights, and our Constitution inspired them in their struggle for freedom, despite the fact that the documents are over 200 years old. Addressing a joint session of Congress, Walesa stated:

"The world remembers the wonderful principle of the American democracy: 'government of the people, by the people, for the people.' . . . in fact the principles and values—reminiscent of Abraham Lincoln and the Founding Fathers of the American Republic, and also of the principles and ideas of the American Declaration of Independence and the American constitution—that are pursued by the great movement of the Polish Solidarity; a movement that is effective." (Address delivered to the Joint Session of Congress, November 15, 1989.)

The moral principles of the historical documents guiding our nation are grounded in the true values of life and in the hopes and aspirations that govern a nation's destiny. The only success that can be expected from applying moral principles is that of making life on this globe more tolerable. As Judge Learned Hand expressed it, "We shall have to be content with short steps; . . . but we shall have gone forward, if we bring to our task . . . patience, understanding, sympathy, forbearance, generosity, fortitude, and above all inflexible determination."

The proper purpose of inflexible determination is not only the preservation of human existence through securing the means of life but also the preservation of reasons for living, which is a matter of spirituality. The recognition of this truth leads to the conclusion reached by Cicero and described above, that human action cannot be morally right without being expedient, and no action can be expedient without being morally right.

# MORALITY AND THE RULE OF LAW
# IN THE FOREIGN POLICY
# OF THE DEMOCRACIES

by

John Norton Moore

## John Norton Moore

*John Norton Moore is Walter L. Brown Professor of Law at the University of Virginia, where he is Director of the Graduate Law Program and also Director of the Center for Oceans Law and Policy and the Center for Law and National Security. He was appointed by Presidents Reagan and Bush and confirmed by the United States Senate as the Chairman of the Board of Directors of the United States Institute of Peace. Also by presidential appointment, he has served as Chairman of the National Security Council Interagency Task Force on the Law of the Sea and as United States Ambassador and Deputy Special Representative of the President to the Law of the Sea Conference.*

*In addition, Professor Moore is a consultant to the nation's Arms Control and Disarmament Agency. He has served as a Counselor on International Law for the Department of State and a consultant to the President's Intelligence Oversight Board. He was also a member of the U.S. delegation to the Conference on Security and Cooperation in Europe in Athens in 1984, Chairman of the American Bar Association Standing Committee on Law and National Security in 1982–1986, and Co-Chairman of the United States–USSR talks on the Rule of Law.*

*Professor Moore earned his B.A. at Drew University, an LL.B. at Duke Law School, and an LL.M. at the University of Illinois. He was a Fellow at Yale Law School in 1965–1966.*

*In addition to many articles, Professor Moore has written and edited nine books. These include* Law and the Indo-China War *(1972),* Law and the Grenada Mission *(1984), and* The Secret War in Central America *(1986).*

# MORALITY AND THE RULE OF LAW IN THE FOREIGN POLICY OF THE DEMOCRACIES

by

John Norton Moore

"Recent history has shown how much ideas count. The Cold War was, in its decisive aspects, a war of ideas."

> The White House, *National Security Strategy of the United States, August 1991*, U.S. Government Printing Office, 1991, p. 14, col 1.

## Introduction

Ideas, morality, and law not only matter in foreign policy; to an extent not yet fully appreciated, they are of central importance. We see the truth of this proposition in many events that have recently been occurring throughout the world, but nowhere more than in the Soviet Union. The highly visible postcoup Soviet revolution of August 23, 1991, reflects a longer process of revolution that has been under way since *perestroika* and *glasnost* began. The world dramatically changed as this revolution, driven by ideas, progressed, and the postrevolution world will be fundamentally different. As this new world evolves, it will be accompanied by a search for a "new world order." But what will—or should—be the characteristics of this new world order? What goals and new approaches will principally characterize it? How might those goals be more effectively implemented? And how do ideas, morality, and law fit into the new world order?

125

In this exciting and challenging setting, it is appropriate that we examine anew how morality and law play a role in international life. It is the thesis of this paper that a centerpiece of the new world order must be a vigorous effort to support the rule of law and the political morality of "liberal democracy" on a worldwide basis. This is not simply because liberal democracy is *the* principal revolution now affecting the globe, as the Soviet revolution of 1991 reminds us. Nor is it because liberal democracy is the American system or that we now have a more effective opportunity to persuade others of its significance, which we do. Rather, liberal democracy and the rule of law (in the broadest sense) are valuable to the new world order centrally and fundamentally because an impressive body of human knowledge now tells us unmistakably that there is a *direct* correlation between these concepts and a number of highly desirable values in a society: a regard for human rights, the avoidance of government-sponsored "democide" (the massive killing of a nation's own population and the most extreme human rights failure of government), vigorous economic progress, and the avoidance of a synergy that has produced the major international wars of this century. In short, the spread of liberal democracy, or at least the minimization of totalitarianism, is of the greatest importance in realizing fundamental human aspirations.

## The Role of Morality and Law in Foreign Policy

Before examining this thesis, it may be instructive to recall and discard some earlier common myopia concerning the role of morality and law in foreign policy. In this connection, it should be recalled that an earlier generation of realpolitik foreign affairs experts focused almost exclusively on power, or the balance of power, as the determinant in foreign policy. In this view, as illustrated by the work of Professor Hans Morgenthau, morality and law were simply incidental factors in foreign policy. (See *Politics Among Nations: The Struggle for Power and Peace*, 3d ed., Alfred A. Knopf, 1966, pp. 230-231.) George Kennan's now infamous phrase also reflects this view:

> "Morality, then, as the channel to individual self-fulfillment—yes. Morality as the foundation of civic virtue, and accordingly as a condition precedent to successful democracy—yes. Morality in governmental method, as a matter of conscience and preference on the part of our people—yes. But morality as a general criterion for the determination of the behavior of states and above all as a criterion for measuring and comparing the behavior of different states—no. Here other criteria, sadder, more limited, more practical, must be allowed to prevail." *(Realities of American Foreign Policy*, Princeton University Press, 1954, p. 49.)

Today we know that this view was wrong in many different ways. First, as Professors Myres McDougal and David Little, and many others, have shown, for foreign affairs—of all mankind's activities—to be freed from moral or legal appraisal has never been remotely sensible. (McDougal, "Law and Power," *American Journal of International Law*, Vol. 46, No. 1, January 1952, p. 102; Little, *American Foreign Policy and Moral Rhetoric: The Example of Vietnam*, Council on Religion and International Affairs Special Studies, No. 206, 1969, p. 19. See also McDougal, "International Law, Power and Policy: A Contemporary Conception," *Recueil des Cours*, Hague Academy of International Law, Vol. 82, 1953, p. 133. See generally J.N. Moore, "The Legal Tradition and the Management of National Security," in *Toward World Order and Human Dignity: Essays in Honor of Myres S. McDougal*, ed. by W.M. Reisman and B.H. Weston, Free Press, 1976, p. 321; and H. Dillard, "Some Aspects of Law and Diplomacy," *Recueil des Cours*, Vol. 91, 1957, p. 447.)

Second, this view neglected the critical role that ideas, including morality and law, played in influencing the behavior of nations as well as that of the people forming those nations. It is a common philosophical error to believe that the only reality is an objective reality, or things, and that ideas or subjectivities have no reality or real-world effect. But a moment's reflection indicates that the history of ideas and political movements, including liberal democracy, communism, naziism, fascism, nationalism, religion, human rights, and many other "subjectivities," have profoundly influenced this world and its international relations. I would argue, as would others I know who have focused on the issue, that, most recently, the movement toward the internationalization of minimum guarantees of human rights, and particularly the manifestations of this movement within the Helsinki Process, almost certainly had more to do with promoting the movement toward democratization in the Soviet Union than did the entire history of arms control efforts with the Soviet Union. Yet for years we believed—and acted upon this belief as the centerpiece of United States policy toward the Soviet Union—that regulation of the "objective" hardware of nuclear weaponry was the holy grail for peace.

George Weigel, the president of the Ethics and Public Policy Center, suggests a balanced view of the importance of ideas in foreign policy:

> "The alternative to conventional Realism is not utopianism or an idealism run riot. The alternative is an approach to foreign policy that takes ideas and values seriously as motivators of men and nations, and thus instruments for change. This is the age of Lenin, Hitler, Mao, and Pol Pot; of Gandhi and the teachers at the London School of Economics in the 1930s; of Churchill and the founders of the State of Israel; of Havel, Michnik, and Wojtyla. One would have thought that, at this late stage, the importance and power of ideas in the shaping of history would have become, in Mr. Jefferson's idiom, self-evidently clear." (Weigel, *American Purpose*, Vol. 5, September 1991, pp. 54–55.)

## Why Is "Rule of Law Engagement" an Important Component of Foreign Policy?

Granted that ideas, morality, law, and other subjectivities have enormous ability to influence events, why should "rule of law engagement" or a vigorous effort to promote liberal democracy become a centerpiece of the new world order? The answer is simple and compelling: Now we know that liberal democracy and its core principles of the rule of law are critical components for the realization of human rights, peace, and more rapid economic development, while also, not incidentally, better protecting environmental interests.

Twenty years ago it was argued that certain statist totalitarian models would achieve superior economic growth
or more effectively meet the needs of working-class citizens. Ten years ago political rhetoric could still hail the
alleged extraordinary progress in controlling infant
mortality in Fidel Castro's Cuba. Even today, an influential segment of intellectual opinion sees no relationship
between peace and liberal democracy. But for all who
are not blinded by self-imposed political filters capable
only of permitting data that reinforces their own images
of the real world to pass through, the evidence is now
overwhelming on all fronts.

Totalitarian systems that kill human economic freedom kill their own engine of economic progress. The
London School of Economics, which reportedly for years
taught the contrary to Third World leaders, can no longer
escape the overwhelming economic data from the real
world. You may be interested in one revealing vignette
told to me by a high-ranking former Soviet economic
minister. At an important conference of "socialist"
states, he was impressed by the Cuban data on progress
in dealing with infant mortality. After the meeting, he
approached the Cuban official and said, "Your progress
in controlling infant mortality is impressive. What do
you do that we might copy in the Soviet Union?" The
Cuban official replied, "It is simple. We wait until the
children are one year old before registering their birth."

As with economic freedom, human rights are not ran-
domly distributed across a spectrum of forms of government. Rather, as the framers of the United States Constitution knew, and as the "new thinkers" in Eastern
Europe and the Soviet Union know full well, the realization of critical human rights depends upon meaning-

ful human rights guarantees and is directly related to governmental structures. It was simply never possible to fully promote "human rights" internationally without simultaneously seeking to promote the liberal democratic governments capable of supporting them. Of necessity, the next step in any serious effort to internationalize concern for human rights had to focus on governmental structures.

More ominously, in recent years a body of impressive data has emerged linking totalitarian regimes with the democide of their own populations. (See R.J. Rummel, *Lethal Politics: Soviet Genocides and Mass Murders Since 1917*, Transaction Publishers, 1990; and R.J. Rummel, "The Rule of Law: Towards Eliminating War and Democide," speech prepared for presentation to the American Bar Association Standing Committee on Law and National Security, Washington, D.C., October 10–11, 1991.) In its magnitude, such killing in this century certainly exceeds the total of deaths in *all* wars of the twentieth century. Indeed, the principal scholar in this area believes that the figure is over 148 million killed, or roughly four times the number of all persons killed in wars in the same time frame. (R.J. Rummel, "The Rule of Law: Towards Eliminating War and Democide,"*ibid.)* Democide, the ultimate human rights failure, is illustrated by the nazi holocaust (the most intense example), Stalinist and other governmentally ordered killing of the Soviet population (probably the most extensive example—and largely effected through the gulag death camps), and Pol Pot's killing of perhaps a third of the entire population of Cambodia (Kampuchea) in an ideologically driven return to nature mandated by iron Leninist discipline. Sadly, all forms of government have committed violations of human rights, but massive democide is exclusively a feature of totalitarian governments. The underlying political reality, which also was fully understood by the political geniuses who gave us the United States Constitution, is that power corrupts, and absolute power corrupts absolutely. Thus, a governmental structure of checks and balances and some degree of separation of powers seems essential to avoid megadeaths by governments.

Finally, with respect to the relation to peace, an impressive body of data also suggests that encouraging the spread of liberal democracy and regimes that guarantee fundamental human rights is one of the most important real-world factors in reducing major wars. There are, of course, many competing models that seek to explain the origins of war. Moreover, there are many different kinds of violent conflict, and, therefore, the issue of war is somewhat analogous to that of cancer. That is, the many different kinds require many different solutions. Nevertheless, after spending five years reviewing the best scientific thinking about war and peace as the Chairman of the Board of the United States Institute of Peace, I have concluded that a major causative model of the principal international wars in the twentieth century consists of a synergy between a nondemocratic regime bent on the aggressive use of force to propagate its value system and an overall, systemwide failure to deter such aggression—thinking of the deterrence process in the broadest context, including the relevant international political and legal systems, economic interdependencies, and military power and alliance systems, as well as the necessity for clear communication in delivering and receiving deterrent messages.

Until recently, it was thought that World War I did not fit this model, but the most recent data suggests that the war may indeed have been principally caused by a synergy of the aggressive German war aims and the failure of Great Britain to indicate that it would join the allies against Germany in the event of a German attack. World War II, the Korean War, and, most recently, the Gulf conflict are paradigms of this model. The most recent data suggests that the Indo-China conflict also fits this model in major ways, contrary to prevailing mythology at the time.

If this model *is* pointing the way to the causative elements in the most serious form of war, then clearly what is needed to reduce the risk of war is a combination of measures that will encourage the end of totalitarianism and promote deterrence by means of clear deterrent signals against such regimes. A vigorous and consistent rule of law engagement effort thus becomes a critical component of a foreign policy seriously aimed at war prevention.

## The Meaning of "Rule of Law Engagement"

It is important that we examine what the objective is in "rule of law engagement." Procedurally, rule of law engagement is not a strategy to impose democratic regimes by force of arms. Rather, it is a strategy similar to that of the "human rights engagement" from the Helsinki Process that played such a momentous role in changing the human rights and, ultimately, the political landscape in Eastern Europe and the Soviet Union. Substantively, the rule of law is *not* an effort to promote narrow legality by which the legal niceties are followed on the way to the gulag. Rather, it stands for the most important precepts of liberal democracy, particularly mechanisms to prevent unchecked political power, assure accountability to the people, and protect the individual citizen against the state.

The concept of the rule of law and its major tenets are described in the overview paper of the United States delegation to the Moscow-Leningrad talks on the rule of law, which I presented in Moscow in March 1990:

"The 'rule of law' collectively symbolizes the most important features of democratic governance. Its core meaning is that governmental decisions must be rooted in the consent of the governed, acting only through structures and procedures designed to prevent individual oppression or governmental tyranny, which protect fundamental rights and freedoms, and which are subject to appraisal by an independent judiciary rendering judgments based on law. It stands in contrast to decisions based on naked power, arbitrary fiat, political expediency or personal gain. But most meaningfully, it encompasses much more than simply the opposite of these negative images. Individual judgments differ as to the core underpinnings of the rule of law, but I believe there are at least five principal tenets—each with a number of fundamental sub-tenets. These five highest-level tenets are:

• government of the people, by the people, and for the people; (For the origin of this phrasing, see President Abraham Lincoln's Gettysburg Address, November 19, 1863.) (*See also* the French Constitution.)

- separation of powers and checks and balances;

- representative democracy and procedural and substantive limits on governmental action against the individual (the protection of human freedom and dignity);

- limited government and federalism; and

- review by an independent judiciary as a central mechanism for constitutional enforcement." (Moore, "The Rule of Law: An Overview," paper presented to the Seminar on the Rule of Law, Moscow and Leningrad, USSR, March 19–23, 1990 [USIA translation to Russian for conference proceedings publication, forthcoming 1992, Progress Press, USSR].)

This overview paper, which examines in detail these major tenets, as well as "Some Essential Components of Limited Government and Protection of Individual Rights and Freedoms in a Representative Democracy," "Some Essential Components of the Rule of Law Within an Independent and Democratic Judicial Process," and "The Rule of Law in International Affairs," is set out as an Afterword in this paper.

In defining the broad meaning of the rule of law, it is instructive to consider the famous Hart-Fuller debate about the meaning of law. Professor H.L.A. Hart, with characteristic English clarity, maintained that it is essential to keep the term "law" free from any particular content, without judging whether it is good or bad law. (Hart, "Positivism and the Separation of Law and Morals," *Harvard Law Review*, Vol. 71, 1958, p. 593.) Professor Lon Fuller, on the other hand, equally strenuously insisted that, in order to be most meaningful and to produce the effect we seek in the real world, the word "law" must be used only when the system embodies certain fundamental internal principles of "morality" by which a good legal system operates. (Fuller, "Positivism and Fidelity to Law—A Reply to Professor Hart," *Harvard Law Review*, Vol. 71, 1958, p. 630.)

Without taking sides in this debate (and both assertions may be correct depending on the reason one asks, what is law?), I think it may be imperative to have a phrase standing for *all* of the fundamental principles we regard as essential to liberal democracy and a good rule of law. I propose that we use the phrase "the rule of law" for this, as indeed it has begun to be adopted internationally.

"Rule of law engagement" also has a second meaning. The first, as discussed, involves an effort to encourage through a multiplicity of foreign policy devices and arenas, the spread of liberal democracy as a governing basis for nation-states. At the least, the effort should be made to move totalitarian regimes toward the more authoritarian portion of the governmental spectrum that poses a greatly decreased risk of democide and war. Ultimately, of course, the objective is, in fact, to promote liberal democracy built around checks and balances on power.

The second meaning, however, involves a *major* and consistent effort in foreign policy to promote the rule of law in international relations. Most important, this means a major foreign policy effort to strengthen international condemnation of both democide and aggressive attack and, of equal importance in avoiding war, to strengthen assistance to defense against aggressive attack from the international community, whether that aggression takes the form of open invasion or covert hostage taking, terrorism, or other "low-intensity" aggression. Significantly, it is the *differential* between the international community's treatment of aggression and its treatment of defense that can add to effective deterrence against agression, and *not* simply a condemnation of all use of force, as is frequently assumed. Paradoxically, as the condemnation of all use of force has gained de facto dominance in international relations, fueled by scholars and statesmen who strongly believed this was the route to peace, we have simultaneously largely destroyed the effectiveness of law in deterring aggression, thus eroding the most important principle for world order of the United Nations Charter. The reason for this unfortunate result is simple, obvious, and hugely neglected: Law will not help to *deter* an aggressor if its cost to the defender is perceived to be equal to or greater than its cost to the aggressor.

## Objections to "Rule of Law" and "Liberal Democracy" Engagement

We are all familiar with a host of conventional objections to rule of law engagement and vigorous efforts at "democracy building." I believe that such objections are the "old thinking" that must be set aside if we are as serious as we should be in our foreign policy about seeking to promote human rights and economic development and to end democide and major war.

The first objection is simply a misinterpretation of what is meant by the rule of law. As used in this paper, the rule of law is *not* a phrase signifying narrow legalities. Rather, it stands for fundamental principles of good government that seem strongly linked by the empirical data to protection of human rights, economic development, and avoidance of democide and major war. Although it can be argued that phrases such as "democracy building" would better convey the important content here, "rule of law" is achieving considerable international success as a rallying cry; and, moreover, the term "democracy" has been frequently borrowed by the worst kinds of totalitarian regimes.

The second objection to rule of law and liberal democracy engagement is that we should not seek to impose our system on others; governmental structures should reflect local conditions and aspirations. This objection has force because it reflects sensitivity to differing conditions and to self-determination. Although it is true, of course, that we should not impose our system on others, if read too broadly, this objection becomes an argument for *not* sharing with others what we believe to be the most important component of our own success: our democratic governmental structures. It is somewhat paradoxical that we would be willing to share health or computer technology with others and yet believe that it is impermissible to share the most important fundaments of our system. Moreover, this approach ignores the extraordinary eagerness for assistance in building liberal democracy that we now see arising from much of the world.

The objection that we should not seek to impose our system on others is, in its most extreme form, also too relativistic. Human experience does *not* record that all governments are fungible. Rather, the data *strongly* shows a correlation between totalitarian systems and human rights violations, democide, and even major aggressive attacks. This objection may also inadvertently reveal a chauvinism in the objector, who may believe that a concept such as "government of the people, by the people, and for the people" is peculiarly American. The French, of course, would dispute this vigorously. The reality is that liberal democracy shares broad international origins.

Furthermore, for years we have accepted the "new thinking" in human rights engagement. No one today could effectively argue that we should not interfere in the cultural choices of nations that chose to commit major human rights abuses or slaughter their populations. The real world shows that a powerful correlation *does* exist between forms of government and the achievement of human rights. Thus, if we are serious about human rights, it is inevitable that we move forward to engagement on governmental structures.

A third common objection to rule of law engagement is a variant of the second, only this one focuses on pointing out the flaws and imperfections in our own system or in liberal democracy as a model. Flaws and imperfections there are and have been, but to dwell on them is to miss the enormous comparative success of the democracies measured by virtually every major standard. In a comparative sense, these objections usually reveal that the critic is more aware of the imperfections of his or her own culture than of the extraordinary abuses by totalitarian regimes. No government is completely benign. Indeed, that reality is a major premise of liberal democracy, which is rooted in checks and balances and protection for the individual against the state. Thus, not surprisingly, the record of democracies as opposed to that of totalitarian regimes is as different as day is to night. The "new thinkers" in Eastern Europe and the Soviet Union

who have personally experienced totalitarianism understand this better than critics who have experienced only
liberal democracy.

A fourth objection, which might be more properly described as a "confusion," has involved dismissing efforts
at human rights and rule of law engagement as inconsistent or unattainable in a foreign policy environment
where difficult choices must all too frequently be made
in working, or maintaining relations, with less than perfect regimes. To defeat Hitler, the United States assisted
Stalin. To resist totalitarianism during a half-century-
long struggle, the democracies have repeatedly aided
authoritarian regimes, some of which have had quite
poor human rights records. No policy can relieve us of
the necessity of making difficult choices in real-world
settings when United States foreign policy goals do not
all cut neatly in the same direction, and no policy will be
self-defining about its best application in the real world.

For example, these problems of choice and application
form the essence of the debate about United States policy
toward the People's Republic of China following the
events of 1989 in Tiananmen Square. What is the best
way to approach China and move it toward human rights,
the rule of law, and a new world order? A policy of rule of
law engagement does not automatically define the best
method (including isolation) for such engagement at any
particular time. Concerning this objection, Lawrence
Harrison writes in his generally favorable review of
Joshua Muravchik's recent book:

"The streak of idealistic purism in *Exporting Democracy* surfaces again when Muravchik says, '... the
[nonconfrontational] policy of the Bush administra-

tion toward China has been . . . incomprehensible.' The Bush policy may or may not be wrong, but it is surely comprehensible. It raises an age-old diplomatic dilemma: if I publicly confront this government, it may change its policies as I wish. But if it doesn't, then the diplomatic dialogue is over, and I've lost access and influence. The dilemma, reminiscent of the debates over our posture toward South Africa, is underscored by events since *Exporting Democracy* was published. What would have been the consequences in the Persian Gulf—on key U.N. votes, for example—if the United States had alienated China? I note in passing that neither any Western nation nor Japan is pursuing the kind of policy Muravchik counsels, in part, I'm sure, because of concern about future economic relationships with the world's most populous country.

"Promotion of democracy can and should—and probably now does—receive a higher priority than it has previously. But there will always be currents and realities influencing U.S. foreign policy that may conflict with the promotion of democracy and simply cannot be ignored...." (Harrison, "Nurturing Democracy Abroad," *Freedom Review*, Vol. 22, September–October 1991, p.42 at col. 3, a review of Joshua Muravchik, *Exporting Democracy: Fulfilling America's Destiny*, AEI Press, 1991.)

Finally, as I mentioned above, political "realists" and "realpolitik" thinkers for a long time have relegated ideas, morality, and law to a subsidiary role in foreign policy. They have viewed foreign policy as a field properly concerned with power; and considerations of ideas, morality, and law were regarded as the playthings of generally benign but fussy or irrelevant thinkers.

With some caveats, one might also view these objections in "left-right" terms. The political right (or, in this case, the conventional foreign policy wisdom) has dismissed ideas such as liberal democracy and the rule of law in foreign policy as of little relevance in a realpolitik model. The political left has focused on flaws in the liberal democracies to conclude wrongly that all existing governmental systems are fungible or even that totalitarian systems based on communitarian ideals hold promise for the future despite their "imperfections." Dave McCurdy examines this theme, writing:

> "[C]ynicism may be the biggest illusion we suffer from in foreign affairs. . . . Some on the right believe that America's history and institutions make us and our West European friends uniquely suited to democracy. For other peoples, they imply, the best to be hoped for is 'stability.' . . .
>
> "Realism of a different kind was found on the left. Those enchanted with heroic promises made by revolutionaries in Latin America, Africa and Southeast Asia warned that the United States would be fighting the inevitable tide of history if we let scruples about human rights and democracy turn us against the 'people's liberation' movements. . . . Ironically, realism in foreign policy was where cynicism of the right—cynicism about foreigners' capacity for democracy—converged with cynicism of the left— cynicism toward American-style democracy."

(McCurdy,"Bad Week for 'Realism,'" *Washington Post*, September 2, 1991, p. A23, cols. 2-3.)

## Modes of Implementation of Rule of Law Engagement

If we assume that rule of law engagement and an approach built on assistance rooted in the moral foundations of liberal democracy make sense as central (not just important) components of foreign policy, how do we put these concepts into practice?

First, it should be noted that the most important step has already been taken. Under the leadership of Ambassador Max Kampelman, the June 1990 meeting in Copenhagen of the Conference on Security and Cooperation in Europe (CSCE) adopted an extraordinary document about the rule of law. This Copenhagen Document is one of the most important documents in human history, yet it has received little press attention. It is, by analogy, the "rule of law" or "governmental structures" counterpart to the Helsinki "human rights basket" that played so great a role in human rights engagement. Perhaps an even more powerful analogy is that just as the Magna Carta recognized certain obligations of the English government to its people, the Copenhagen Document has *internationalized* a detailed code of obligations concerning *governmental structures* and the rule of law. Henceforth, a requirement such as "political parties will not be merged with the State" is a legitimate subject of *international concern*. ("Document of the Copenhagen Meeting of the Conference on the Human Dimension of the CSCE, June 1990," U.S. Commission on Security and Cooperation in Europe, Washington, D.C., I[5.4].)

The Copenhagen Document contains principles agreed to and accepted by North Atlantic Treaty Organization states, the Soviet Union (even prior to the August 1991 revolution), Eastern European states, and the neutral and non-aligned nations of Europe. Examples of these principles include:

"The participating States express their conviction that the protection and promotion of human rights and fundamental freedoms is one of the basic purposes of government, and reaffirm that the recognition of these rights and freedoms constitutes the foundation of freedom, justice and peace.

"They are determined to support and advance those principles of justice which form the basis of the rule of law. They consider that the rule of law does not mean merely a formal legality which assures regularity and consistency in the achievement and enforcement of democratic order, but justice based on the recognition and full acceptance of the supreme value of the human personality and guaranteed by institutions providing a framework for its fullest expression.

"They reaffirm that democracy is an inherent element of the rule of law. They recognize the importance of pluralism with regard to political organizations.

"They confirm that they will respect each other's right freely to choose and develop, in accordance with international human rights standards, their political, social, economic and cultural systems. In exercising this right, they will ensure that their laws, regulations, practices and policies conform with their obligations under international law and are brought into harmony with the provisions of the Declaration on Principles and other CSCE commitments." ("Document of the Copenhagen Meeting," I(1) through I(4) [paragraph numbers omitted]. Because of the great importance of the Copenhagen Document, please review the more extensive excerpts of these principles that are provided in Appendix I of this paper.)

Clearly, the Copenhagen Document is a milestone in the internationalization of the rule of law and human progress toward genuine democratic principles. This process must be vigorously continued within the CSCE and possibly elsewhere.

Illustrative suggestions for further modalities in rule of law engagement include the following:

1.  We should create an interagency task force on implementing rule of law engagement and place someone such as Ambassador Richard Schifter or Ambassador Max Kampelman in charge. This paper begins with an excerpt from the 1991 *National Security Strategy* report that shows that rule of law engagement has already been incorporated into United States foreign policy. That same report's three-paragraph treatment of the subject illustrates, however, that its potential as a *major* component of U.S. foreign policy has not yet been fully internalized by the foreign policy process. (See The White House, *National Security Strategy of the United States, August 1991*, U.S. Government Printing Office, 1991, p. 14, col. 1.)

2. We should seek to coordinate rule of law engagement modalities with our allies. The issue should be on every Summit agenda, and perhaps we should begin a rule of law caucusing group within the United Nations system.

3. We should vigorously encourage exchange programs and educational programs of every type focused on constitutionalism, human rights, and the rule of law.

4. We should seek to promote regional counterparts to the CSCE process for Asia, Africa, Latin America, and the Middle East. Such regional CSCE processes should then focus on rule of law and human rights engagement as well as confidence-building measures.

5. Just as with human rights engagement, we should carefully explore appropriate linkages for promoting rule of law objectives.

## Conclusion

As Lawrence E. Harrison has written, "Surely, the priority of the pro-democracy component of our foreign policy merits upgrading at this turning point in history." *(Id.*, pp. 42, 44.) One of the most important approaches in our foreign policy, that of human rights engagement, was resisted by the conventional foreign policy process. The thinking behind the conventional process mistakenly assumed that issues of morality and ideas were "soft" and unimportant in a rough-and-tumble foreign policy world dominated by power. Moreover, conventional foreign policy maintained that it was impermissible to try to tell states how to treat their own citizens and that such an attempt would surely backfire and add new tensions to our foreign policy. The cornerstone of war prevention was perceived as nuclear arms control with the Soviet Union.

We now know that one of the most important foreign policy initiatives has been the general human rights engagement arising almost by accident from the Helsinki human rights basket. This experience (and an impressive body of data about the behavior of governments) suggests that, as the next step, rule of law engagement has great promise to work for human rights and peace in our international relations.

Ideas, morality, and law certainly do matter. They are of *fundamental* importance as we seek to shape our foreign policy for a new world order. We must ensure that this reality is *internalized* within the foreign policy process of the democracies.

## Afterword on the Rule of Law

> "[W]hile the laws shall be obeyed all will be safe."
>
> Thomas Jefferson, Original draft of first Inaugural Address, March 4, 1801.

On March 19–23, 1990, a Seminar on the Rule of Law was held in Moscow and Leningrad, where delegations from the United States and the Soviet Union joined in discussing the full meaning of the rule of law. Serving as Co-Chairman, with the U.S. Deputy Attorney General, for the American Delegation, I presented the overview paper for the delegation, which is provided in this After-word, with the omission of the introductory paragraphs. (Moore, "The Rule of Law: An Overview," paper presented to the Seminar on the Rule of Law, Moscow and Leningrad, USSR, March 19-23, 1990 [USIA translation to Russian for conference proceedings publication, forthcoming 1992, Progress Press, USSR].)

## I. Introduction

. . . . .

The overview discussion which follows will first set forth what I believe to be major tenets of the rule of law. It will then consider some essential components of limited government and individual rights and freedoms in a representative democracy and some essential components of the rule of law within an independent and democratic judicial process. Finally, it will note the importance of the rule of law in international affairs and of a robust legal profession. Throughout, this paper is guided by a spirit of candor, irrespective of any possible philosophical differences perceived between and possibly even within delegations.

## II.  Major Tenets of the Rule of Law

The "rule of law" collectively symbolizes the most important features of democratic governance. Its core meaning is that governmental decisions must be rooted in the consent of the governed, acting only through structures and procedures designed to prevent individual oppression or governmental tyranny, which protect fundamental rights and freedoms, and which are subject to appraisal by an independent judiciary rendering judgments based on law. It stands in contrast to decisions based on naked power, arbitrary fiat, political expediency or personal gain. But most meaningfully, it encompasses much more than simply the opposite of these negative images. Individual judgments differ as to the core underpinnings of the rule of law, but I believe there are at least five principal tenets—each with a number of fundamental sub-tenets. These five highest-level tenets are:

- government of the people, by the people, and for the people; (For the origin of this phrasing, see President Abraham Lincoln's Gettysburg Address, November 19, 1863.)
- separation of powers and checks and balances;
- representative democracy and procedural and substantive limits on governmental action against the individual (the protection of human freedom and dignity);
- limited government and federalism; and
- review by an independent judiciary as a central mechanism for constitutional enforcement.

Let us review each of these basic general tenets in turn.

### Government of the People, by the People, and for the People

Overwhelmingly, philosophers and political theorists have rooted the authority of *democratic* governance in the people—not in the few or an assumed elite. Thus, to Aristotle: "[I]n democracies the people are supreme. . . ."

(Aristotle, *Politics* [ca. 325 B.C.].) John Locke viewed government as being based on popular consent and wrote that governmental actions exceeding the laws are "without authority." (J. Locke, *Second Treatise of Civil Government* [1690].) In a famous phrase discussing abuse of power, he concluded: "Wherever law ends, tyranny begins. . . ." (*Id.*) Echoing these premises, the American Declaration of Independence provides:

> "We hold these truths to be self-evident, that all men are created equal; that they are endowed by their Creator with certain unalienable rights; that among these are life, liberty, and the pursuit of happiness. That, to secure these rights, governments are instituted among men, deriving their just powers from the consent of the governed . . . ." (The Declaration of Independence [U.S. July 4, 1776].)

Adopted less than three weeks earlier, the Virginia Bill of Rights provides "[t]hat all power is vested in, and consequently derived from, the people." (From Article 2 of the Virginia Bill of Rights [June 12, 1776].) This is emphatically not the concept of the unchallengeable general will underlying the philosophy of Jean Jacques Rousseau under which "the public must be taught to know what it wants." (J.J. Rousseau, *The Social Contract* [1762].) Needless to say, the Western democratic conception of "government of the people, by the people, and for the people" also is emphatically *not* the inverted social contract of Rousseau as reflected in his social contract oath for his proposed Constitution for Corsica, which provides: "I join myself, body, goods, will and all my powers, to the Corsican nation, granting her ownership of me, of myself and all who depend on me." (Printed in 2 *The Political Writings of Rousseau* 250 [C.R. Vaughan ed., 2 vols., Cambridge 1915]. *See also* Chapter 1 in P. Johnson, *Intellectuals* [1988].)

Collaries of this first principle that the authority of law comes from the governed include the following:

- Constitutions should embody the fundamental compact with the people—such constitutions should serve as the highest form of law to which all other laws and governmental actions must conform. As such, constitutions should embody the *fundamental* precepts of a democratic society rather than serving to incorporate ever-changing laws more appropriately dealt with by statute. Similarly, governmental structures and actions should *seriously* conform with constitutional norms, and constitutions should not be mere ceremonial or aspirational documents.

- Legislatures and chief executives should be popularly elected under a system which will ensure frequent accountability. Elections must in practice be fully fair, open and meaningful. Mechanisms, such as initiative and recall, might be devised to keep elected officials close to the people.

- There should be no merger of a political party with the State or control of the electoral process by a political party. It is the freely elected representatives of the people, acting through *governmental* structures such as the legislative and executive branches, which should govern the State.

- The constitutional system should provide for reasonable change and amendment as conditions and the popular will change.

*Separation of Powers and Checks and Balances*

A principal underpinning of much writing on democratic governance and the rule of law is that governmental structures should be constructed through a separation of powers and checks and balances to prevent governmental tyranny. Thus, Montesquieu wrote in *The Spirit of the Laws* in 1748:

> "The political liberty of the subject is a tranquillity of mind, arising from the opinion each person has of his safety. In order to have this liberty, it is requisite the government be so constituted as one man need not be afraid of another.
>
> "When the legislative and executive powers are united in the same person, or in the same body of magistrates, there can be no liberty; because apprehensions may arise, lest the same monarch or senate should enact tyrannical laws, to execute them in a tyrannical manner.
>
> "Again, there is no liberty, if the judicial power be not separated from the legislative and executive. Were it joined with the legislative, the life and liberty of the subject would be exposed to arbitrary control; for the judge would be then the legislator. Were it joined to the executive power, the judge might behave with all the violence of an oppressor." Montesquieu, *The Spirit of the Laws* [1748].)

The connection between this principle of separation of powers and the rule of law was vividly reflected in the Constitution of the State of Massachusetts adopted in 1780:

> "In the government of this Commonwealth, the legislative department shall never exercise the executive and judicial powers, or either of them: The executive shall never exercise the legislative and judicial powers, or either of them: The judicial shall never exercise the legislative and executive powers, or either of them: to the end it may be a government of laws and not of men." (The Constitution of the Commonwealth of Massachusetts, "Part the First," art. XXX [1780], *reprinted in* M. Connolly, *The Constitution of the Commonwealth of Massachusetts* 3, 10 [1984].)

And this principle was a major underpinning of the United States Constitution. As James Madison wrote in *The Federalist* papers, explaining the new Constitution:

> "No political truth is certainly of greater intrinsic value or is stamped with the authority of more enlightened patrons of liberty than that on which the objection is founded. The accumulation of all powers legislative, executive and judiciary in the same hands, whether of one, a few or many, and whether hereditary, self appointed, or elective, may justly be pronounced the very definition of tyranny. Were the federal constitution therefore really chargeable with this accumulation of power or with a mixture of powers having a dangerous tendency to such an ac-

cumulation, no further arguments would be necessary to inspire a universal reprobation of the system."
(*The Federalist* No. 47, at 324 [J. Madison] [J. Cooke
ed. 1961].)

Similarly this principle was a fundamental tenet of
the 1789 French Declaration of the Rights of Man, where
it was said: "Any society in which the guarantee of the
rights is not secured, or the separation of powers not determined, has no constitution at all." (Article 16 of the
Declaration of the Rights of Man and the Citizen [Aug.
26, 1789].)

It should be noted that the principle of separation of
powers does not stand in opposition to a strong legislature or a strong executive. Indeed, it is partly rooted in
the functional attributes and efficiencies of each branch
in respectively making, applying and enforcing the laws
(as well as the executive role in foreign affairs). And it is
critically complemented by checks and balances, such
as, for example, in the American system, the right of the
Executive to veto legislation, the right of the Senate to
withhold advice and consent to a treaty, and the requirement that Congress rather than the Executive "declare
War" and "raise and support Armies." It should also be
noted that an independent judiciary is a major corollary
of this principle of separation of powers. Moreover, the
Framers of the United States Constitution, recognizing
the potential great power of the legislature in making
laws, provided checks and balances even within the legislature by providing for a bicameral legislature elected
by differing constituencies and for different terms. Finally, it should be noted that if separation of powers and
checks and balances are avoided by unitary party con-

trol of all branches of government then the benefits of this fundamental underpinning of the rule of law could be easily lost. This is yet another reason for avoiding a merger of a political party with the State.

*Representative Democracy and Procedural and Substantive Limits on Governmental Action Against the Individual (The Protection of Human Freedom and Dignity)*

Every democracy faces the problem of how to protect fundamental human freedom and dignity against governmental action—whether arbitrary or mandated by a majority. The most important and recurrent answer to this issue has been to provide constitutional guarantees of basic human freedoms—frequently denominated as a "bill of rights." Other partial answers, however, involve building in checks against factionalism and hasty laws through *representative* democracy, *bicameralism* and *cautious modes of legislative deliberation and action,* as well as endowing government only with *limited authority* not extending to compromising such basic freedoms. Among other examples of a "bill of rights" approach, in 1215, the Magna Carta extracted a series of rights as pledges from a reluctant King John. This included these rights:

> "No free man shall be taken or imprisoned or dispossessed, or outlawed, or banished, or in any way destroyed, nor will we go upon him, nor send upon him, except by the legal judgment of his peers or by the law of the land.

"To no one will we sell, to no one will we deny, or delay right or justice." (Magna Carta, nos. 39 & 40 [1215].)

Similarly, following the revolution of 1688, the British Parliament extracted a "bill of rights" from the Crown. The State of Virginia adopted the Virginia Bill of Rights in 1776; in 1789 during the early months of the French Revolution, the National Constituent Assembly formulated a "Declaration of the Rights of Man and of the Citizen"; and following a major debate about the new Constitution, the first Congress of the United States formulated the Bill of Rights that was ratified by the states effective December 15, 1791. In 1991, America will celebrate the bicentennial of this Bill of Rights of fundamental freedoms. Time has confirmed their importance to an enduring democratic government.

It should also be noted that the protection of fundamental rights extends both to substantive and procedural rights, including essential procedural elements incorporated in American law in the concept of due process of law. The cornerstone of the criminal justice system, as well as of administrative law, is these concepts of procedural due process. Finally, it should be noted that protection of fundamental liberties is seen as sufficiently essential to democratic governance and the rule of law that many political theorists have stressed the protection of such freedoms as a fundamental objective of democratic governance without which no government can be just. Aristotle wrote in *Politics:* "The basis of a democratic state is liberty; which, according to the common opinion of men, can only be enjoyed in such a state;—this they affirm to be the great end of every democracy."

(Aristotle, *Politics* [ca. 325 B.C.].) The Declaration of Independence speaks of securing "life, liberty, and the pursuit of happiness" as the very reason for government, and the preamble of the United States Constitution includes among the reasons for establishing the Constitution that it is to "secure the Blessings of Liberty to ourselves and our Posterity." Certainly there can be no meaningful rule of law which does not protect fundamental human freedom and dignity *as a very reason for government.*

## Limited Government and Federalism

Yet another underpinning of the rule of law is the related principles of limited government and federalism. As has just been discussed, the principle of a limited government of enumerated powers has been one partial answer to the protection of fundamental freedoms. Indeed, in *The Federalist* papers, Alexander Hamilton urged that the limited powers of the new federal constitution made a specific bill of rights unnecessary.

Limited central government, however, serves another important function in the rule of law in maximizing regional and local control of governmental functions principally affecting peoples at a local level. In this context, limited government and federalism divide governmental authority between a central government, which should have authority in issues of defense, foreign policy, interstate commerce and other issues of governance affecting citizens on a national basis, and regional and local governmental authorities, which should have authority in issues of governance such as municipal services and education primarily affecting citizens on a more local basis. This principle simultaneously makes government more responsive to and controllable by the people and encourages a diversity in public policies adopted within different regions according to local conditions, needs, traditions and desires. It directly incorporates an insight of participatory democracy that groups affected by decisions should have a voice in those decisions. As correctly perceived, it does not detract from strong federal authority in the areas where authority must be and is centralized in a national government.

Adjusting the boundaries between the federal and regional governmental units and maintaining a proper balance is necessarily the essence of a large body of law in any federal system. Federalism, of course, assumes an at least initial voluntary acceptance by constituent units.

*Judicial Review by an Independent Judiciary*
*as a Central Mechanism for Constitutional Enforcement*

An independent judiciary is a critical component of the principle of separation of powers, as well as of an effective principle of constitutionalism in embodying and realizing the major conditions of the consent of the governed. The "Introduction" to *Judicial Review and American Democracy* roots judicial review in "the belief that the Constitution is the Supreme expression of the people's will." Thus, it says:

"The ultimate and necessary foundation upon which judicial review rests is the belief that the Constitution is the supreme expression of the people's will. Since it results from the acts of the people in their constituent capacity, it is fundamental law embody-

ing the people's determination of the proper division
and extent of governing authority between the various branches of the national government; between
the central government and the state governments;
between the national government and individuals;
and, especially under the expanded application of the
Fourteenth Amendment, between state governments
and individuals." (Melone and Mace, *Judicial Review
and American Democracy* 3 [1988]. *The Federalist*
No. 78 [Hamilton] provides perhaps the strongest indication in constitutional history that the Framers
contemplated judicial review concerning issues of
constitutional consistency.)

Because of the *great* importance of judicial review as a
central mechanism for constitutional enforcement and
for maintenance of the rule of law, however, I believe
that it should be considered a fundamental principle in
its own right. Indeed, no principle in the American experience has been more important in maintaining the
integrity of the major constitutional underpinnings of
the rule of law than has the principle of independent
judicial review. Thus, the Supreme Court, in the 1962
reappointment decision of *Baker v. Carr*, has sought to
police the integrity of the "one person one vote" principle
underlying government of the people, by the people, and
for the people. (Baker v. Carr, 369 U.S. 186 [1962].) In
major decisions such as *INS v. Chadha*, in which the
Court in 1983 struck down the so-called "legislative
veto," the Court has policed the critical workings of
separation of powers and checks and balances. (INS v.
Chadha, 462 U.S. 919 [1983].)

The Court has since its earliest days been repeatedly concerned with maintaining a proper balance in issues of federalism. And perhaps its most vital role has been in protecting the fundamental rights and freedoms of individuals against encroachment by federal and state action. As the Framers correctly foresaw, the judicial power could not be subsumed within the executive or legislative branches consistent with effective exercise of the judicial role in policing these principles of the rule of law. Indeed, judicial review by an independent judiciary may be the only way to *effectively* ensure the supremacy of the Constitution. The realization of this point was an essential element in the reasoning of Chief Justice John Marshall in the landmark decision of the Supreme Court in the 1803 case of *Marbury v. Madison*, setting out the doctrine of "judicial review" by declaring for the first time an act of Congress unconstitutional. (Marbury v. Madison, 5 U.S. 137 [1803].) Thus, Marshall wrote:

"Certainly all those who have framed written constitutions contemplate them as forming the fundamental and paramount law of the nation, and, consequently, the theory of every such government must be, that an act of the legislature, repugnant to the constitution, is void.

"This theory is essentially attached to a written constitution, and is, consequently, to be considered, by this court, as one of the fundamental principles of our society. It is not therefore to be lost sight of in the further consideration of this subject.

"If an act of the legislature, repugnant to the constitution, is void, does it, notwithstanding its invalidity, bind the courts, and oblige them to give it effect?

Or, in other words, though it be not law, does it constitute a rule as operative as if it was a law? This would be to overthrow in fact what was established in theory; and would seem, at first view, an absurdity too gross to be insisted on. It shall, however, receive a more attentive consideration.

"It is emphatically the province and duty of the judicial department to say what the law is. Those who apply the rule to particular cases, must of necessity expound and interpret that rule. If two laws conflict with each other, the courts must decide on the operation of each.

"So if a law be in opposition to the constitution; if both the law and the constitution apply to a particular case, so that the court must either decide that case conformably to the law, disregarding the constitution; or conformably to the constitution, disregarding the law; the court must determine which of these conflicting rules governs the case. This is of the very essence of judicial duty.

"If, then, the courts are to regard the constitution, and the constitution is superior to any ordinary act of the legislature, the constitution, and not such ordinary act, must govern the case to which they both apply.

"Those, then, who controvert the principle that the constitution is to be considered, in court, as a paramount law, are reduced to the necessity of maintaining that courts must close their eyes on the constitution, and see only the law.

"This doctrine would subvert the very foundation of all written constitutions. It would declare that an act which, according to the principles and theory of our government, is entirely void, is yet, in practice, completely obligatory. It would declare that if the legislature shall do what is expressly forbidden, such act, notwithstanding the express prohibition, is in reality effectual. It would be giving to the legislature a practical and real omnipotence, with the same breath which professes to restrict their powers within narrow limits. It is prescribing limits, and declaring that those limits may be passed at pleasure." *(Id.* at 176–78 [Opinion of the Court].)

A genuinely independent judiciary, of course, requires not only a doctrine of judicial review but also scrupulous protection of the independence of the judiciary in form and in fact. Details of appointment, tenure, salary, status, training and removal must all be resolved to preserve and strengthen that independence. Similarly, the selection of judiciary must not be on a partisan basis and should ensure the selection of the most qualified legal experts. And the legal profession, as well as the government and society as a whole, must internalize the independence of the judiciary and the important reasons for it.

## III. Some Essential Components of Limited Government and Protection of Individual Rights and Freedoms in a Representative Democracy

As has been discussed, major tenets of the rule of law in a representative democracy include limited government and constitutional limits on governmental action against the individual. In turn, these tenets include a broad range of substantive and procedural components.

Some such components widely regarded as essential include: preserving a climate of free discussion and opinion; fairness in criminal process; protection of religious freedom; protection of civil rights; accountability of governmental officials and protection of governmental processes; protection of the rights of workers; civilian control of the military; protecting the environment; and protecting economic freedom and entitlements. The following discussion of this list is emphatically *not* a complete inventory of fundamental components of the major tenets of limited government and constitutional limits on governmental action against the individual. (The rights to travel and emigrate and the right to privacy, for example, are also fundamental.)

*Preserving a Climate of Free Discussion and Opinion*

Nothing is more essential to the proper functioning of representative democracy than maintaining a climate of free discussion and opinion. This requires maintenance of freedom of speech; freedom of assembly; free and vital television, radio and newspaper media; freedom to petition government for redress of grievances; a free and vital publishing industry; academic freedom in institutions of higher learning; protection of exchange in the legislative process and depoliticization of governmental information efforts. Ultimately, an informed and involved citizenry is the lifeblood of democracy. As the writing of Thomas Jefferson reminds us:

"If a nation expects to be ignorant and free, in a state of civilization, it expects what never was and never will be." ("Letter to Colonel Charles Yancey, January

6, 1816," in 11 *The Works of Thomas Jefferson* 497
[P. Ford ed. 1905].)

Protecting the necessary climate of free discussion and
opinion is a crucial role of the rule of law.

### Fairness in Criminal Process

An essential element in the relationship of government to its citizens is the maintenance and operation of
a criminal process. Protection of the fairness and integrity of that process is an essential element of the rule of
law. The Magna Carta and numerous bills of rights
throughout human history attest to the importance of
such fairness. Indeed, the fourth, fifth, sixth and eighth
amendments in the Bill of Rights to the United States
Constitution directly relate to the fairness of criminal
processes, including requirements concerning search
and seizure (the fourth amendment); protection against
double-jeopardy and self-incrimination (the fifth amendment); the rights to a speedy and public trial by an impartial jury, to be informed of all charges, to be confronted
with adverse witnesses, to have compulsory process for
obtaining witnesses and to have the assistance of counsel
in defense (the sixth amendment); and prohibition of excessive bail or fines and of cruel and unusual punishment
(the eighth amendment).

Perhaps the most important guarantee undergirding
the protection of the individual against the State in criminal trials, however, is the presumption of innocence until
proven guilty. Similarly, the right of *habeas corpus*, ap-
pellate review of criminal convictions, and fairness in
sentencing and subsequent treatment are also vital. Also

of great concern, the criminal process must not be politicized or used for the punishment of political dissidents. Fairness in criminal process is not a monopoly of systems rooted in either common or civil law traditions. It is, however, a function of adherence to certain minimum standards such as advance promulgation of law, protection against unreasonable searches and seizures or unreasonable criminal charges, a high standard of proof by the finder of fact such as proof beyond a reasonable doubt, an impartial trial with an opportunity for an adequate defense, a right to independent advice of defense counsel, a strict separation of prosecutorial and judging functions, independent judges, and reasonable and proportional sentencing.

While all traditions can be rooted in the rule of law, I prefer the adversarial process of the common law tradition as providing greater protection for an accused and a more vigorous search for the truth, among other advantages. Of possible interest, a growing body of empirical social science evidence seems to support popular preference for an adversarial process involving a genuinely independent adversarial defense over an inquisitorial model. (See, e.g., E.A. Lind & T.R. Tyler, *The Social Psychology of Procedural Justice* [1988]. Cross-cultural aspects of this research indicate key findings are likely applicable to European conditions. *Id.* at 129–45.)

## Protection of Religious Freedom

The maintenance of religious freedom is one of the oldest and most important components of individual freedom. Thus, ensuring religious freedom is an essential component of the rule of law. Again, the importance of such freedom is attested throughout human history. It is a central component of, among other historic indicators, the Magna Carta in 1215, Roger Williams' "Bloudy Tenent of Persecution for Course of Conscience" in 1644, the Maryland Toleration Act of 1649, the Virginia Bill of Rights of 1776, Thomas Jefferson's masterful Virginia Statute for Religious Freedom in 1786, and the first amendment to the United States Constitution as ratified in 1791. The importance in Thomas Jefferson's mind of the Statute of Virginia for Religious Freedom is reflected in the epitaph he chose for his tombstone:

Here was buried
Thomas Jefferson
Author of the Declaration of American Independence
of the Statute of Virginia for religious freedom
& Father of the University of Virginia.

Religious freedom encompasses at least two vital and interrelated principles—the free exercise of religion and the non-establishment of religion. To avoid interference with the free exercise of religion, as well as to maintain consistency with the underlying purposes of non-establishment of religion, it would seem essential also that government not establish a doctrine of non-religion, just as it must not establish a particular religion. Finally, the full protection of religious freedom may require strong and effective civil rights laws to protect against discrimination on religious grounds.

*Protection of Civil Rights*

A democratic society must ensure equality before the

law and the protection of minority and even disadvantaged majority populations. The United States fought a civil war in the long struggle for effective realization of this principle, and with the Supreme Court leading the way in *Brown v. Board of Education* in 1954, the United States has taken this principle to heart. (*Brown v. Board of Education of Topeka*, 347 U.S. 483 [1954].) Today such civil rights, including protection against discrimination based on race, gender, or religion, are protected not only against abusive governmental action by constitutional principle, but also against both State and private action by a growing network of civil rights laws. Such laws are a vital component of the rule of law in a modern democratic society.

*Accountability of Governmental*
*Officials and Protection of Governmental Processes*

Any modern democratic society must have a vital network of laws to ensure accountability of governmental officials and protection of governmental processes and rational decision. Such laws may include measures to facilitate petition of government for redress of grievances, "freedom of information" laws, "sunshine" laws, private suits against government or government officials in certain cases, agency inspectors general, "whistle blower" laws, "impact statements" required before decision (used particularly in the environmental area), ombudsmen, conflict of interest laws, administrative remedies and appeals, and even independent counsel (though this check remains controversial in the United States).

## Protection of the Rights of Workers

Certainly every genuine democracy should seek to protect the rights of workers. Indeed, that is a major philosophical premise underlying the Soviet system. Yet, as the emergence of "solidarity" in Poland illustrates, the rights of workers can be abridged by the State at least as thoroughly as by private employers. The developed nations have created a detailed labor law centering on the rights of workers to organize and bargain collectively and on the maintenance of a safe and healthy work environment. The development and enforcement of such a body of labor law would seem an important component of the rule of law in a modern democratic society.

## Civilian Control of the Military

Many democratic societies have stressed the essential nature of civilian control of the military. In the United States this is guaranteed not only by important constitutional provisions concerning legislative control over military appropriations and appointments, but is also an essential element of the military's own code of professionalism. Similarly, the military follows a tradition that is nonpolitical. And, of course, this principle of civilian control of the military also applies to civilian control of intelligence agencies. (See generally Chapter 19 in *National Security Law* [J. Moore, R. Turner and F. Tipson eds. 1990] for measures ensuring civilian control of intelligence agencies within the United States and the operation of such agencies within the rule of law.) Both military and intelligence agencies must operate under the rule of law and constitutional structures.

## Protecting the Environment

One major reason for governmental intervention in a market economy is protection against "externalities" such as environmental damage. Because of the potentially great societal cost of environmental damage, insuring that environmental costs will be adequately considered and that high standards of environmental protection are met is an essential role of modern democratic governance. Moreover, because governmental actions and projects, if not directly accountable and if identified with government itself, have an equal if not greater potential for ignoring environmental costs than private sector actions, vigorous protection of the environment is essential in all systems.

## Protecting Economic Freedom and Entitlements

Perhaps no issue in the past has proceeded as thoroughly on different philosophical premises as the protection of economic freedom and property rights. The developed democracies, with a tradition of John Locke and market-oriented economies, have traditionally protected economic freedom and individual property rights. The Soviet system, however, has followed Marx and Engels in the abolition of many forms of private property. Thus, John Locke, in his *Second Treatise of Civil Government* in 1690, wrote at length in support "of property." And the breadth of support for this principle is illustrated by the 1789 French Declaration of the Rights of Man, which begins article 17 with the preamble "Property being a sacred and inviolable right. . . ." Yet the Communist Manifesto provides in relation to certain private property that "the theory of the Communists may be summed up in the single sentence: Abolition of private property."

Clearly, market-oriented economies are a major feature of the rule of law in developed societies based on Western democratic values. The economic success of those societies, not only in enhancing overall production of goods and services, but also in broadly delivering consumer goods and services, speaks with the normative force of facts. Increasingly, however, the literature in the West has also shown a powerful connection between economic freedom generally, including private property rights, and both individual freedom and overall societal levels of freedom and success of governmental structures. Thus, property rights and freedom in the economic sphere are increasingly recognized as essential components of human freedom. For if tight control of property enables pervasive State control of the individual, then freedom can be lost as effectively as through the denial of civil and political freedoms. Indeed, Professor Charles A. Reich writes in a famous article on "The New Property" that "[t]he institution called property guards the troubled boundary between individual man and the state." (C. Reich, "The New Property," 73 *Yale L.J.* 733 [1964].) And further:

> "At the very least, it is time to reconsider the theories under which new forms of wealth are regulated, and by which governmental power over them is measured. It is time to recognize that "the public interest" is all too often a reassuring platitude that covers up sharp clashes of conflicting values, and hides fundamental choices. It is time to see that the 'privilege" or 'gratuity' concept, as applied to wealth dis-

pensed by government, is not much different from the absolute right of ownership that private capital once invoked to justify arbitrary power over employees and the public.

"Above all, the time has come for us to remember what the framers of the Constitution knew so well— that 'a power over a man's subsistence amounts to a power over his will.' We cannot safely entrust our livelihoods and our rights to the discretion of authorities, examiners, boards of control, character committees, regents, or license commissioners. We cannot permit any official or agency to pretend to sole knowledge of the public good. We cannot put the independence of any man . . . wholly in the power of other men." (*Id.* at 787.)

Of particular relevance concerning a system in which the individual must rely heavily on government "entitlements," a central thrust of this article by Professor Reich is the importance of protecting these State-controlled "entitlements" as "the new property" against arbitrary or politicized government denial. Moreover, the roles of private property in providing individual incentive and as a prerequisite for voluntary exchange, which is the basic mechanism of decentralized market systems, has long been recognized in the developed democracies. Indeed, there is a growing feeling among many in the West that political systems which broadly limit private property rights may not be able to adopt more open governmental processes without also adopting greater economic freedom—going far beyond efforts at greater decentralization of governmental planning. The reason is that the resulting inefficiencies in relatively centralized governmental setting of prices, as opposed to the decentralized actions of markets, may inevitably lead either to popular efforts at fundamental change in government structures or to massive emigration, as was most recently evident in the events in the German Democratic Republic following the courageous and internationally applauded dismantlement of the Berlin Wall. A discussion of this potential linkage between freedom in the economic sphere and freedom elsewhere appears in the *Economic Report of the President* transmitted to the United States Congress in February 1982. Chapter Two of this report on "Government and the Economy" begins:

"Political freedom and economic freedom are closely related. Any comparison among contemporary nations or examination of the historical record demonstrates two important relationships between the nature of the political system and the nature of the economic system:

"• All nations which have broad-based representative government and civil liberties have most of their economic activity organized by the market.

"• Economic conditions in market economies are generally superior to those in nations (with a comparable culture and a comparable resource base) in which the government has the dominant economic role.

"The evidence is striking. No nation in which the government has the dominant economic role (as measured by the proportion of gross national product originating in the government sector) has maintained broad political freedom; economic conditions in such countries are generally inferior to those in comparable nations with a predominantly market economy. Voluntary migration, sometimes at high personal cost, is uniformly to nations with both more political freedom and more economic freedom.

"The reasons for these two relationships between political and economic systems are simple but not widely understood. Everyone would prefer higher prices for goods sold and lower prices for goods bought. Since the farmer's wheat is the consumer's bread, however, both parties cannot achieve all they want. The most fundamental difference among economic systems is how these conflicting preferences are resolved.

"A market system resolves these conflicts by allowing the seller to get the highest price at which others will buy and the buyer to get the lowest price at which others will sell, by consensual exchanges that are expected to benefit both parties. Any attempt by one party to improve his outcome relative to the market outcome requires a coercive activity at the expense of some other party. The politicization of price decisions—whether of wages, commodities, or interest rates—tends to reduce both the breadth of popular support for the government and the efficiency of the economy. A rich nation can tolerate a good bit of such mischief, but not an unlimited amount. One should not be surprised that all nations in which the government has dominant control of the economy are run by a narrow oligarchy and in most economic conditions are relatively poor. In the absence of limits on the economic role of government, the erosion of economic freedom destroys both political freedom and economic performance.

"Only a few dozen nations now guarantee their citizens both political and economic freedom. The economic role of government in these nations differs widely, without serious jeopardy to political freedom. Within the range of experience of the United States and the other free nations, the relation between the political system and the government's economic role is more subtle. Expansion of the economic role of the government tends to reduce both the level of agreement on government policies and the inclination to engage in political dissent. The link between political and economic freedom is important. Increasing economic freedom will also provide greater assurance of our political freedom.

"A major objective of this Administration's economic program is to reduce the Federal Government's role in economic decisionmaking while strengthening the economic role of individuals, private organizations, and State and local governments. This shift will entail substantial reductions in the size and number of Federal spending programs, significant reductions in both personal and business Federal tax rates, major reforms of Federal regulatory activities, and a reduced rate of money growth. While an important element in this redefinition of the Federal Government's economic role is a political judgment about the appropriate relationship among individuals, the States, and the Federal Government, this redefinition also is supported by an extensive body of economic analysis." (Chapter 2 "Government and the

Economy," from the "Annual Report of the Council of Economic Advisers," in *Economic Report of the President, Transmitted to the Congress February 1982*, at 27–28 [1982].)

Chapter Two also contains a good summary statement of the macroeconomic case for limited governmental intervention in private markets, including the concepts of: "externalities" (positive and negative), "monopoly," "public goods," "income redistribution" and "macroeconomic stability." And this chapter contains an interesting discussion of the theoretical reasons for "government failure" as opposed to "market failure" dealt with above as settings for limited government intervention. These reasons include the political process as "overly responsive to special interest groups," inefficiencies in "supply by government agencies," a failure to maximize responses to "diversity of conditions and preferences," "limits on information" and the over-discounting by government decisionmakers of programs which impose costs today in return for future benefits. (See *id.* at 29–42.)

As these theoretical points illustrate, modern democratic governance in a market economy has ample latitude for taxation and regulatory intervention (exercise of the "police power") to protect workers, consumers, investors and the environment without banning or overburdening the market economy itself.

Similarly, Justice Antonin Scalia, now of the United States Supreme Court, wrote in a book published in 1987:

"I know no society, today or in any era of history, in which high degrees of intellectual and political freedom have flourished side by side with a high degree of state control over the relevant citizen's economic life. The free market, which presupposes relatively broad economic freedom, has historically been the cradle of broad political freedom, and in modern times the demise of economic freedom has been the grave of political freedom as well." (A. Scalia, "Economic Affairs as Human Affairs," in *Economic Liberties and the Judiciary* 31, 32 [J. Dorn & H. Manne eds. 1987].)

Finally, quite apart from the considerable issues of necessity and of the costs to individual freedom and governmental systems from any such effort, questions are being raised in the West concerning the internal consistency of efforts to avoid exploitation of man by man through a denial of private property rights and economic freedom. That is, it has been argued that any thoroughgoing effort to ensure approximate economic equality requires the socialization of both economic success and economic failure. But, if that is so, then, in turn, does it not mean that inevitably there will be systematic exploitation of some groups (the economically successful) by others (the economically unsuccessful), and, moreover, that public officials, who have a major role in directing the economy in a non-market system, will have power, motive, and opportunity to do some exploiting of their own in a more direct way? (See generally S. Arnold, *Marx's Radical Critique of Capitalist Society: A Reconstruction and Critical Evaluation* [1990].)

Whatever the answers to these questions may be, it is increasingly clear that the protection of economic freedom is an essential component of the rule of law in a modern democratic society. I believe that addressing this issue fully and progressively is as important as any element in the overall process of "perestroika." (What is liberalized directly, of course, should not be banned indirectly through continuing criminalization of "profit," vaguely defined "speculation," or pervasive bureaucratic control.)

## IV. Some Essential Components of The Rule of Law Within an Independent and Democratic Judicial Process

One can also speak of essential components of the rule of law within a democratic *legislative* process. These would certainly include a presumption of openness in publication of draft laws, debate before adoption, and other measures concerning due process within the legislative process, as well as anti-corruption measures, among others. (For a general discussion of the legislative process, see J. Davies, *Legislative Law and Process* [2d ed. 1986]; W. Eskridge & P. Frickey, *Cases and Materials on Legislation: Statutes and the Creation of Public Policy* [1988]; and C. Nutting & R. Dickerson, *Cases and Materials on Legislation* [5th ed. 1978].)

Just as the fundamental tenets of limited government and protection of individual rights and freedoms depend importantly on a number of essential components, so, too, the rule of law within an independent judicial process depends on a number of essential components. These include:

- The supremacy of constitutional guarantees within the judicial process.

- The principle, *"nullum crimen, nulla poena, sine lege"* (literally meaning that without a law, there can be no crime and no punishment), that there can be no penalty without prior, publicly known and reasonably specific laws.

A seemingly similar statement was apparently made by President Mikhail Gorbachev at the Nineteenth Party Conference: "[W]e must adhere strictly to the principle that everything that is not prohibited by law is permitted." ("Gorbachev Report Sizes Up Restructuring," 40:26 *Current Dig. of the Soviet Press 7*, 19 [Jul. 27, 1988].)

Professor John Jeffries of the University of Virginia says of the rule of law in the context of the "vagueness" issue in this tenet:

> "The evils to be retarded are caprice and whim, the misuse of government power for private ends, and the unacknowledged reliance on illegitimate criteria of selection. The goals to be advanced are regularity and evenhandedness in the administration of justice and accountability in the use of government power. In short, the 'rule of law' designates the cluster of values associated with conformity to law by government." (Jeffries, *Legality, Vagueness, and the Construction of Penal Statutes, 71 U. Virginia L. Rev. 189*, 212–13 [1985].)

It should be emphasized that secret laws and regulations, unknown to those to whom they will be applied, are fundamentally inconsistent with the rule of law.

- The principle of decisions based on law, stemming from an analysis of the functional intent of the lawmaker as opposed to political factors, party affiliation, personal gain or arbitrary fiat. The essence of an independent judicial process is judging based on rational analysis of the law and its underlying policies as applied in a specific case.

- The principle that "like cases should be treated alike."
- The principle that reasons should be given for decisions, that the reasons given should be candid for appraisal by others, and that such opinions should be published and made widely available to lawyers and in specialized libraries.
- The principle that judges should defer to clear higher authority within a system, whether it is a constitution, a legislative enactment, or a higher court within an overall judicial system. That is, in constitutional interpretation the judge is not superior to the Constitution, in statutory interpretation the judge is not superior to a clear intent of the legislature, and a judge is bound to follow a ruling on point of a higher judge within an overall judicial system.

These and other principles underlying the judicial process, including principles of interpretation, are not self-defining, and a rich body of jurisprudential writing addresses their meaning and effect. In particular, the legal realists have taught us that judicial decisionmaking is inevitably a process involving choice in rule selection, fact selection, and semantic and syntactic interpretation. (See, *e.g.*, Holmes, "The Path of the Law," 10 *Harv. L. Rev.* 457 (1897); Cardozo, *The Growth of Law* [1924]; K.N. Llewellyn, *The Common Law Tradition* [1960];

Allen & Caldwell, *"Modern Logic and Judicial Decision Making: A Sketch of One View,"* 28 *L. & Contemp. Problems* 213–24 [1963]. See also for a discussion of "the inner morality of law" in the new natural law tradition, Fuller, "Positivism and Fidelity to Law—A Reply to Professor Hart," 71 *Harv. L. Rev.* 630 [1958].) While opinions differ as to the precise content and effect of such principles, however, there is widespread agreement on their importance to the rule of law.

### V.  The Rule of Law in International Affairs

Just as the rule of law is an essential component in national life, so, too, it is an essential component in international life. As John Jay wrote in *The Federalist:*

> "It is of high importance to the peace of America, that she observe the laws of nations . . . ." (*The Federalist* No. 3, at 14 [J. Jay] [J. Cooke ed. 1961].)

And, as Thomas Jefferson wrote in 1790:

> "I think with others, that nations are to be governed with regard to their own interests, but I am convinced that it is their interest, in the long run, to be . . . faithful to their engagements, even in the worst of circumstances, and honorable and generous always." ("Letter to The Marquis De Lafayette, April 2, 1790," in 8 *The Writings of Thomas Jefferson* 12 [Mem. Ed. 1903].)

One fundamental principle in international affairs is, of course, that nations should follow the rules of treaty and customary international law binding on them. Perhaps the essential principle of world order, however, is that nations must adhere to the United Nations Charter obligation not to use force aggressively in international relations. In this connection the peoples of the democracies applaud the decision by President Gorbachev to repudiate the Brezhnev doctrine and to permit genuine self-determination in the countries of Eastern Europe.

Perhaps one area for future discussion might be an approach to "world peace accountability" that would highlight the critical importance of strict adherence to the Charter prohibition against aggressive use of force in international relations and would seek to raise public awareness of these issues much as the Helsinki process has raised public awareness of human rights issues. Indeed, one of the interesting paradoxes of beginning major international accountability with human rights accountability is that a whole network of practices and institutions has grown up around such human rights accountability, while there is no such network surrounding accountability for another central thrust of the United Nations Charter, the prohibition in Article 2(4) against the threat or use of aggressive force. (There is, of course, obviously a loose international network of claims and counterclaims and some degree of international institutions devoted to such accountability but, strikingly, nothing similar to human rights accountability as it has evolved in the Helsinki process.) Accountability to this great principle, however, is, like human rights, of obvious concern to all nations as they struggle for a world that is free from the aggressive use of force. Indeed, in an age in which legal scholars can debate the "death" of Article 2(4) of the Charter, something badly needs to be done, if possible, to revitalize this fundamental principle. Moreover, the recent statement by President Mikhail Gorbachev before the United Nations, in which he emphasized the impermissibility of the use of aggressive force in international relations, thus verbally recognizing this Charter principle as a cornerstone of world order, suggests an important opportunity to strengthen this principle through enhanced accountability.

## VI. A Robust Legal Profession

The rule of law inevitably requires a healthy and robust legal *profession*. This, in turn, requires high-quality legal education in a climate of academic freedom, a vital and independent organized bar, a tradition of understanding and protection for the lawyer's role in representing unpopular as well as popular clients and causes, an independent and learned judiciary, a code of professional ethics rooted in the independence and integrity of the judicial process, and a reliable and effective system of legal reporting and public dissemination of laws. Of necessity, the rule of law requires an adequate number of well-trained and professional lawyers and judges to provide defense counsel in criminal proceedings, to staff a genuinely independent judiciary, to provide advice on the law, and to carry out the myriad of other services performed by a professional bar. Resources, status, salaries and other incentives must be adequate to develop such a bar. A robust legal profession can also be assisted by enhancing support for institutions devoted to the recommendation and appraisal of individual laws and the operation of the legal system as a whole.

## Appendix I

*Excerpts from the Commission on
Security and Cooperation in Europe
"Document of the Copenhagen Meeting"*

("Document of the Copenhagen Meeting of the Conference on the Human Dimension of the CSCE, June 1990," U.S. Commission on Security and Cooperation in Europe, Washington, D.C., I(1)–I(8), III(26) & III(27).

I

(1)  The participating States express their conviction that the protection and promotion of human rights and fundamental freedoms is one of the basic purposes of government, and reaffirm that the recognition of these rights and freedoms constitutes the foundation of freedom, justice and peace.

(2)  They are determined to support and advance those principles of justice which form the basis of the rule of law. They consider that the rule of law does not mean merely a formal legality which assures regularity and consistency in the achievement and enforcement of democratic order, but justice based on the recognition and full acceptance of the supreme value of the human personality and guaranteed by institutions providing a framework for its fullest expression.

(3)  They reaffirm that democracy is an inherent element of the rule of law. They recognize the importance of pluralism with regard to political organizations.

(4)  They confirm that they will respect each other's right freely to choose and develop, in accordance with international human rights standards, their political, social, economic and cultural systems. In exercising this right, they will ensure that their laws, regula-

tions, practices and policies conform with their obligations under international law and are brought into harmony with the provisions of the Declaration on Principles and other CSCE commitments.

(5)        They solemnly declare that among those elements of justice which are essential to the full expression of the inherent dignity and of the equal and inalienable rights of all human beings are the following:

(5.1)    — free elections that will be held at reasonable intervals by secret ballot or by equivalent free voting procedure, under conditions which ensure in practice the free expression of the opinion of the electors in the choice of their representatives;

(5.2)    — a form of government that is representative in character, in which the executive is accountable to the elected legislature or the electorate;

(5.3)    — the duty of the government and public authorities to comply with the constitution and to act in a manner consistent with law;

(5.4)    — a clear separation between the State and political parties; in particular, political parties will not be merged with the State;

(5.5)    — the activity of the government and the administration as well as that of the judiciary will be exercised in accordance with the system established by law. Respect for that system must be ensured;

(5.6)    — military forces and the police will be under the control of, and accountable to, the civil authorities;

(5.7)    — human rights and fundamental freedoms will be guaranteed by law and in accordance with their obligations under international law;

(5.8)    — legislation, adopted at the end of a public procedure, and regulations will be published, that being the condition for their applicability. Those texts will be accessible to everyone;

(5.9) — all persons are equal before the law and are entitled without any discrimination to the equal protection of the law. In this respect, the law will prohibit any discrimination and guarantee to all persons equal and effective protection against discrimination on any grounds;

(5.10) — everyone will have an effective means of redress against administrative decisions, so as to guarantee respect for fundamental rights and ensure legal integrity;

(5.11) — administrative decisions against a person must be fully justifiable and must as a rule indicate the usual remedies available;

(5.12) — the independence of judges and the impartial operation of the public judicial service will be ensured;

(5.13) — the independence of legal practitioners will be recognized and protected, in particular as regards conditions for recruitment and practice;

(5.14) — the rules relating to criminal procedure will contain a clear definition of powers in relation to prosecution and the measures preceding and accompanying prosecution;

(5.15) — any person arrested or detained on a criminal charge will have the right, so that the lawfulness of his arrest or detention can be decided, to be brought promptly before a judge or other officer authorized by law to exercise this function;

(5.16) — in the determination of any criminal charge against him, or of his rights and obligations in a suit at law, everyone will be entitled to a fair and public hearing by a competent, independent and impartial tribunal established by law;

(5.17)   — any person prosecuted will have the right to defend himself in person or through prompt legal assistance of his own choosing or, if he does not have sufficient means to pay for legal assistance, to be given it free when the interests of justice so require;

(5.18)   — no one will be charged with, tried for or convicted of any criminal offence unless the offence is provided for by a law which defines the elements of the offence with clarity and precision;

(5.19)   — everyone will be presumed innocent until proved guilty according to law;

(5.20)   — considering the important contribution of international instruments in the field of human rights to the rule of law at a national level, the participating States reaffirm that they will consider acceding to the International Covenant on Civil and Political Rights, the International Covenant on Economic, Social and Cultural Rights and other relevant international instruments, if they have not yet done so;

(5.21)   — in order to supplement domestic remedies and better to ensure that the participating States respect the international obligations they have undertaken, the participating States will consider acceding to a regional or global international convention concerning the protection of human rights, such as the European Convention on Human Rights or the Optional Protocol to the International Covenant on Civil and Political Rights, which provide for procedures of individual recourse to international bodies.

The participating States declare that the will of the people, freely and fairly expressed through periodic and genuine elections, is the basis of the authority and legitimacy of all government. The participating States will accordingly respect the right of their citizens to take part in the governing of their country, either directly or through representatives freely chosen by them through fair electoral processes. They recognize their responsibility to defend and protect, in accordance with their laws, their international human rights obligations and their international commitments, the democratic order freely established through the will of the people against the activities of persons, groups or organizations that engage in or refuse to renounce terrorism or violence aimed at the overthrow of that order or of that of another participating State.

(7)     To ensure that the will of the people serves as the basis of the authority of government, the participating States will

(7.1)   — hold free elections at reasonable intervals, as established by law;

(7.2)   — permit all seats in at least one chamber of the national legislature to be freely contested in a popular vote;

(7.3)   — guarantee universal and equal suffrage to adult citizens;

(7.4)   — ensure that votes are cast by secret ballot or by equivalent free voting procedure, and that they are counted and reported honestly with the official results made public;

(7.5)   — respect the right of citizens to seek political or public office, individually or as representatives of political parties or organizations, without discrimination;

(7.6)   — respect the right of individuals and groups to establish, in full freedom, their own political parties or other political organizations and provide such political parties and organizations with the necessary

legal guarantees to enable them to compete with
each other on a basis of equal treatment before the
law and by the authorities;

(7.7)    —ensure that law and public policy work to permit
political campaigning to be conducted in a fair and
free atmosphere in which neither administrative
action, violence nor intimidation bars the parties
and the candidates from freely presenting their
views and qualifications, or prevents the voters
from learning and discussing them or from casting
their vote free of fear of retribution;

(7.8)    —provide that no legal or administrative obstacle
stands in the way of unimpeded access to the media
on a nondiscriminatory basis for all political group-
ings and individuals wishing to participate in the
electoral process;

(7.9)    —ensure that candidates who obtain the necessary
number of votes required by law are duly installed
in office and are permitted to remain in office until
their term expires or is otherwise brought to an end
in a manner that is regulated by law in conformity
with democratic parliamentary and constitutional
procedures.

(8)      The participating States consider that the presence of observers, both foreign and domestic, can enhance the electoral process for States in which elections are taking place. They therefore invite observers
from any other CSCE participating States and
any appropriate private institutions and organizations
who may wish to do so to observe the course of their
national election proceedings, to the extent permitted
by law. They will also endeavour to facilitate similar
access for election proceedings held below the national
level. Such observers will undertake not to interfere
in the electoral proceedings.

. . . . .

### III

(26)     The participating States recognize that vigorous democracy depends on the existence as an integral part of national life of democratic values and practices as well as an extensive range of democratic institutions. They will therefore encourage, facilitate and, where appropriate, support practical co-operative endeavours and the sharing of information, ideas and expertise among themselves and by direct contacts and co-operation between individuals, groups and organizations in areas including the following:

— constitutional law, reform and development,
— electoral legislation, administration and observation,
— establishment and management of courts and legal systems,
— the development of an impartial and effective public service where recruitment and advancement are based on a merit system,
— law enforcement,
— local government and decentralization,
— access to information and protection of privacy,
— developing political parties and their role in pluralistic societies,
— free and independent trade unions,
— co-operative movements,
— developing other forms of free associations and public interest groups,
— journalism, independent media, and intellectual and cultural life,
— the teaching of democratic values, institutions and practices in educational institutions and the fostering of an atmosphere of free enquiry.

Such endeavors may cover the range of co-operation encompassed in the human dimension of the CSCE, including training, exchange of information, books and instructional materials, co-operative programmes and projects, academic and professional exchanges and conferences, scholarships, research grants, provision of expertise and advice, business and scientific contacts and programmes.

(27)     The participating States will also facilitate the establishment and strengthening of independent national institutions in the area of human rights and the rule of law, which may also serve as focal points for co-ordination and collaboration between such institutions in the participating States. They propose that co-operation be encouraged between parliamentarians from participating States, including through existing inter-parliamentary associations and, *inter alia*, through joint commissions, television debates involving parliamentarians, meetings and round-table discussions. They will also encourage existing institutions, such as organizations within the United Nations system and the Council of Europe, to continue and expand the work they have begun in this area.

# RULE OF LAW IN
# A NEW CENTURY

by

Frederick Quinn

## Frederick Quinn

*Frederick Quinn is a retired member of the Senior Foreign Service, having held the rank of Minister-Counselor, and is presently an international consultant. His overseas assignments included Cameroon, Vietnam, Haiti, Burkina Faso, Morocco, and Czechoslovakia. In Czechoslovakia he was the American embassy's principal contact with the Charter 77 dissident movement. He also served as Deputy Assistant Secretary of Transportation for Public Affairs from 1983 to 1985.*

*Mr. Quinn worked closely with Chief Justice Warren E. Burger as International Coordinator for the celebration of the Bicentennial of the U.S. Constitution. Based in the director's office of the U.S. Information Agency, this program sent hundreds of leading American judges, lawyers, and legal scholars abroad to meet with counterparts in over 50 countries. The program also translated the Constitution into at least fourteen major world languages and organized radio and television interviews, seminars, and study grants.*

*Mr. Quinn received his undergraduate degree from Allegheny College and holds three advanced degrees, including a Ph.D. in modern European history, from the University of California at Los Angeles. He is also an ordained clergyman in the Episcopal Church and has chaired the Environment Committee of the Episcopal Diocese of Washington, D.C.*

*In addition to serving as editor of* Diplomacy for the 70s, A Program of Management Reform for the Department of State *(1970), Mr. Quinn has contributed to such books as* African Therapeutic Systems *(1978),* Black Men in a White Man's War: African Manpower Questions in World War I *(1986), and* Introduction to the History of Cameroon *(1989). He has published articles and book reviews in many scholarly and professional journals, including* Legal Times, American Historical Review, Africa, African Arts, *and* The Christian Century.

# RULE OF LAW IN
# A NEW CENTURY

by

Frederick Quinn

Harold Nicolson wrote:

> "No, it was not the telephone that, from 1919 onwards, brought about the transition from the old diplomacy to the new. It was the belief that it was possible to apply to the conduct of *external* affairs the ideas and practices which, in the conduct of *internal* affairs, had for generations been regarded as the essentials of liberal democracy." (*The Evolution of Diplomatic Method*, Cassell, 1954, p. 84.)

The technological explosion is important, but even more significant is the international impact of what Nicolson calls "the essentials of liberal democracy," which a contemporary audience would identify as issues of human rights, rule of law, and constitutionalism. The telephone of Nicolson's era has been replaced by satellite communications, fax and telephone answering machines, the Voice of America, and Cable News Network. I spoke recently with a Polish human rights lawyer who kept alive the investigation into the state-sponsored murder of a Roman Catholic cleric, Jerzy Popieluszko. The Warsaw lawyer requested material on American Bill of Rights law and asked, "Can you fax it to me?" I knew Bronislaw Geremek, Solidarity intellectual and leader of the Polish parliament, when he was a scholar at the

193

Woodrow Wilson Center in 1978. We both studied French
history and recalled our early exposure to the *les Annales*
writers. Geremek described his delight in having unrestricted access to a photocopying machine, something
denied Central Europeans at home for economic and
security reasons. While others sampled the culture of
Washington on weekends, he copied materials on gypsies
in the Middle Ages and commentaries on how democracies face their political agendas. The scientific explosion that transfers information so quickly has played
a part in the recent changes in Central and Eastern
Europe; but the ideas of freedom spread by the successors to Nicolson's telephone have played an even greater
role.

A new international landscape is forming, and fresh
diplomatic responses, including those based on rule of
law, are needed, both to assure this country's national
interest and to create a world order where disputes are
settled through legal rather than military means.

America's overseas military presence diminishes and
foreign aid monies shrink as Cold War bipolar political-
military confrontation subsides and acrimonious regional and global issues dominate embassy cable traffic.
Regional issues include conflict between Balkan ethnic
groups, Arabs and Jews, Czechs and Slovaks, rural parts
of the Philippines and the Manila government, and
Chinese human rights activists and the central state.
While intensely local in character, such problems have
strong international dimensions, and their solution often
defies local possibilities.

Today's transnational problems, likewise, cannot be
solved by unilateral action of individual states. The
issues include growing world armaments, the global

environment, terrorism, the recrudescence of fundamentalist movements, an endemic presence of hunger, a destructive world narcotics traffic, the exponential rise of world population, a growing disparity between debtor and creditor nations, and a new face of world crime as money, including drug transaction profits, moves globally like a stream through a sandy delta. Max M. Kampelman writes, "The requirements of our evolving technology are increasingly turning national boundaries into patterns of lace through which flow ideas, money, people, crime, terrorism, ballistic missiles—all of which know no national boundaries." ("Politics Must Catch Up to Scientific Advance," Cosmos Club Bulletin, Washington, D.C., June 1991, p. 7.)

The list of conflicts is long; protracted negotiations may resolve some issues, but the process will remain one of extinguishing individual brushfires unless laws and legal institutions are in place providing means to reach a just resolution of disputes in a timely, equitable manner. Building institutions to resolve such issues through legal rather than military means is a task for American foreign policy in the decades ahead rivaling the complexity and commitment of America's earlier response to Cold War issues. Future international order depends on the willingness of states to cooperate with each other to prevent or moderate conflict, correct global economic imbalances, and respond to disenfranchised peoples' appeals for justice. Peter Vaky asks, "Will nations be able to cooperate creatively to bring about order and stability absent a central threat like the Cold War? No one really knows." ("International Relations, a New Era," unpublished manuscript, 1991, p. 6.)

## The Advantages of the Rule of Law

There are distinct reasons why support of rule of law initiatives is in the American national interest. First, increasingly the United States and other countries face complex issues lending themselves to legal rather than traditional diplomatic solutions. One example is the new visage of international crime. Money, information, and people move about the globe, mixing sophisticated technology and ancient greed. The Bank of Credit and Commerce International (BCCI) and Colombian drug cartels are but two examples of such groups. Second, it is easier for the United States to conduct productive relations with stable democracies than with totalitarian regimes. American businesses seek equal protection in local courts to resolve commercial disputes; Americans living or visiting abroad will value the right to due process in a foreign court, should they be accused of wrongdoing. Finally, there is an altruistic reason: Helping others build stable governments is a long-standing, albeit sometimes submerged, component of American foreign policy. The State Department's Legal Advisor, Edwin D. Williamson, argues that acceptance of rule of law principles is important to the United States

> "simply on humanitarian grounds. The singular innovation of the American constitution was to establish that the state was not the ultimate sovereign power, but merely derived its enumerated powers from the will of the people. I contend that this notion, more than any other, lies at the heart of the newfound enthusiasm for rule of law." ("Theoretical Basis for Rule of Law Engagement in Foreign Pol-

icy," ABA Committee on Law and National Security, Washington, D.C., October 10, 1991, p. 2.)

## The Issue of Values in the Foreign Policy Process

Americans should not be uncomfortable about introducing this country's political values, as expressed in its legal tradition, into the foreign policy process. Immense energies go into exporting athletic shoes, laptop computers, credit cards, jet aircraft, videotapes, and soft drinks. At the same time, countries ask us increasingly about the institutions and values that make such commerce possible. Without being cultural imperialists, is it not possible to respond to the aspirations of others and share the wellsprings of our democratic society with them? A useful distinction must be made between including moral issues in the foreign policy process and moralism, the zealous advocacy of a particular ideological stance, which would be inappropriate and unworkable in the foreign policy process.

I am aware, as both a historian and a Foreign Service officer, that suggesting the possibility of institutional legal change to other countries would be taboo to many diplomats. Even such a prescient observer as George F. Kennan is ambiguous on the subject. Traditional diplomatic textbooks would probably relegate advocating institutional change to the "soft" side of diplomacy. A rereading of authors of the Hans Morgenthau and Henry Kissinger generation revisits ideas of realpolitik, balance of power, and classic military-political confrontation as the tools of statecraft. But times have changed, and so have issues. For many years, Americans believed in, and poured billions of dollars into, a military confrontation with the Soviet Union. But the real engine of change triggering the collapse of the repressive system was holding it up to the clear light of day and the reflective mirror of the Conference on Security Cooperation in Europe (CSCE) provisions. This came from the determined effort of human rights advocates, dissident intellectuals, disaffected members of the various governments, and sustained contact with the West from exchange programs, the CSCE community, Radio Free Europe, Voice of America, and groups like Helsinki Watch and Amnesty International. This represents, once more in history, the triumph of ideas, not weapons.

## Objections to Rule of Law

Some would argue that the injustices and imperfections in our own legal system are so widespread that we should clean house first before exporting democracy. Such arguments do not appreciate the grimly repressive nature of totalitarian societies. A political scientist has tabulated the number of persons killed by totalitarian regimes in this century. R.J. Rummel's working numbers suggest over 148 million persons killed, roughly quadruple the number of all persons slain in wars during the same period. Clearly such dictatorial states are vastly different from the likable despots in a Graham Greene novel. ("The Rule of Law: Towards Eliminating War and Democide," speech prepared for presentation to the American Bar Association Standing Committee on Law and National Security, Washington, D.C., October 10–11, 1991.)

Traditional diplomatists also might object to including rule of law provisions among the tools of statecraft because they are not always enforceable, especially in troubled countries and in regions where alliances are sometimes necessary with unsavory governments. The argument is, why raise human rights or rule of law issues when traditional political-economic relations represent the only real possibilities for bilateral relations? Difficult choices are a fact of international life, witness our relations with the Duvaliers and Mobutus of this world. Still, if rule of law issues cannot always be a major theme in bilateral relations with repressive governments, they can remain a secondary subject, always part of the total composition, ready to be raised at an appropriate moment.

## The Wellsprings of Democratic Belief

Globally, countries undergo fundamental political, social, and economic change. Many codify that change through constitutional reforms, and some ask Americans to share with them what endures from our constitutional experience.

Late one night in Warsaw, I watched the local news and Russian parliamentary debates about where power should reside as both countries wrestled with legal reforms. I recalled an American newspaper, a 1787 New York broadside called the *Independent Journal*, printed by handset type on rag paper. Page one carried an ad about a horse for sale and another about a landlord renting rooms in his small house on Wall Street. Between them was a column identified only by the caption "Federalist 10." Hamilton, Madison, and Jay faced the same questions Russian and Central European constitution writers debate: ethnic divisions, regional interests, issues of where power lies, how to contain conflict.

The Federalists were not graduates of the Moscow Institute of International Affairs, the Sorbonne, or the London School of Economics. They were businessmen, farmers, planters, and lawyers, mostly in their 30s and 40s. Neither cynics nor idealists, they held a hopeful but pragmatic vision. Having seen human nature in the public square, they experienced both its frailty and its aspirations. They knew, as the English historian R.H. Tawney wrote, "The heart of man holds mysteries of contradiction which live together in vigorous incompatibility." Madison put it differently: "[I]t is of great importance in a republic not only to guard the society against the oppression of its rulers, but to guard one part of the society against the injustice of the other part."

**Madison, the Hopeful Realist**

Madison wrote in the wake of Shays's Rebellion, in which armed small landholders and farmers with deeply felt legitimate grievances took power in their own hands. Madison warned of the dangers of factional democracies, "spectacles of turbulence and contentions." Hamilton feared "an infinity of little, jealous, clashing, tumultuous commonwealths, the wretched nurseries of unceasing discord."

Madison knew the American republic's fragility, just as contemporary constitution writers are aware of the vulnerability of emerging democracies. Madison saw building order and containing factions as the constitutionalist's task. In *Federalist 10* he defined factions as a "number of citizens, whether amounting to a majority of the whole," united "by some common impulse of passion, or of interest, adverse to the right of other citizens, or to the permanent and aggregate interest of the community." The roots of ethnic, regional, social, religious, or economic factions are "sown in the nature of man . . . we see them everywhere . . . a zeal for different opinions concerning religions, concerning government."

"If men were angels, no government would be necessary," *Federalist 51* states; but humans are not angels, and governments are needed to provide for the common good and to keep any one political interest group from seizing total power.

## The Individual vs. Society

Designers of rule of law programs can appreciate the basic conflict between institutions and individual human rights. Institutions, even with well-intentioned laws and leaders, move slowly and are given to compromise. Institutions often present a broad, diffuse vision of a problem, where the individual litigant or voice in the wilderness seeking justice has a sharp, focused cry. There is no way to solve this problem effectively; ambiguity and tension are part of life under rule of law. It would be unwise for constitution writers to deny that recurrent conflict between individuals and institutions is an ingredient of political life or to deny its proponents access to justice and public expressions of grievances. When the doors of justice are barred, the walls of society crumble, as Warsaw Pact political leaders learned.

There will always be a Martin Luther King, Andrey Sakharov, or Vaslav Havel, a Clarence Gideon, Dred Scott, John Brown, or Toyosaburo Korematsu to chal-

lenge a country's basic legal beliefs. Holding in balance
both the individual justice-seeker and the social institution responsible for dispensing justice is the enduring
challenge to rule of law proponents anywhere. It is a difficult but not impossible task, for the problem goes back
to the wellsprings of our society. Before Madison and
Jefferson, Magna Carta and Aristotle, there were the
Hebrew prophets and jurists, whose injunction to society
was, like that of Amos, to "let justice flow on like a river
and righteousness like a never-failing torrent" or like
that enigmatic figure in Second Isaiah, not unlike some
human rights activists, whose goal was to "establish justice among the nations" and who "will never falter or be
crushed until he sees justice on earth." (42:1–4.)

### What Is Rule of Law?

Rule of law means the conduct of international relations through agreed-upon laws and legal institutions. It
also means strengthening individual countries' legal
bodies through mutually accepted goals and specific
institution-building programs. Rule of law has theoretical foundations and practical applications. It is more
than enacting specific laws; it is building judicial institutions and promoting respect for and acceptance of a
legal culture within a country and among nations.

A distinction should be made between rule of law and
international law in the international system. International law is just that, the law of international organizations and, increasingly, international commercial law.
International law can function more efficiently in a
world with heightened support for broader rule of law
initiatives. "A people and a government that support

strict adherence to the rule of law are more likely to support the principles outlined in the United Nations Charter," Williamson states, adding, "and [are] less likely to engage in unlawful aggression or to otherwise commit acts that disturb international peace and security." (Williamson, p. 2.) Support of rule of law does not mean diminishing the United Nations' role. If rule of law programs are in place worldwide, it will help create a climate allowing the United Nations to realize its potential more fully.

Also, rule of law is not a program to export the American judicial system as an act of political imperialism, that is, the ugly American in judicial robes. Rather, it is contributing to the growing global judicial culture already in existence. In this international legal community, participants will have much to learn from each other and are already in active contact. One American contribution can be the experience of the world's oldest working constitution, with features, including separation of powers, an independent judiciary with the right of judicial review, and a written, enforceable Bill of Rights, that have safeguarded our system and may serve as models for others. William W. Schwarzer, an American jurist with overseas contacts, cautions, "Much as we admire our own Bill of Rights . . . our aim must not be to try to transplant it. While in some respects it reflects universal values, we cannot assume it will suit other societies." ("American Judges and the Rule of Law Abroad," unpublished manuscript, October 1991, p. 7.)

Rule of law offers no panacea; it is not a magician's wand. Rule of law is devising constitutions, other laws, and legal codes and strengthening the judicial institutions needed for their realization. While this discussion focuses on the judiciary, the judiciary is not a tranquil island set in a roiling sea. It will soon collapse if the law enforcement institutions around it are weak. Each country needs an honest, well-equipped, decently paid police force; just prosecutors; humanely run prisons; and other services, such as public defenders and an independent bar association, providing to each segment of society access to justice.

Commenting on the need to assist new democracies in establishing law enforcement and judicial infrastructures, Robert S. Ross, Jr., head of international programs for the Department of Justice, notes:

> "A critical step in the introduction of democracy in eastern Europe and the Soviet Union has been the abolition of internal security forces such as the Stasi and the KGB. These police organizations are usually the first to go because they were the old governments' tools of repression. They also were responsible for the eradication of crime. As a consequence, these fledgling democracies are left with very inexperienced law enforcement institutions that must struggle with ordinary crime. Sophisticated, international crime is well beyond their capabilities." ("Building the Law Enforcement and Judicial Infrastructure of a Democracy," unpublished manuscript, October 10, 1991.)

Rule of law, in short, does not mean imposing one country's legal system on another nation; each country will adopt its legal system in response to the unique problems of its historical, geographical, social, and economic setting.

A.E. Dick Howard, who has advised many countries on constitution writing, notes:

> "A nation needs good laws, but laws can only do so much in assuring that citizens enjoy peace, prosperity, opportunity, and the benefits of civilization. Likewise, a good constitution can foster but cannot assure the benefits implicit in the concept of constitutionalism. Belligerent neighbors may wage war, a country's own military leader may refuse to accept civilian oversight, ethnic quarrels may rend the social fabric, political leadership may prove inept, poverty and economic ills may make constitutional government impossible." (*Democracy's Dawn*, University of Virginia Press, 1991, p. 4.)

### Components of Rule of Law

What follows is a prescriptive list of guidelines for the content of a rule of law program, based on meetings with jurists in Europe, Asia, Africa, and Latin America, and with American Supreme Court judges and other legal experts during the period of the Bicentennial of the U.S. Constitution commemorations from 1987 to 1991, when a wide range of substantive international exchange programs took place.

### A. Limited Government

The underpinning of rule of law is limited government arrived at through the consent of the governed. This differs from the idea of state supremacy as the wellspring of law. It introduces an untidy tension between "government of the people, by the people, and for the people," as Abraham Lincoln described it, and rulers who seek to run states without being held accountable. Individuals criticize the state in a democracy. State bureaucracies regret that their efforts are not appreciated more fully. Still, a tension between coequals is preferable to the endemic frustration experienced in authoritarian regimes, where critical voices are labeled treasonous or seditious. One such example in modern times is the Philippines under Ferdinand Marcos, who abrogated the country's constitution, telling the people to leave their governance to him and to God.

## B. Separation of Powers

Limited government is realized institutionally through a clear separation of powers between the legislative, executive, and judicial branches, and such separation of powers is stabilized through checks and balances. Checks and balances can take several forms, including the executive's right to veto a legislative act, the right of the legislature not to ratify a treaty, and the right of one branch to propose a budget and expenditure of public monies and of another branch to concur or dissent. Some countries will find a bicameral legislature, with powers divided between an upper and a lower chamber, a further instrument for diffusing power.

Lord Acton said power corrupts and absolute power corrupts absolutely. "You trust your mother, but you cut the cards," a popular adage states. Modern countries, like those of Central and Eastern Europe, wrestle with the question of a strong executive or a strong legislative branch. In either case, the need for an institutionalized separation of powers is clear. According to Chief Justice Warren E. Burger, international jurists visiting him as Chairman of the Commission on the Bicentennial of the U.S. Constitution asked more questions about the workability of separation of powers than about any other single topic.

## C. An Independent Judiciary

Equally important is establishing an independent judiciary with the right to originate judicial review over actions taken by the executive and legislative branches. No single contribution from the American legal tradition is more important than judicial review. This provides a way of breaking legal impasses and resolving differences between contending parties. It also represents the source of people's access to justice through courts.

The courts will gain popular respect only if they are independent and are not agents of the executive. Judges should be well educated and well paid; "learned in the law," as they once were described; appointed for long terms if not for life; provided with wages that will remove the temptation to corruption; and given clerks, secretaries, and other court officials to make the administration of justice possible. In India, it takes twenty years for a case to work its way through the appeals process and the Supreme Court. The old adage "justice delayed is justice denied" holds true. There must be provisions to remove judges in case of corruption or incompetence, but not because they hand down courageous, unpopular decisions.

## D. Containing Conflict

Contemporary Eastern European constitution writers and reformers of authoritarian governments frequently express frustration about responding to public criticism. Flag-burning and obscenity cases tax the patience of American courts. In many countries, political cartoons, such as appear daily on the editorial pages of American newspapers, are considered treasonous. Although many people find some of these actions deeply offensive, a country committed to free speech will have a much healthier political climate than one restrictive of its citizens' free expression. In Eastern Europe, the precedents for robust political discussion are few. In old Russia, the triumvirate of God, Czar, and Motherland was all-inclusive. The only avenue for opposition was the revolutionary cell. Lenin and Stalin, in the name of abolishing the former regime, introduced an ever more grimly monolithic structure. Today's Russian rule of law proponents speak of limited government with possibilities for dissent, free speech, petition, and assembly as ingredients in a society governed by law. Add to that the necessity of keeping political parties free and distinct from the government. Freely elected officials must act through the government, not the party, in their role as agents of the people.

## E. Building a Civic Culture

Rule of law programs will only work where there is a civic culture respecting the political principles on which the country is based. In fragile democracies, cynicism is as destructive as terrorism in destroying public confidence in institutions. Thus, fundamental laws must be justiciable. Lofty provisions that cannot be interpreted into law and enforced provide a rhetorical, not a legal, foundation for society. Likewise, for a civic culture to exist, there must be an independent bar, as well as law schools and media protected by rights to free speech, assembly, and petition.

Laws must be reported and disseminated. I have spoken with many practitioners in legal systems where this basic assumption of rule of law did not hold true. A West African jurist expressed frustration in trying to ascertain what the high court had decided since an overly occupied court clerk took unusable notes on several high court decisions. An Asian barrister was angry at being unable to appeal a case because an entire shelf of supreme court opinions was removed from the court library, presumably by an opposing party.

One of the drafters of a new constitution for South Africa spoke poignantly of the attention given to human rights and due process in the new document and yet of the public cynicism with which it was greeted in a country where access to justice was systematically denied to large segments of the population for most of this century and where intransigence and racial distrust characterized the civic culture.

Citizens must trust the system to deliver justice fairly and quickly. This requires trained judges paid enough to reduce the lure of corruption. In the Philippines, the average judge makes less than $4,000 a year; the average new partner in a major Manila firm, more than $40,000 a year. Judges, in turn, require efficient court offices, clerks, adequate secretarial support, and information retrieval systems to track court records.

## F. Defendants' Rights

No issue is more important in establishing rule of law than fairness and individual protection in the criminal process. The basic provision in criminal trials should be the presumption of innocence until proven guilty. This was recognized in the Bill of Rights to the United States Constitution, especially in the articles on search and seizure, protection against double jeopardy and self-incrimination, the right to a speedy trial by jury, access to all charges and witnesses, and the assistance of counsel if required, plus a restriction against excessive bail or fines and against cruel and unusual punishment. The ancient injunction that "without a law, there can be no crime and no punishments" holds as true today as it did historically.

## G. Religious Freedom

A central issue facing any country is protection of religious freedom, an especially difficult question in countries with a dominant faith with its own legal system, as in the Islamic *sharia*. Each country has religious groups, some with many adherents, others with fewer, all expressing deep-felt convictions with visible civic ramifications. The American experience, expressed in the First Amendment, may prove helpful. The free exercise of religion is guaranteed to all groups, and the nonestablishment of any religious group is assured. These provisions are the result of an acrimonious history, including the active persecution of dissenters, such as Roger Williams in the 1640s, and the moral bankruptcy of the established church in Virginia.

If any group is favored with public funds or tax credits or with access to public buildings to the exclusion of others, a basic disruption of the body politic is created.

Also, religious questions have a way of reappearing frequently in courts and not being settled to the satisfaction of all parties. This is not an unhealthy sign in a society; better to have lively contention than deadening repression.

## H. Economic Rights

Chief Justice Burger has said that when people think of the Bill of Rights, they should consider an additional fundamental right expressed in the Commerce Clause, the brief notation in Article I, Section 8, that Congress shall have power "to regulate commerce with foreign nations, and among the several states, and with the Indian tribes."

No less important is the clause giving rise to intellectual property law in the provision "to promote the progress of science and useful arts, by securing for limited times to authors and inventors the exclusive right to their respective writings and discoveries." (Article I, Section 7.)

The importance of constitutionally assuring the framework for economic freedom cannot be overstated, for unless a country has economic stability, there is little likelihood that free political institutions will flourish. The emergence of a market-oriented economy is central to societies in the Western democratic tradition. Private property, fair competition, and a market economy are the yeast allowing political institutions to function.

## I. Bills of Rights

Bills of Rights range from a short enumeration of ten articles, as in the American example, to several pages of carefully spelled out rights, as in the Chilean constitution. Some constitutions contain first-, second-, and third-generation rights. First-generation rights belong to individuals, second-generation rights belong to social groups, and third-generation rights are more general, dealing with the use of natural resources and the rights to a minimal quality of life, with appropriate education and health care. Some countries adopt lengthy constitutions enumerating legal provisions more properly contained in civil, criminal, commercial, and other codes. The Chilean constitution, for instance, contains an article that all guano deposits belong to the state. Although seafowl deposits are a valuable source of fertilizer and revenues, the provision could more easily fit in a commercial code. One result of packing too much into a constitution is that such documents are not enduring fundamental laws on which a country's legal system can be built, but represent tactical politician compromises of the present legislative moment. They are outdated as soon as they are passed, quickly becoming footnotes in a country's legal history. One estimate is that the average Latin American constitution lasts less than eight years. This wreaks havoc with the fabric of society. The key consideration for Bill of Rights drafters is not the lofty prose, but an answer to the question, Are these rights enforceable?

## The CSCE Accords As Model

In contemporary East-West relations, the period of most intense diffusion of rule of law questions came during the mid-1970s CSCE deliberations. The Soviet Union's then-ruler, Leonid Brezhnev, was obsessed with obtaining an agreement acknowledging his country's borders and hegemony over Central Europe. The United States, without accepting the document as legally binding, signed it as long as Basket III was included. Basket III was a feast for human rights and rule of law advocates: It provided for the free flow of information, immigration, and observers at political trials. These issues were long a part of the domestic agenda of the Western democracies. In one comprehensive, tightly crafted package, they became an agenda item for the Western democracies to negotiate with Warsaw Pact members. It has taken Harold Nicolson's insight a half-century to move from Versailles to Prague, but the ideas and practices of the Western democracies became a battleground over which a political conflict was waged.

### In Prague, 1975–1978

I was Press and Cultural Counselor at the American Embassy in Prague in 1975–1978 when CSCE Basket III became a mainstream component of American foreign policy. We provided Charter 77 dissidents with books and records and showed contemporary American films at our apartment for Czechoslovak writers and artists. I made frequent representations to the Foreign Ministry and to government newspapers like *Red Rights, Our Soldier,* and *Young Socialist.* I asked, "When will you let

citizens travel freely?" "When can artists display their
work without prior approval by the communist party?"
"When will Western publications circulate in bookstores
and magazine stands?" During this time, 800 subscrip-
tion copies of *National Geographic* were confiscated by
censors because a story on the Danube River contained
unfavorable references to Iron Curtain border guards.

The rule of law agenda was not crystalline. Some embassy officers were more enthusiastic than others in
promoting the CSCE agenda. The State Department
Human Rights bureau was often more vigorous an advocate than were its geographic counterparts. Among
Czechoslovaks, a few Foreign Ministry officials private-
ly expressed satisfaction at Western pressures for enforcing Basket III provisions; others echoed a traditional
party line. Charter 77 participants initially had no consistent strategy beyond opening a broad dialogue with
the government on realizing the CSCE provisions. What
they and we were doing in the late 1970s, without being
fully aware of it, was making an international issue out
of many of the constitutional provisions long a part of
the Western democracies' internal agendas.

One December night in 1976, a Czech dissident economist visited our apartment in Prague, bringing a pine
bough and a copy of Charter 77. It was a brief document,
a smudged carbon copy of about two pages. Later
editions were longer. Czechoslovaks did not have access
to photocopying machines; even the one in the Foreign
Ministry was locked and guarded. Most *samizdat* documents (published unofficially and underground) were
typed in six copies; that was all Czechoslovak carbon
paper would allow. The CSCE Helsinki Accords had
been signed earlier that year. The communist govern-

ment was perplexed about how to deal with them. Some Foreign Ministry hardliners believed Basket III provisions could destabilize the rigidly controlled society. "I'm not sure we knew what we were getting in for," a younger Foreign Ministry official confided as we walked down the hall, free of microphones.

Meanwhile, antigovernment intellectuals, disaffected communists, and others saw the CSCE provisions as a rallying point. "The government signed the Helsinki Accords. Now we want to see what the government will do about them," said the economist, who had been dismissed from his university position when a Cuban student denounced him for holding heterodox views. During the next decade, dissidents were jailed, books and records were confiscated, show trials were held, but the freedom movements intensified until they caused the whole monolithic structure of communism to fall, like the giant statue of Stalin that once loomed from a hill overlooking the Vltava and was finally pulled down by Czechs celebrating their new-found freedoms.

Proponents of international rule of law initiatives will find a useful model in provisions of the Helsinki and Copenhagen meetings of the Conference on the Human Dimension of the CSCE. Delegates from thirty-five nations met in June 1990, stating their determination to advance the principles of rule of law.

> "They consider that the rule of law does not mean merely a formal legality which assures regularity and consistency in the achievement and enforcement of democratic order, but justice based on the recognition and full acceptance of the supreme value of the human personality and guaranteed by institutions

that provide a framework for its fullest expression."
("Document of the Copenhagen Meeting of the Con-
ference on the Human Dimension of the CSCE,"
Copenhagen, Denmark, June 29, 1990.)


The CSCE document is a comprehensive enumeration
in which "the participating states express their conviction that the protection and promotion of human rights
and fundamental freedoms is one of the basic purposes of
government, and reaffirms that the recognition of these
rights and freedoms constitutes the foundation of freedom, justice and peace." Other major provisions include
free and periodic elections by secret ballot, representative government, accountability to an elected legislature
or to the electorate, and a clear separation between the
state and political parties.

Military and police forces will be accountable to civil
authorities: Human rights will be guaranteed by law,
the independence of judges will be ensured, defendants
will be presumed innocent until proven guilty, and habeas corpus provisions will be enforced.

There are provisions against torture and in support of
conscientious objectors, strong provisions for freedom of
media and expression, and promotion of the rights of
minorities, including migrant workers. The document is
explicit; for example, participating states "clearly and
unequivocally condemn totalitarianism, racial and ethnic hatred, anti-semitism, xenophobia and discrimination against anyone as well as persecution on religious
and ideological grounds. In this context they also recognize the particular problem of Roma [gypsies]."

While some would argue that the CSCE provisions represent a regional accord, hammered out in the crucible of a unique historical context, many of its provisions have universal applicability.

### *"We Don't Trust the Courts"*

Today, like many other people in Eastern Europe, the Czechoslovaks are writing a new constitution; several Western constitutionalists have met with them to discuss its contents. There are difficulties, including Czech and Slovak nationalism, the absence of a federal ministry of justice, and a grim legal inheritance. "We don't trust the courts," a jurist remarked, noting the country's Austro-Hungarian, Nazi, and communist periods of rule.

One evening I saw a riveting example of a citizen's experience with communist justice. Oldrich Kulhanek is an internationally recognized graphics artist. In 1968, a Czechoslovak arts jury selected eleven of his works for an exposition in Japan. When the prints arrived in Tokyo, a political guardian at the embassy found them objectionable, and a two-year investigation followed. In 1971, Kulhanek was tried, was jailed, and, after being freed, was subject to lengthy secret police interrogations every other Saturday for the next two years. His lawyer, a well-known human rights advocate, could raise only procedural issues during the trial.

At one point, President Gustav Husak declared an amnesty of provisions under which Kulhanek was sentenced, so he was released. But the three-judge court let stand an order to liquidate his art. This usually meant burning books or paintings in the Ministry of Justice courtyard.

*The Trial*

The trial's substance was kafkaesque. (Czechs see much humor in Franz Kafka's dark world.) The trial illustrates why there is no healthy judicial culture in Czechoslovakia and why it is so difficult to build rule of law programs.

During pretrial proceedings this exchange took place between Kulhanek and the interrogators. The documents were obtained following the velvet revolution.

> "Look here, you needn't put on this intellectual play-acting for me. This is pornography in print. Here our Comrade Ambassador to Japan, Kozesnik, testifies that the female comrades at the embassy were outraged by the size of the sex organs when he showed them the prints."
>
> "O.K. I can't help it if the female comrades at the embassy don't like big sex organs."
>
> "But the female comrades were outraged!"
>
> "Yes, then why did the ambassador show them?"
>
> "You are not here to ask questions. Admit that you have been producing pornography."
>
> "No, I'll not admit that. The genitals are not excessively big."
>
> "They are. The female comrades said so."

It was difficult to bring political charges against the artist, whose work was filled with fantasy detail, but the Ministry of Interior pressed its case that the work "reviled the representatives of a friendly state," that is, the Soviet Union.

Interrogator: "Why has the child in the bottom right corner a hole in his head the shape of a five-point star?"

"O.K. that is not true, the hole is not in the shape of a five-point star."

"We know it is! Admit it! If Stalin were here now, I should not be talking to you like this. The working class would make short work of you. . . . Look here, we know everything. We know very well what you are thinking. Admit it and you will be left in peace and I too. Do you think I enjoy this? I know absolutely nothing about art."

A skilled interrogator will look for accomplices, especially foreigners. The prosecution asks, "Who is Hieronymus Bosch? Who is Hugo van der Goes? Who is Hans Memling? Inform us of their addresses, when and where you met them, their profession, and the names of their employers. Denying will not help you. We know everything. One after the other, in turn. Who is Hieronymus Bosch? When and where did you meet him?"

Answer: "Hieronymus Bosch was a Dutch painter. He was born in 1450. I became acquainted with his work in Bruges."

Interrogator: "That will do! I should like his address and the name of his employer."

## A Kafkaesque Ending

The case's closing could indeed have been written by Kafka. Policemen seized the eleven offensive prints, but not the plates from which they were printed. Later, the artist encountered one of the judges and asked how the liquidation order was carried out. "Oh, we divided the works among ourselves," the judge replied.

Kulhanek translated his prison experience into four world-quality graphic prints. They represent an eloquent statement about the absence of democratic values and the rule of law in post-World War II Czechoslovakia; thousands of others have suffered in silence.

Now we face new times. The political, economic, and intellectual monolith of state communism has crumbled. How does the West respond coherently?

**What Is To Be Done?**

There is no White House or National Security directive making rule of law a component of America's foreign policy, and one is needed. Meanwhile, scattered rule of law initiatives grow like topsy among government agencies in response to the internationalization of legal programs and the spread of international interests into what was once a domestic arena. The Department of Justice has over 700 employees stationed abroad, most of them in law-enforcement activities. It would like to increase that number sizably. The Federal Judicial Center, a training center for federal judges, plays an increasingly important role in receiving delegations of overseas jurists. The Agency for International Development (AID), traditionally focused on "Give us the tools, we'll finish the job" economic development programs, has a democratization mandate, as does the U.S. Information Agency (USIA). The World Bank, a sometime Cinderella's stepsister among international agencies, could make rule of law requirements part of its lending policies. The U.S. Patent Office, in response to international interest in American intellectual property law and to increased global litigation on this topic, has expanded its international programs. Other government agencies, such as the Institute of Peace and the National Institute for Democracy, support international programs, as do universities and professional associations like the American Bar Association. A major Washington, D.C., area law school that has international programs, is located near the national capital, and has numerous faculty resources would be an ideal venue for an international rule of law center. Such a center would serve as a catalyst for rule of law initiatives, hold conferences, house visitors from here and abroad, and issue publications and program materials. A helpful first step would be a survey, similar to the Institute of Peace's report on constitution writing in the Soviet Union and Eastern Europe, answering the questions, What are the present rule of law programs of governmental and non-governmental groups? How extensive are they? Who are the players? With which overseas countries?

In recent years, the Department of State has launched rule of law programs. State has an impressive policy mandate but lacks funds for actual programs. The architects require other agencies to turn the blueprints into realized structures supporting the national interest. Discussing the need for a meaningful exchange program, Richard Schifter said:

"A three-day conference in the United States or in a foreign country won't do. What we need are extended visits, by eastern Europeans to the United States and by Americans to eastern Europe. Programs need to be developed which would give eastern European

judges, lawyers, government officials, police administrators a true understanding of the role of the law in
a democratic society. It is up to us, trained in the law,
to enlist in this effort which will strengthen the Rule
of Law and thus the cause of democracy and human
rights worldwide." ("The Rule of Law," address delivered at the Center for National Security Law,
University of Virginia Law School, Charlottesville,
Va., February 22, 1991, pp. 4-5.)

If rule of law is to take its place as an active instrument
of American foreign policy, there must be a clear presidential directive saying so. Next, where should such
programs be based? How broad a mandate should that
office hold? How large should the staff be? What kinds
of program monies will be needed? What should be its
coordinating role with other agencies and the private
sector? A skilled Cartesian logician could argue effectively that either the Department of State or the Department of Justice should house such an initiative. Possibly
a struggle, like the State-Commerce conflict over control
of international economic policy and the officer corps
to carry it out, could be avoided by a clear presidential
policy statement. Still, turf battles are as much a feature
of Washington bureaucratic life as is overgrowth in
Rock Creek Park. Regardless of where the power rods
are deposited, several agencies should play significant
roles in realizing the programs. The Federal Judicial
Center could expand programs to include international
seminars, consultancies, study groups, media programs,
visitor grants, and publications. AID, USIA, the Madison Foundation, a university law school, an independent
commission, or a group with international activities,

such as the American Bar Association, could originate concrete rule of law programs. Each embassy abroad should report regularly on rule of law issues and design a specific rule of law annual plan for that country, complete with goals, programs, and funding requirements. The congressional foreign affairs and judicial committees should have a role in this deliberative process.

## Toward Tomorrow

This century's final years represent an opportune time for a detached look at both issues facing American foreign policy and the instruments used to respond to them. The century's middle years were characterized by tireless human rights advocacy on behalf of individuals and minority groups. Laudable and heartrending as this activity is, without liberal democratic governments, or governmental structures receptive to due process, such initiatives will remain episodic. The contemporary world scene is one in which an increasing number of issues can best be solved through legal means, yet neither the policy nor the structure is in place to launch a clearly articulated, finely honed rule of law initiative as an instrument of American foreign policy. The time has come to move from conceptualization to action. During the last five years, rule of law ideas have entered the common vocabulary of many Washington policy makers, academics, and members of the international legal and diplomatic community.

During the period of the Bicentennial of the U.S. Constitution, many leading American jurists spoke in overseas laws schools and ministries of justice, and thousands of foreign judges and constitutional experts came to the

United States, where they met with Chief Justice Burger; visited public defenders; and asked federal judges, "How do you run your court?" and newspaper editors, "How much can you get away with?" We have translated the Constitution into major world languages; held seminars and radio and television conferences; sent the Corpus Juris Secondum, at their request, to members of the High Court of Pakistan; and sent a complete set of *U.S. Reports* and other law books to the new Supreme Court of Namibia. The range of such activities is extensive, but such programs now need consolidation, a permanent institutional home, a budget, and incorporation into a wider rule of law initiative.

The global democratic revolution that Harold Nicolson described is complex, its full political impact only just arriving around the world. The idea and practice of rule of law, shaped in the crucible of Western democracies' domestic politics, now seeks a lasting place in the discourse of nations.

# READJUSTING OUR MORAL COMPASS: OPPORTUNITIES FOR U.S.-SOVIET RELATIONS AFTER COMMUNISM

by

Nicolai N. Petro

## Nicolai N. Petro

*Nicolai N. Petro received a B.A. with a* summa cum laude *in history in 1980, an M.A. in public administration in 1982, and a Ph.D. in foreign affairs in 1984, all from the University of Virginia. He taught at the Monterey Institute of International Studies, where he became the founding Director of the Center for Contemporary Russian Studies. Last year he taught political science and international relations at the University of Pennsylvania, and he is presently teaching political science at the University of Rhode Island. He is also an Associate Scholar of the Foreign Policy Research Institute and Visiting Research Associate at the Center for Foreign Policy Development at Brown University.*

*From 1988 to 1989, Professor Petro was Thornton D. Hooper Fellow in International Affairs at the Foreign Policy Research Institute in Philadelphia. From 1989 to 1990, he was International Affairs Fellow of the Council on Foreign Relations. In this capacity he served as Special Assistant for Policy in the Office of Soviet Union Affairs at the U.S. Department of State and as temporary political attaché at the U.S. Embassy in Moscow. While in the Soviet Union he was an observer of local elections in several republics.*

*Dr. Petro has been a postdoctoral fellow at the Kennan Institute for Advanced Russian Studies, the Institute for Global Conflict and Cooperation at the University of California, the Hoover Institution at Stanford University, and the Miller Center of Public Affairs at the University of Virginia. He has published in such journals as* The Wilson Quarterly; Comparative Strategy; Studies in Comparative Communism; Global Affairs; Orbis; *the monthly of the Russian Supreme Soviet,* Rodina; *and the social sciences journal of the USSR Academy of Sciences,* Obshchestvennye nauki i sovremennost'. *He is the author of* The Predicament of Human Rights *and the editor of* Christianity and Russian Culture in Soviet Society. *He also edits a series for Westview Press on change in contemporary Soviet society.*

# READJUSTING OUR MORAL COMPASS: OPPORTUNITIES FOR U.S.-SOVIET RELATIONS AFTER COMMUNISM

by

Nicolai N. Petro

> "Everything has changed
> except our way of thinking."
> Albert Einstein

Whether we recognize it yet or not, our relationship with the region of the world traditionally known as the USSR has been profoundly transformed. We are witnesses to a drastic alteration of the political realities governing U.S.-Soviet relations, a shift as profound in its political consequences as a shift in the earth's axis would be to our very notions of geography. This is not merely an episodic transformation of the earth's surface, such as an earthquake, however severe, might produce. Rather, our very sense of direction has been affected, and the first imperative before charting a new foreign policy course in the postcommunist era is to reestablish our bearings.

The degree of change can be measured by the fact that before 1986 any scenario predicting the withdrawal of Soviet forces from Eastern Europe, the collapse of communist ideology and institutions in Russia, and the emergence of both a popularly elected Russian leader committed to privatization and a multiparty democracy based on the rule of law would surely have been viewed by our most eminent experts as preposterous ravings. Today, however, we face precisely such a reality, with all the opportunities and dangers it represents. (Please note that when I contrast "Russia" to the Soviet Union, I mean to point out the enduring characteristics and qualities of the Russian people, not to refer to the Russian Republic, formerly a part of the Soviet Union, as a political entity.)

The comforting certainties that undergirded the U.S. approach to Russia have all collapsed. The noted historian of Russia James H. Billington, currently the Librarian of Congress, aptly summarized the conventional wisdom of the American foreign policy establishment during the Cold War: (1) The Soviet system is immutable and rooted in Russian tradition; (2) it will never permit change in Eastern Europe, least of all in East Germany; (3) popular political movements like Solidarity in Poland are hopelessly romantic and foredoomed; and (4) the only hope for countering the Soviet threat is to appeal to the realpolitik of the existing political leadership.

These assumptions, while shifting in nuance, remained basically unchanged over the past fifty years, lending tremendous continuity to U.S. policy toward the Soviet Union after World War II. Historian John Lewis Gaddis aptly refers to all postwar American policies toward the Soviet Union as "strategies of containment."

Such certainty is no longer possible. Indeed, it is completely inappropriate, given the magnitude of the changes occurring within the Soviet Union. I am not referring to the superficial alterations of governmental structure, or even to the territorial adjustments that the secession of segments of the empire will produce. Rather, I refer both to the attempt under way to forge a new social contract between the state and civil society in Russia and to the revival of concepts of the Russian national interest that have been submerged, but not forgotten, during the past seventy years. Only if we understand that what is occurring is a sea change in Russian history are we likely to recognize our own need to reevaluate many fundamental assumptions about Russian political culture and readjust our vision of what is possible in our relations with the Soviet Union's successor.

The past five years have shown that many widely held assumptions regarding the popularity and stability of communism in Russia proper were false. It was these assumptions, along with the very real issues of conflict that emerged between the superpowers after World War II, that set the pattern of Cold War thinking and the American response of containment. With the disappearance of most objective issues of conflict in recent years, however, these assumptions have remained largely intact among Sovietologists. The almost universal assumption of essential continuity between Russian and Soviet political cultures has prevented subjecting this thesis to timely scrutiny. And the reluctance of many prominent analysts to view the collapse of the Soviet system as a fundamental transformation of social relations is no more than a reflection of the common wisdom that Russian history offers no opportunities for democracy and civic participation.

Today, it is primarily this constrained vision of Russian political culture that is the primary obstacle to establishing a new pattern of relations with a postcommunist Russia. We need a postcontainment policy to chart a new course and a new vision of the opportunities of our relationship with Russia, but we are unlikely to get either without first reexamining the faulty assump-

tions about Russian political culture that have dominated our thinking for the past three generations.

## The Limitations of Sovietology and U.S. Foreign Policy

The place to begin understanding post-Sovietology is,
obviously, with a critique of traditional Soviet analysis.
We should begin by asking, as Martin Malia correctly
suggests, why the field of Soviet studies was dominated
for so long by what were, in fact, false and misleading
questions. It would be patently unfair, of course, to
blame any political analyst for not anticipating the precise course of events or the breakneck speed at which
they took place. But it seems valid to criticize the dominant theoretical premises that prevented us from anticipating these developments.

It is worth noting, for example, the remarkable degree
of consensus among Sovietologists on the stability and
longevity of the Soviet political system. This consensus
rested on three assumptions: first, that communist political values had been accepted as legitimate by the majority of the peoples within the Soviet Union, beginning
with the Russians; second, that the populace attributed
any improvement in their standard of living to the present regime; and third, that there was no functional
memory of alternative values that could undermine the
present value system, much less pose any threat to Soviet
rule. With only two major universities—Harvard and
Columbia—responsible for producing more than two-
thirds of current faculty in this discipline throughout the
country, the field of Soviet studies was perhaps more
prone than most to propagate the conventional wisdom.

Current opinion polls, however, reveal both that the vast majority of people in the Soviet Union have long felt that that political system suffered from considerable malaise and that a considerable number of them can best be described as latent anticommunists. It strains credulity to believe that such a dramatic shift in political beliefs could occur in just a few short years. It is much more likely that we drastically misread the sentiments of the population and hence were totally unprepared for the rapidity of social transformations and the popular support they enjoy.

The presumption of stability and popularity of the Soviet political system had a notable impact on U.S. foreign policy. As the other major nuclear power, the Soviet Union clearly posed a threat to the United States. Hence the belief grew that, while the aggressiveness of the Soviet Union needed to be kept in check, it would be best not to challenge the system so directly that the USSR would see no alternative but to strike back. In his anonymous article signed "X" in *Foreign Affairs*, the young George F. Kennan discussed a strategy for containing Soviet expansion while at the same time lessening the risk of outright confrontation.

Policy makers focused their immediate attention on matters of strategy, but it was Kennan's view of Russian history that provided the intellectual foundation for containment and would prove to be the most durable component of his influence on policy. For Kennan, Russian history was a dismal succession of failed opportunities, of rulers distant and unresponsive to the needs of their population, and of a populace that, though worthy of our compassion and sympathy, was largely incapable of effecting changes. To a considerable extent, it might even be presumed sympathetic to the government's arguments on the need to isolate Russia and increase its repressive characteristics. Throughout his article, Kennan emphasizes Russia's "Asiatic" worldview in order to distinguish the assumptions of what he perceived as a political tradition alien and hostile to the West. Kennan purposefully referred to "Russian" and "Soviet" interchangeably, in contravention of academic standards of the time, precisely to convey a sense of fundamental continuity between the Russian political tradition and the current Soviet system.

To reinforce the dichotomy between the West and the "Russian or oriental mind," Kennan stressed the passivity and sterility of Russian political traditions. He viewed the populace as rather pitiable spectators in the political process, lacking the intellectual or spiritual resources with which to undermine the regime. It is noteworthy that when Kennan spoke of containment ultimately eroding the communist regime, he anticipated that this would be through external pressures upon the Soviet leaders, not through popular discontent.

Hence, the perception of the Soviet threat to our survival and the perceived lack of alternatives to communist rule became the linchpins of containment, dominating the thinking of all postwar American administrations. The remarkable degree of consensus that existed among prominent advisers to both Republican and Democratic administrations is, in no small measure, attributable to the consensus view on Russian history and Russian political culture that Kennan and others helped form. Scholars as diverse in their politics as Richard Pipes and Marshall Shulman, to name just two prominent examples, nevertheless subscribed to the view that Russia lacked any viable civic culture or any functional democratic tradition and believed that the communist regime could rely on a reserve of popularity rooted in Russian nationalism. It was this constrained view of Russian political culture and history, the belief that prospects for democracy in Russia were slim at best, that continued to provide intellectual cohesiveness for containment even after serious disagreements had erupted over the size of the Soviet strategic arsenal, defense spending, and military strategy. It remained the only viable policy for successive American administrations because no one could seriously challenge its assessment of Russian political culture. And despite Secretary of State John Foster Dulles's brief-lived exhortations to "roll back" communism, ultimately no administration was willing to enact a policy based on Russian democratic forces that no one believed existed.

This constrained reluctance lingers on today as a serious impediment to formulating a postcontainment foreign policy strategy. It is the primary reason, in my judgment, why senior officials in the Bush administration clung so desperately to the notion that Mikhail Gorbachev was essential to reform even after months of political indecisiveness had weakened him domestically and after the crackdown of January 1991 had led to a precipitous drop in his popularity within the USSR. Moreover, we are now witnessing the truly odd policy of a U.S. President concerned with shoring up the prestige of the Soviet central leadership, just when that central leadership has become irrelevant to the political process in the USSR. Future historians will surely wonder at the astounding malleability of a policy that, after forty years of rhetorical anticommunism, now clings desperately to communism's last vestiges rather than embracing democratic alternatives.

The Bush administration's policy is less surprising than one might think, however, because to most analysts of the Soviet Union it was simply inconceivable that they could be witnessing a social transformation promoted by independent social forces. So accustomed were they to viewing Soviet society as run from the top that trying to identify popular alternatives to Gorbachev was not even considered. As one senior State Department official told me cryptically when asked why we paid so much attention to Gorbachev despite the evidence of other sociopolitical forces, "Gorbachev is the best Russian we are likely to get."

To be sure, there were many valid arguments for the policy of containment. I believe that political and ideological hostility limited the opportunities available for improving U.S.-Soviet relations during the Cold War. But as the arms race shifts full gear into reverse, as the Soviets withdraw from territories they have occupied and cease supporting client communist states around the world, our own limited appreciation of the diversity of Russian history looms ever larger as a constraint upon our ability to redefine our relationship with the Soviet Union.

One defining characteristic of containment, particularly as espoused by George Kennan and Henry Kissinger, was the extent to which the Soviet nuclear threat limited our moral opportunities in international relations. This was a common refrain of the "realist" school—one used quite effectively by Kissinger and Marshall Shulman to argue against raising human rights concerns with Soviet leaders. If this assumption was indeed valid, then conversely such opportunities to promote moral values must now be expanding dramatically, but they are not being utilized fully because of a constrained vision of the opportunities afforded by Russian political culture. I am afraid that we do not have a consensus on a postcontainment policy because there has been no sufficiently compelling intellectual reappraisal of Russian political culture, one that would allow us to envision the possibility of a stable, pluralistic Russian society. Yet without such a vision, I believe we are unlikely ever to forge any such consensus.

## The Argument for a Usable Past

While the need for a new postcommunist, postcontainment foreign policy consensus is widely acknowledged, the prerequisites for it are strikingly absent. I believe this can be remedied only by revisiting one of the sharpest debates in Soviet studies: the continuity, or lack thereof, between Soviet and Russian political culture.

Sometime in the 1960s, the majority of Sovietologists concluded that the most militant aspect of the Soviet regime had succumbed to the influence of Russian nationalism. After Stalin's death the regime restrained its attacks on the Russian heritage and in return became more legitimate in the eyes of the populace. The result, according to this view, was a much more stable and popular Soviet regime, in large part a result of the continuity of fundamental aspects of Russian political culture both before and after the October Revolution of 1917. As the director of the Harvard Russian Research Center, Adam Ulam, put it, "Soviet patriotism is a veneer on

Russian nationalism," and, according to this view, the stability of the Soviet regime rests on the popular acceptance of this fact.

True, a remnant, including such notables as Leonard Schapiro, Hugh Seton-Watson, Alain Besancon, Bertram D. Wolfe, and the late Mikhail Karpovich, clung stubbornly to the notion that the October Revolution had resulted in a fundamental break with traditional Russian political and social values. They believed that the regime perceived Russian political culture not as an ally but as an enemy to be eradicated. The Soviet system had supplanted authentic Russian patriotism with a perverse brand of "Soviet internationalism." The result, says the distinguished British historian Hugh Seton-Watson, was "a culturally mutilated Russian nationalism" where imperial ambitions and proletarian internationalism became inextricably intertwined.

Despite Stalin's late embrace of popular Russian national symbols to bolster popular opposition to the German invasion, this remnant felt that the regime never succeeded in gaining the people's confidence, but continued to rule through increasingly sophisticated mechanisms of oppression.

What is most striking about this minority view in Western Sovietology is faith of its adherents that this type of regime would never be able to gain popular support and must eventually succumb to indomitable forces inherent in the human spirit and in Russian culture. In prophetic remarks at Oxford on four decades of Soviet despotism, Wolfe remarked:

"We have seen that forty years of *Gleischaltung,* corruption and terror have not rooted out of the artist the ineradicable notion that sincerity to his creative vision is more to be desired than *partiinost* and *ideinost*. We have seen that the youth, though the faint-hearted thought they would be turned off the con-veyer-belt as 'little monsters,' are still born young, and therefore plastic, receptive, doubting, capable of illusion and disillusion, capable of 'youthful idealism' and youthful questioning of the elders and of the established, and of youthful rebellion. . . .

"Nor, finally, have I ever for a moment ceased to cast about for grounds of hope: that weaker heirs might make less efficient use of the terrible engines of total power; that a struggle, or succession of strug-gles for the succession, might compel a contender to go outside the inner circles and summon social forces in the lower ranks of the party or outside of it into some sort of independent existence; that the army, disgraced as no other in all history by the charge that it gave birth to traitors by the thousands in its general staff, might develop the independence from the party sufficient to make it a rival power center or an organ-ized pressure body; that intellectuals, that techni-cians, that students, might somehow break through the barriers that hinder the conversion of discontent into an organized, independent force." (*Communist Totalitarianism*, Westview Encore Press, 1985, pp. 290–291.)

It is quite remarkable, and a credit to the first genera-tion of American students of the Soviet Union, that they so clearly foresaw the inevitable rise of a dissident move-ment inside the Soviet Union and saw the dissidents as playing a significant role in social transformations.

By contrast, little more than a decade later, the majority of Western analysts would dismiss these dissidents as a noble but quixotic band of estranged intellectuals. It was commonly assumed that their appeals for the rule of law, restraints on state power, and the need to fundamentally reshape the social contract between rulers and ruled fell on deaf ears.

*Glasnost* has shown us that these assumptions were false. Dissident literature, or *samizdat*, received much wider circulation than was ever thought possible. Most important, it was tremendously influential in shaping the worldview of the generation born in the 1960s. The dissident experience, far from isolating the intellectual elite from the populace, was the tilling of the soil necessary to the fruition of broad-based popular fronts and opposition parties in just two to three years.

It has been a long and difficult gestation, but one that the emerging political leadership of postcommunist Russia acknowledges was vital to the popular acceptance of the radical reform agenda. The consistent victories of the proponents of radical change at the polls, the election of former political dissidents to leadership positions at every level of government, serves as confirmation of their enduring link with broad sectors of the populace.

This enduring link is what Fred Starr, president of Oberlin College, referred to hopefully as Russia's "usable past." What we are witnessing today is the revival of the Russian culture that Aleksandr Solzhenitsyn, Andrey Sakharov, Wolfe, Schapiro, and others predicted. With it we are seeing a new definition emerging of the Russian national interest, with profound implications for American foreign policy.

## Reasserting the Russian National Interest

One of the most famous epigrams about the Soviet Union is attributed to Winston Churchill: "I cannot forecast to you the action of Russia. It is a riddle, wrapped in a mystery inside an enigma; but perhaps there is a key. That key is Russian national interest." The elusive search for the determinants of Russia's national interest has kept generations of scholars busy. But perhaps *perestroika* and *glasnost* have afforded us the opportunity to conclude this debate once and for all.

Until quite recently, one's view of Soviet foreign policy objectives was determined by one of two contradictory interpretations of the origins of the Soviet national interest: the ideological interpretation and the continuity interpretation. The ideological interpretation held that Marxism-Leninism had distorted true Russian national interest. This interpretation was consonant with the broader view of the October Revolution as a break in Russian political culture. By contrast, the continuity interpretation held that the only plausible definition of national interest was that given by the government at the moment. Other options were mere wishful thinking. It flowed from a view of Soviet policies as, by and large, a continuation of Tsarist political aspirations but was also shaped by the assumption that failure to acknowledge the durability of the Soviet state left no option to American foreign policy but intractable hostility and probable nuclear confrontation. Moreover, the supporters of continuity often suspected that their opponents, many of whom had in middle age abandoned their youthful enthusiasm about socialism, were now blinded by their ideological hostility to communist ideology.

Now into this fray come contemporary Soviet diplomats and diplomatic historians siding overwhelmingly
with the ideological interpretation. Their arguments have
not received as wide an acceptance in this country as one
might expect (the dispute, after all, was supposed to be
about what actually motivated foreign policy decision
making on the other side—now the other side is telling
us). The reason, I suspect, has more to do with a reluctance to countenance arguments that sound like justi-
fications for the policies of the Cold War. As Martin
Malia has perceptively pointed out:

> "No Western historian, therefore, can write about
> the Russian Revolution without commenting indirect-
> ly on the West, and none can keep his Western world-
> view out of an analysis of Russia. Ever since 1917,
> whenever the Soviet experiment seemed headed for
> success, the Western Right has been automatically
> deflated; and if it veered toward failure, the Western
> Left has been correspondingly diminished. And so
> the Russian Revolution became the great polarizing
> event in the 20th century politics." ("The Hunt for
> True October," *Commentary*, October 1991, p. 21.)

Our domestic political differences should not blind us,
however, to the fact that the new Russian foreign policy
is now clearly being constructed under the imperative
of discarding the ideological constraints of Soviet foreign policy. The contours of the new Russian foreign
policy are already quite clear: It is to be a pragmatic,
nonideological, nonsectarian interpretation of the Russian
national interest, in direct contrast to the guiding principles of Marxism-Leninism, which are seen to have sub-

ordinated the formulation of a sound foreign policy based on the national interest to utopian aspirations.

It is the removal of the ideological yoke (which so many Western Sovietologists refused even to acknowledge) that has allowed for a redefinition of Soviet interests in arms control, Cuba, Afghanistan, the Kurile Islands, even relations with the Baltic states. Most specifically, it is the ability now to view Western actions as not endemically hostile to Russian interests. It is certainly true to say that Soviet commitments abroad were a burden to the economy, but this rationale would never by itself have sufficed to so dramatically alter the course of Soviet foreign policy.

The present period in Russian history is so dramatic not because the changes may lead to reduction of arms, new treaties, or agreements on withdrawal of Soviet armed forces from points of strategic interest to the United States, desirable as those outcomes may be. Such agreements, after all, were reached with past Soviet leaders. They are dramatic because they represent a redefinition of the national interest by the very peoples of the Soviet Union. This is not merely a shift in priorities; it is a sea change in a nation's worldview, in its assumptions about itself. The current leadership of the Russian and other republics is attempting, as Thomas Paine once observed about the American nation, "to make the world anew." This attempt may fail, but the magnitude of the undertaking is cause for a serious reexamination of our previous assumptions.

This situation, of course, does not imply that there will no longer be conflict between the U.S. and the successor state to the USSR. Tensions between sovereign states seem to be in the same category as death and taxes in personal life. But the same conflict can be viewed quite differently, depending on the general tenor of relations between states. For instance, European thinkers in the nineteenth century commonly assumed that Germany and France could not prosper simultaneously, hence tension between the two nations was endemic. Yet today we are seeing high-level discussions on the creation of joint Franco-German armed forces!

Likewise, while many points of disagreement remain between Japan and the United States, particularly in matters of trade, the changes in Japanese society after World War II now make it implausible that a war between the two nations will erupt over these issues. The quality of conflict and its degree of resolvability depend on the ability of nations to limit their definition of national interest to pragmatic, nonutopian considerations.

History remains our best guide as to what issues of conflict might arise between a pragmatically guided United States and Soviet Union. Here it is worth noting that the 130 years of diplomatic history between the Russian empire and the United States were generally cordial. The factors most often credited for this were distance, the lack of territorial conflict, modest trade, and Tsar Alexander II's sympathy for the North during the Civil War. Lincoln likewise held the tsar in high esteem for liberating the serfs four years before slaves were freed in the United States.

The one issue that soured relations and led to the abrogation of the Treaty of Commerce and Friendship of 1832 was the treatment of Jews in the Russian empire, or what we would now call a human rights question. Through revolutions and changes of government, this issue has remained a stumbling block toward the establishment of fully cordial relations between the two nations. It looms large not only in Russian-American relations but also in our image of ourselves and of our conduct of foreign policy. It is at this intersection of foreign policy with ethical concerns, therefore, that I see the possibility for continued conflict arising, unless our policy is adjusted to reflect the new realities of Russian domestic politics.

## Ethical Interdependence in the Postcontainment Era

In the spring of 1980, Nobel prize winner Aleksandr Solzhenitsyn published a seminal article in *Foreign Affairs*, one of the bastions of traditional American foreign policy. Provocatively entitled "Misconceptions about Russia Are a Threat to America," Solzhenitsyn's paper suggested that the United States had lost its "ethical compass" and as a result was pursuing an amoral policy with regard to the Soviet Union and other communist countries. The loss of this solid moral foundation, Solzhenitsyn argued, had led to a foreign policy of expediency—satisfactory only to the most minimal objectives over the shortest period of time. These problems could be corrected, he suggested, if American foreign policy became more farsighted and more concerned with the ethical plight of those who live under communist rule. Such concern must begin by recognizing a sharp distinction between Russian values and communism, between the terms "Russian" and "Soviet."

Solzhenitsyn's essay was widely criticized by the American foreign policy establishment. Influential *Washington Post* columnist Joseph Kraft dismissed his

prescriptions as mere "personal morality." Henry Kissinger warned that such an approach would be tanta-
mount to advocating the overthrow of the Soviet government. Stanford Sovietologist Alexander Dallin cautioned
that following Solzhenitsyn's advice "would preclude a
coherent policy toward the Soviet Union."

But while Solzhenitsyn was faulted for exaggerating
the problems of his country and for failing to accept the
established view that Soviet and Russian interests largely
coincided, most critics ignored his central point: that a
foreign policy not anchored in a coherent, long-term
ethical vision of the world will constantly be derailed by
the winds of political expediency.

Now that the transformations that Solzhenitsyn and
others augured have occurred, it is worth dusting off
this decade-old argument to ask why the alternatives to
containment proposed by Solzhenitsyn were so roundly
rejected. What have we learned in the intervening decade, and can this knowledge help us to establish a postcontainment strategy?

Upon closer reflection, the distance between Solzhenitsyn and his critics on the appropriate criteria for foreign
policy success is not as great as the rhetoric might indicate. The solution to the superpower impasse, he suggests,
is avoiding the pitfalls of "legal rationalism" in foreign
affairs, with its simplistic assumption that the creation
of laws means the achievement of justice. This is certainly an argument familiar to the students of Hans J.
Morgenthau and George F. Kennan, the father of American realism.

Second, Solzhenitsyn mistrusts what he calls moralism, or the application of a single moral standard to the
conduct of nations. This would not allow, he says, for

"the complex, distinct, and unrepeatable organisms" of society essential to man's freedom.

Third, while the West should be held accountable for counterproductive and unethical behavior, the burden of liberation rests squarely on the shoulders of the people under the communist yoke. Freedom cannot be imposed from without but will result only from what Solzhenitsyn termed, back in 1974, a "personal moral revolution." The recognition of both the limits of external assistance and the importance of self-reliance fit comfortably within the traditional American foreign policy mainstream.

Indeed, now that events in Russia are sweeping aside the last ideological obstacles to reform, there remains but one serious point of disagreement between mainstream American realists and the new Russian realists advocating a narrower definition of the national interest—the debate over the continuity between Russian and Soviet political values. And here it seems to me that Solzhenitsyn was right and his critics were wrong.

The distinction between "Russian" and "Soviet," which Solzhenitsyn saw as fundamental to understanding Russian national aspirations, became much clearer in 1991. We saw with our own eyes how the populace adopted the tricolor Russian flag as their symbol of resistance to tyranny during the heady days of August and how the voters in the birthplace of the October Revolution chose to restore to Leningrad the venerated name of St. Petersburg. This distinction, indeed, must be the centerpiece of any effort to shape an intellectually sound postcontainment strategy.

Solzhenitsyn's main injunction has been to cease viewing the world as divided into isolated regions with little impact on each other. While American political scientists have contributed a great deal to the literature on economic interdependence and the limitations on sovereignty, particularly in the less-developed countries (LDCs), Solzhenitsyn extends this notion to the spiritual realm and argues that there is a comparable sphere of ethical interdependence among nations. Those leaders who appreciate its importance will be more successful in their foreign policy; those who ignore it risk isolation, misunderstanding, and failure.

The idea of an ethical interdependence among nations must seem strange to the modern Western political analyst, steeped in a secular vision of political judgments and quantifiable measures of success. But it was certainly not unknown to previous statesmen. Some, like William Gladstone, Woodrow Wilson, or even Otto von Bismarck, often reflected on the importance of having a national policy attuned to supreme ethical standards, for practical as well as moral reasons. Bismarck was probably reflecting on how the two were linked when he wrote that "the statesman cannot create the stream of time, he can only navigate upon it . . . he must try and reach for the hem when he hears the garment of God rustling through events."

More recently, Sissela Bok in her latest book *A Strategy for Peace* has written of trust as an essential international good. But such trust presumes an understanding and appreciation of shared values. Sounding at times very much like Solzhenitsyn, Bok argues that without a minimum of mutual and verifiable trust, nations would be in a state of "mere truce."

"This would be just a suspension of hostilities rather than a peace—a cold war. A truce between countries armed to the teeth, caught up in that atmosphere of mutual distrust which stems from long-standing policies of hostility, deceit, and treachery [,] could hardly end in anything but another war." (*A Strategy for Peace: Human Values and the Threat of War*, Vintage Books, 1990, pp. 42-43.)

Ethical interdependence would have an immediate impact on our approach to human rights, which has been the most visible expression of our concern for morality in foreign policy. Traditionally, this policy has had two objectives: the first, to secure the emigration of oppressed national minorities, primarily Jews; the second, to encourage respect for fundamental human rights principles inside the Soviet Union. Recent events have made these two issues largely obsolete. While there may still be technical difficulties for those wishing to emigrate from the Soviet Union, a more serious problem now is finding a Western country willing to take them. Likewise, with the passage of new legislation, the registration of independent political parties, and an increasingly assertive press and judiciary, Soviet citizens are gaining confidence that grievances against the system can be addressed through indigenous institutions. In a word, the human rights agenda of the past twenty years is obsolete. The task now is to refine that agenda so that human rights, and ethical issues in general, become less of an obstacle in our relations with a democratic Russia.

A significant part of the problem has been our approach on human rights, traditionally one of intercession, which is typically viewed by foreign countries as intervention. While Democratic and Republican administrations have differed on matters of style, both viewed in-

tervention as entirely appropriate, much as a surgeon
might intervene to save a sick patient or a fireman might
enter a burning building to save the inhabitants. It was
assumed that the doctor or the fireman knew best what
needed to be done. Indeed, senior human rights officials
in the Carter administration would wearily refer to their
task as "firefighting."

But now that the infrastructures of democracy are
taking root in the Soviet Union, we should rethink this
relationship. Today that patient is able to cure or save
himself and has his own sense of which remedies to pursue and which to reject. And above all, the patient should
be respected for that choice *even when we disagree with
it.*

There is among democratic countries considerable diversity of interpretation, for example, on the definition
of rights and on the proper mixture of socioeconomic and
political rights. It is entirely plausible that the distinct
Russian mix of values may ultimately come to resemble
that of Japan or Germany more than it does that of the
United States.

On a practical level, a recognition of ethical interdependence should lead to a human rights policy that en-
gages in vigorous debate and promotion of those aspects
of civil society that we consider fundamental to democratic government. It should include such initiatives as
sponsoring colloquia on the rule of law and on local government administration like the ones currently in place.
But it would also be mindful of the fact that institution
building does not mean mimicry of the West and that the
quickest way to taint a good idea is to present it as a
Western invention to be adopted wholesale. The best way
to ensure the adoption of such institutions and ideas is to

look for previous examples in Russian history and to build upon them, forging links between indigenous institutions and ideas and Western ones. We should inform ourselves about ideas, thinkers, and traditions in Russian culture that resonate with our own. These traditions are there; we are simply unaware of them.

The absence of major items of substantive conflict has left the field wide open for intellectual engagement. At present, Soviet intellectuals are starved for information, starved for fresh ideas. The Western world, its intellectual heritage and experiences are the subject of immense interest and debate. Yet I would hesitate to call the fascination with novelty the triumph of the West or the "end of history." Previous encounters between the West and more traditional cultures such as Meiji Japan, imperial China, and Ataturk's Turkey have seen what appeared to be equally decisive victories emerge into virulent anti-Western reactions. One of the foremost tasks of a post-containment human rights effort should therefore be to minimize the potential of such an anti-Western reaction while maximizing the opportunities for appreciating the common aspects of our heritage. The thing to avoid at all costs, and that has unfortunately been synonymous with our human rights efforts in the past, is a preachy, know-it-all attitude of the morally superior toward the morally inferior. A "patronizing attitude toward the older, unfamiliar Eastern cultures," James Billington notes, has been a fixture in all the mistaken conventional wisdom about Russia.

A good place to start searching for the common cultural thread between the Western liberal tradition and the Russian liberal tradition is in the writings of Aleksandr Solzhenitsyn, especially his most recent essay, *Rebuild-*

*ing Russia* (1991). It is symptomatic of our sense of misdirection when looking at the Russian political spectrum that while Solzhenitsyn is perceived as conservative, even reactionary, in the United States, it may be more appropriate to place him in the tradition of what the late Leonard Schapiro termed Russian "liberal conservatives." This group, Schapiro argues, "stood midway between Slavophiles and Westernizers. They accepted the Slavophile veneration of Russian national tradition, while rejecting their romantic idealization of innate Russian virtues as a substitute for the more usual civic virtues." This tradition includes many illustrious scholars and statesmen of the past century, as well as writers and philosophers.

During the late 1970s, Solzhenitsyn hoped that detente would eventually give way to what he called a policy of "an open hand," that is, establishing direct contacts with peoples in communist-dominated areas, thus giving them a chance to grow in their self-awareness and emancipation. Now that this has begun in earnest, the classical Russian liberal traditions of the past are re-emerging, and we should do everything possible to clasp the hand that it is extending toward us.

### Conclusion

The need for a fundamental reappraisal concerning the viability of democracy in Russia is long overdue. The astonishment among Soviet experts at the pace of change, over popular support for reform candidates, and at the popular response to the August 1991 coup attempt are all evidence of an underlying failure to comprehend the changes the populace has undergone. Without radically altering our assumptions about Russian political culture, it is unlikely that we will be able to respond to the opportunities now presenting themselves. If we fail to change, despite overwhelming economic and military superiority, it is unlikely that we will be the ones setting the agenda for U.S.-Soviet relations in the 1990s.

We will likewise fail in our efforts to understand the direction in which these transformations are pushing Russian foreign policy. To redirect our moral compass away from the constrained assumptions of the containment period to a vision of opportunity, we must first acknowledge that opportunities for democracy exist in Russian political culture.

Many would argue that, in late 1991, Russian democracy looks anything but viable. The economy is collapsing, and the Soviet empire is rapidly disintegrating. It is not at all clear what sort of new governments will emerge over there. Civil war seems a more likely prospect than stable democratic government in the Soviet Union.

Political and economic conditions will probably continue to deteriorate in the near future. It will be necessary to deal with a variety of governments, each with distinctive political aspirations, where we once dealt with only one. The argument for caution, however, should not overshadow the need to take seriously the degree of social change that has already taken place and that is by now well documented in polls, nationwide election results, and recent historical events.

Second, focusing on short-term problems is no substitute for asking the crucial question, if the present political situation is unstable, what will stabilize it? What type of social contract, based on what values, will the majority of the populace eventually find acceptable? We already know that the political situation is deteriorating. What we need to figure out is where this erosion will bottom out. Put another way, what values are likely to form the basis for a stable political order?

This is hardly an idle question in the face of imminent social disintegration. Without a tentative answer to the question of what social forces are likely to emerge and construct a consensual political order, any monetary assistance, technical assistance, or any other form of aid will at best be stabs in the dark and may even be counterproductive.

Yet most of our political decision makers seem mesmerized by the question of whether a new governmental structure can be successfully institutionalized, forgetting that the question of what values people will pledge their allegiance to precedes the question of what structures will contain them.

By now there is ample evidence that the standard tools of social science can be helpful in identifying the contours of the new Russian national consensus. Polling information and election results analysis, along with a comprehension of how the diverse strands in Russian political culture are shaping the political debate, can go a long way toward beginning to chart the outlines of a new Russian foreign policy and new social contract upon which it is based. Our failure to do much in this regard has made our policy toward the Soviet Union reactive, unprepared, and overly cautious.

A postcontainment policy guided by considerations of ethical interdependence needs to be constructed gradually, with initiatives in a number of different directions. The first is education. Our base of knowledge is terribly important. The way we have studied Soviet politics has tended to reinforce stereotypical assumptions that the country was run by an untouchable clique, leading to the rather bizarre image, as Moshe Lewin puts it, of "a political system without a social one, a state floating over everything else, over history itself." As scholars we need to go back to the drawing board to determine how we missed so many obvious signals of social discontent.

Second, we need to be aware of the intellectual antecedents of the new generation of Russian political leaders. These leaders did not emerge from thin air. Their popularity rests on the resonance between their political values and those of the populace. A case in point is Boris Yeltsin. Most Western commentators mistakenly attributed his tremendous popularity before the coup to "populism" and "demagoguery." In reality, Yeltsin's popularity is the result of both a decisive commitment to change and a consistent political program. Our misunderstanding of the Yeltsin phenomenon drove our policy toward excessive reliance on Gorbachev, an increasingly unpopular and irrelevant figure in Soviet politics.

Third, we need to encourage joint research by Russian and American think tanks, universities, and foundations on the conditions necessary for markets, rule of law, political stability—in sum, on reconstituting civil society. Right now we have too many missionaries over there seeking converts and too few explorers willing to learn. This leads to a fourth point, raised by Billington, that when we do engage in training we do it with people qualified to put the Western experience in a context understandable to the Soviet listener and that we try to bring people over here, where they can roam around freely and teach themselves.

The sea change in Russian national consciousness has fundamentally transformed the problems we will be facing in the future and the opportunities for establishing a new pattern in our relationship with the Soviet Union. But unless we recognize how fundamentally the lay of the land has changed, we can run into stumbling blocks where none really exist. A good example of this is our inordinate concern for Russian nationalism that, even in its most chauvinistic expression, is no more significant a force in Russian public opinion than the Ku Klux Klan is in the United States.

Soviet history may be over, but a new period in Russian history is just beginning. It brings with it an opportunity to close one of the most dangerous chapters in human history—the Cold War. We should not let this opportunity escape us for, as Gorbachev recently observed, "History punishes those who come late."

# INVESTMENT FROM ABROAD—
# NO LONGER JUST AN OPTION

by

Alexander J. Gillespie, Jr.

## Alexander J. Gillespie, Jr.

*Alexander J. Gillespie, Jr., is Of Counsel to the New York
law firm Breed, Abbott & Morgan. From 1960 to 1989, he was
associated with ASARCO Incorporated, where he served as
Vice Chairman of the Board and General Counsel as well as
Vice Chairman–Legal and Corporate Affairs.*

*Mr. Gillespie graduated from Dartmouth College and the
Fordham University School of Law, where he was Associate
Editor of the* Fordham Law Review *and was awarded the
Senior Class Prize. As a member of the United States Naval
Reserve, he served on a destroyer escort in the Atlantic and
Pacific theaters of World War II and with the China occupa-
tion force.*

*In addition to membership in numerous bar and legal asso-
ciations, Mr. Gillespie serves as an Advisory Board member
both for the International and Comparative Law Center of
The Southwestern Legal Foundation and for the Parker School
of Foreign and Comparative Law of Columbia University.
He has also been an arbitrator for the American Arbitration
Association and the National Association of Security Dealers.
He has lectured at many symposia sponsored by the American
Bar Association, the Practising Law Institute, the Conference
Board, and The Southwestern Legal Foundation and has been
Co-Chairman of the Fordham Corporate Law Institute.*

*In addition to serving numerous national charities, Mr.
Gillespie has been a Director of the Silver Hill Foundation,
the Fordham Law Alumni Association, the Bruce Museum
Associates, and the Brunswick School.*

# INVESTMENT FROM ABROAD—
# NO LONGER JUST AN OPTION

by

## Alexander J. Gillespie, Jr.

In the area of foreign investment the concepts of expediency and morality have never really received equal attention or application, with one frequently existing entirely separate from the other. History more often than not reveals human nature showing its more unattractive aspects when one analyzes the diverse motivations of countries when they have intruded into economies other than their own.

The Roman Empire spread its influence to areas distant from Rome that, even today, are a number of jet-hours away. Ofttimes conquering or invading for strategic advantage or for political purposes, Rome also ventured abroad for commercial and trade reasons. The Old World—Egypt, Greece, Asia Minor, and North Africa—once conquered, provided grain, marble, and lumber, all to supply the increasing demand of the Roman economy. A primary reason for Rome's occupation of Britain was to obtain precious tin for the production of bronze weapons, while the lead mines of Spain sourced the conduits for the quite-sophisticated plumbing of Roman homes. Every area of the eventual Empire held some economic attraction. "Investment" by force of arms, with all of that path's implicit atrocities and excesses, was certainly the order of the day in the first millennium and well into the second.

Circumstances changed over the span of centuries, and the desire for things foreign to, or unavailable in, Europe produced events that are familiar to all. In almost every instance of major exploration and subsequent discovery, however, the romantic aspect of the accomplishment has overshadowed its frequently cruel and ugly sides. We are seeing that today in the variety of recognitions being given to celebrate the five-hundredth anniversary of Columbus's discovery of the Western World. The monarchist conquests in the Western Hemisphere from Mexico and the Antilles to Peru in the search for "Eldorado," the efforts of militant powers in later attempts to colonize North America, and the subsequent efforts to fulfill Manifest Destiny do not constitute stories that should generate much pride today. That is, however, the historical record of early exploration, commercialization, and settlement. These events sometimes had a religious aspect that gave ostensible elements of credence (and morality) to any particular country's attempt to accomplish what were basically pragmatic goals. More often, however, underlying motivations included mixtures of national pride, dynastic perceptions, revenge, politics, and, usually, a substantial degree of economic compulsion. In rare instances, the various sixteenth- and seventeenth-century English-based "commercial companies" (such as the Massachusetts Bay Company and the Virginia Company) were, arguably, on a more altruistic plane—at least initially. Except for the efforts of these companies, the incursions were almost universally expedient, that is to say, appropriate, but largely devoid of principle and without any truly moral motivation.

Are our efforts today more "moral" than those of our ancestors? I believe that they may be, but we are in a different world, with a large proportion of today's good being provided by yesterday's expedience.

This is a fairly long path to follow to arrive at the hypothesis being considered, namely, that commercial dealings among nations—especially investment—while almost always containing *some* element of expediency, many times have other facets, sometimes obscure, and possibly imposed by society or developed over time, that are compatible with moral principle and ethical standards.

By any measure, the last ten years or more have brought sea changes to many economies and governments. More open political systems have been created that have, in turn, provided the basis for free market economies. These political changes have occurred mostly in the underdeveloped and less-developed areas of the world, as well as in the Comintern countries. Great powers, such as the USSR and the People's Republic of China, have been participants, in varying degrees, in this evolution or revolution. The European Economic Community (EEC), while already a basically free political area and an open market economy, is at the threshold of becoming in 1992 an economic system that may well constitute the world's most powerful and cohesive trading bloc.

The USSR has quite recently encountered upheavals that only months ago even the most imaginative fiction writer would have treated as incredible. That situation continues to evolve, and the events comprising it will likely have deep and long-term political, military, and economic significance. Although the area's eventual shape is far from definite at this time, a number of new political systems and free economies appear now to be likely results.

The lesson of the last decade's tumult can lead to several conclusions. One is that drastic and disruptive political and economic change is becoming more the norm than the exception and therefore will continue to produce critical situations. More optimistic thoughts are that the sum of the numerous switches in governments and in basic economic policies has already resulted in a vastly more open, democratic, and market-oriented society; that the populations involved will thereby inherit significant long-range benefits both in their standards of living and in their personal freedom; and that a stabilized era may ensue.

The events in China in the spring of 1989 were exceptions to the general trend toward democratization. With Tienanmen Square and its surrounding elements of repression, China took a giant step backward in its relationship to the rest of the world and in its apparent internal attitude toward individual rights. Despite efforts at rehabilitation and support, notably from the United States, the attractiveness of China as a trading partner or a co-venturer has certainly been tarnished—an important but negative situation for a country containing nearly one-third of the world's population. But China could provide us with surprises as well!

On the positive side of what one could call, in a political sense, the "march of individual freedom," or, in an economic context, "free trade and open markets," some striking examples worth noting have developed in major areas of the world during the last decade.

In the "developed world" the EEC is, as referred to above, pushing toward 1992, the magic year when most, if not all, trade barriers are scheduled to fall and the concept of one Europe will take on additional validity. All EEC objectives, especially the adoption of implementing legislation and the rationalization of monetary transactions, may not be met by 1992, but immense strides will doubtless be made.

In the Western Hemisphere, only one Latin nation, Cuba, clings to a dictatorial and repressive style of "government by personality" and a statist economic regime. One by one, dictators or military juntas have been replaced by political systems having free elections and encouraging personal freedom. Economic reforms have been extensive and almost universal in the area.

Eastern Europe has seen events since 1989 that can be called, at the very least, extraordinary. Who can forget the television broadcast of the actual downfall of Rumania's president—graphically showing the viewing audience the end of a political era—and an evil one for sure? Similar, if less dramatic, scenes and events occurred in Hungary, Czechoslovakia, Poland, and Bulgaria. East Germany's physical destruction of the Berlin Wall and its subsequent legal annexation by Bonn fall in the same category. As an aside, during the summer of 1990, on a voyage up the Danube (on a Bulgarian ship!) the passengers (most of them from the United States) were greeted with a most welcome variation in political graffiti placed along the riverbank near Bratislava—a display of whitewashed stones spelling out, for all to see, "Ivan go home." An equally important message could have been implied: "Individual freedom and open markets—come here." That was and is Eastern Europe's sentiment.

We should not think, however, that the battle in the Eastern bloc countries is won. The difficult part is still ahead. Before they can fully enter the Western world, they must create both new government structures and free economies. The task is immense, with practically the entire populace of each country having lived all, or at least most, of their lives under a socialist/communist repressive regime with a state-controlled market system. While democracy and individual freedom are now the order of the day, how can the members of this large group of humanity make personal freedom and quality of life better and more fulfilling both for themselves and for future generations? Laws must be enacted; structures of jurisprudence, markets, and finance must be built; and, most important, a confident sense of better things to come at some foreseeably near time must be conveyed to the East European citizenry. No instant fix can reverse seventy years of social and economic repression and backwardness. Expectations of better days must be addressed with all dispatch in order to demonstrate to these countries' inhabitants that they have labored for an eminently worthwhile, indeed, *the* most worthwhile, cause.

To improve their generally low living standards, most of these newly constituted governments, wherever located, have embraced market-oriented economics, whether by privatization, the reform of archaic and discriminatory tax regimes, abrogation of repressive and protectionist investment policies, or, particularly in Latin areas, the institution of radical fiscal restructuring to address massive and stifling debt burdens. As a result, the decision about whether these new economies should opt for investment from abroad or cling to statist economies and substitution of imports is no longer on the table—it has become a race to see which country can first attract the foreign investor to its shores.

Vast and unprecedented political and economic changes have occurred and appear to be continuing. Large segments of the world probably will never be the same as, or even similar to, what they were in 1980. Obviously, this paper cannot provide more than a brief comment on some elements of the changes that seem most significant.

The focus here will be on Latin America because of its importance to the U.S. economy and our sociopolitical institutions and also to recognize that region's "quiet revolution." Comments are on particular countries that seem representative of degrees of development, and the viewpoint is that, coexisting with the political freedom that has been on the upswing, there have been, and there continue to be, substantial efforts to enhance basic economic freedoms. It follows that increased investment from abroad is an important, if not crucial, element for the success of the new economic programs. It appears demonstrable that, if properly instituted and executed, pragmatism in investment policies—expediency, if you will—while often a driving and initiating force, can and often does result in substantial benefits to the host country, as well as to the foreign investor.

## Latin America—Its New Economic Challenge

Unlike other basic elements of the free market system, capital has its own strict limitations. It is dissimilar to debt; it cannot be "created" or transformed so as to appear to be something other than what it really is. Accordingly, capital's finite character makes it the object of extreme competition under present world conditions.

The bidding for capital is heating up, with countries of the Pacific rim competing with the Eastern bloc countries and other economic areas for investment funds. Latin America is also emerging as an active bidder for equity and venture participants now that many of its countries have instituted political and economic reform and thus made such bidding both credible and appropriate.

Latin America in the 1960s adopted severe restrictions on foreign investment and encouraged local and inefficient industries by limiting imports; in the 1970s it attempted to substitute foreign borrowing for foreign investment. Consequently, the Latin countries—burdened by huge public debts, generated and promoted in large part by overly active lenders in the United States, Japan, and Europe; by political instability; and by tax and exchange systems that were archaic and stifling—were not to any substantial degree participants in the world's economic growth from the late 1970s to the late 1980s. But it was and is an area also in revolution, albeit a slower and less dramatic one than that experienced in Eastern Europe and now so precipitously in the USSR.

A major advantage that Latin America may validly claim over newly emerging "free" European countries, including Poland, Czechoslovakia, and Hungary, is that it already has available the infrastructure to take advantage of its new economic and political directions. Latin America can offer investors or joint venturers not only a reliable and intelligent work force but legal systems, monetary and central banking facilities, and accounting practices (not to mention stock exchanges) that have been in place for decades. Eastern Europe has yet to construct the systems or come to grips with the economic and social problems engendered by its new situation, and solutions to all these problems will take substantial time. Most Latin countries also have the advantage over other emerging areas of an underclass used to being entrepreneurs in spite of overregulation and statist-driven economies—its activities in fact have constituted an underground economy.

Additionally, Latin America is in the same hemisphere as the United States—a fact of geographic proximity shared only by Canada. Recall the wistful reaction of West Germany's Chancellor Ludwig Erhard at a mid-1960s economic conference in response to a negative diatribe by one of the United States' southern neighbors on the "problems" created by that nation's 2,000-mile common border with the United States: "What we would give for only a mile or two!"

What have the Latin countries done to move themselves out of decades of stagnation and nonattainment and into a position to compete more effectively in world economy? The answer is that they have done much and continue to achieve positive results. Some Latin countries or areas have prospered, some are now on the verge of success, and all except Cuba are in some phase of developing or implementing new economic, and in some cases political, directions. In an effort to understand this area, which is so important to the United States, it would help to look more closely at some initiatives and concepts that are newly adopted or are being considered in several countries representative of various stages of development.

## A. Mexico

Since colonial times, geography has made for an almost constant interchange of populations, commercial dealings, and ideas between Mexico and the United States. Mexico was and is an amalgam of ancient Indian cultures and subsequent substantial infusions of Spanish influence. It has, despite occasional expressions of xenophobia toward its northern neighbor and the latter's gigantic economic and political presence in the hemisphere, a degree of admiration for the United States' technical achievements, for some elements of its culture, and even for its national moral stature. The trend now seems definitely to be toward a more rational and productive relationship.

Mexico's history, especially from the time it became independent from Spain in 1821 until modern days, is replete with economic tragedy and turmoil, with national humiliations, and with almost unbelievable political upheaval. This is so despite a long period of so-called stability under President Porfirio Diaz from 1876 to 1911 (the period known as the Porfiriato) and at least political continuity under various PRI (the Institutional Revolutionary Party, until recently Mexico's only party) administrations for over sixty years to the present. Mexico now seems to be embarking on a new path, but its history remains a factor to recognize and treat with discretion and respect in all contexts.

Mexico's "today" period probably began with the oil economics of the 1970s and the excesses this situation produced. In the middle of the decade, oil, the rising prices of which were bringing about a near collapse of Western and other energy-driven economies, suddenly caused Mexico to become a focus of interest as an other-than-Mideast producer. President José López Portillo, who had come to office in late 1976, increased Mexican oil production three times over, and by 1982 Mexico had become the United States' largest foreign supplier. The world's overproduction of oil in the early to mid-1980s resulted in a continuing fall in its realized price and caused Mexico to suffer extremely in its balance of payments, especially in view of the debt service burden resulting from the huge increase in debt taken on in the 1970s and early 1980s. The debt crisis of August 1982, when the Mexican debt could no longer be serviced, combined with inflation and the nationalization of commercial banks that September, made the economic prospects in Mexico dim indeed as President Miguel de la Madrid took office in December of that year.

His administration instituted directional changes in many aspects of Mexican economic (and political) policy, though various negative events continued to occur throughout almost his entire term. De la Madrid had pledged to make yet another effort (as had Presidents Portillo and Luis Echeverría) to open more dialogue with the United States in trying to improve relations. Serious attempts were made to eliminate local corruption and to move Mexico into the modern and open economic world. Throughout his term, however, episodic low points in U.S. relations and in other areas continued to occur.

In Mexico itself, a series of natural and economic disasters did little to help the president attain positive goals. The Mexico City earthquake in September 1985, the oil price collapse the following year, rampant inflation, and the stock market crash in 1987 all contributed to a crisis situation in the economy. In December 1987 a compact (the *Pacto*) between labor, the private sector, and the government, all pledging (and adhering to) anti-inflationary steps, put a temporary hold on the deteriorating economic situation.

The de la Madrid administration, despite all these traumas, both natural and man-made, was, on balance, more one of success than of failure, at least in getting the country's economic basis on sounder ground. It certainly saw the introduction of dialogue, and in some cases actual accomplishments, in attempts to vary widely what had become ingrained economic concepts and policies tending toward a managed economy. Privatization of state-owned enterprises was initiated and continues today. Expansion of the duty-free assembly plant, or *maquiladora*, concept gave a measure of economic competitiveness to the Mexican economy, and the use of *maquilas* in assembling complex, high-technology componentry gave the world positive evidence of the high quality of Mexican-manufactured products. Entrance into the General Agreement on Tariffs and Trade (GATT), a partial rationalization of foreign debt, innovative use of debt "swaps" and debt/equity, and the enhancement of U.S. trade policies regarding various sectors were additional evidence of Mexico's desire to reach economic maturity. It should be added that much United States financial assistance and the U.S. government's emphatic encouragement aided in solving the debt problems that occurred. The United States also exhibited a good measure of pragmatic maturity in this very substantial effort to assist, for example, by the U.S. Treasury's security prefunding of Mexican zero coupon debt.

When Carlos Salinas de Gortari was elected president in 1988 by the narrowest margin ever attained by the PRI, the cast of the "new" Mexico toward a freer and more market-oriented capitalistic system was already determined. Salinas, as de la Madrid's Secretary of Budget and Planning, had been the conceptual originator of many of that administration's more liberal and outreaching economic policies, including establishing the *Pacto*, joining GATT, putting into place export incentives, eliminating licenses for many products, and substantially reducing government employment.

A critical element of the overall plan for development and liberalization of the Mexican economy during the Salinas presidential administration was and is the attempt to enhance hard currency investment from abroad. This decision came in the context of a history of protectionism and of nationalization, or Mexicanization, of important industrial components, as well as of unhelpful policies and laws dealing with intellectual property and taxation. It was not that there was no foreign investment—there was—but there had been a significant decline of investment by the foreign sector as well as a huge "capital flight" from Mexico involving the funds of thousands of Mexican nationals. Salinas has actively sought foreign investment with a considerable measure of success and has overseen the creation of an economy that continues to attract foreign investment and to reverse the capital flight phenomenon. Some believe that the emergence of the new free political systems and economies in Eastern European countries convinced Salinas early in 1990 that if Mexico was to be a competitor for markets and for investment capital, it had to press full-bore for his underlying program. Within

months of the European political/economic transformation, in addition to encouraging the already commenced retreat from state ownership of industries,
Salinas initiated reprivatization of the banks and
started discussions with United States officials in hopes
of reaching a free trade agreement.

Today the economic picture in Mexico is one that
would have been a very long shot to predict even three
years ago. The tax codes were almost completely re-
vamped and modernized in 1989, eliminating or reducing special tax status segments and broadening the tax
base by a levy on "entrepreneurial assets." The result has
secured a more stable and "evenhanded" business climate. This improved atmosphere, together with elimination of import protection for local industries, has been
helpful in stimulating economic growth and reducing
inflation. Investors seem to have taken note.

New regulations were added in May 1989 to the old
Investment Law (which dated back to 1973) to clarify it
and to reduce the large element of discretion that existed
in its practical application. As a result, the allowable
percentage of ownership by foreign entities has been re-
laxed and clarified, and foreign investors can now invest
in a wider range of investment areas. Thus, foreigners
today may hold 100 percent ownership in some sectors
and may invest in areas, such as petrochemicals, previously forbidden to them. For the benefit of the Mexican
economy and social stability, it is clear that foreign investments that create Mexican job opportunities, provide training skills for employees, and involve fresh
infusions of foreign capital to assist in the Mexican balance of payments will be the ones most certain to be
welcomed. This is a good example of enlightened foreign

investment policy, especially in an area with a history of protectionism and state ownership.

It is not productive to detail here all the many outward-looking accomplishments, initiatives, and participations of the Salinas government. A few should be mentioned, however, including meaningful negotiations on the free-trade agreement with the United States and Canada that might create a North American Trading Association. The June 1991 law dealing with protection and development of industrial (intellectual) property and the increased tempo (and results) in the program to privatize the largest banks, mines, and key industries, previously state controlled, are other important examples of efforts to create an attractive investment ambiance.

A leading financial figure in Mexico, Roberto Hernandez, put it well in August 1991 when he stated in connection with the government having agreed to relinquish control of Banamex, Mexico's largest bank, "This country is changing so quickly that sometimes we don't recognize it. But it's extraordinary. This is a new country."

What all of this means is that the old order has been reversed to provide an attractive investment climate that meets the criteria of stability and confidence that investors outside the national border require, while at the same time creating the distinct probability of bettering the economic health and individual life-style of the Mexican people. An important fact to note is that this has all been done in a democratic and open manner. One should keep in mind, however, that an extraterritorial application of U.S. morality will play a role if this scenario is to have a completely successful result. For instance, the Mexican government must continue to follow through with policy standards of conduct to obviate the application of both the difficult provisions of United States law relating to the environment and the rigorous tests of the FCPA (Foreign Corrupt Practices Act) imposed on United States citizens doing business abroad.

Mexico's democratically constituted political system has enabled the construction and implementation of a free market system. Both systems have a basically moral underpinning, and although actions resulting from them can be viewed as expedient in the short term, they should also have long-lasting and substantial benefits both to the country itself and to those who decide to invest there. We are entitled to be optimistic about Mexico's future.

## B. *Ecuador*

While Mexico seems well embarked on a road to successful economic growth and political stability, as could also be said for Chile and Venezuela, a number of countries in the hemisphere are still struggling (with varying success) to find their way in a rapidly changing world. Ecuador is now a country in that process.

Ecuador is one of the smallest participants in the Southern ·Hemisphere's political/economic scene. Although it gained freedom in 1822 when Antonio José de Sucre, Simón Bolívar's most talented general, defeated the Spanish near Quito, Ecuador did not become totally independent from its neighbors, Colombia and Venezuela (Gran Colombia), until 1830. From that time until the early 1970s, Ecuador was a principally agricultural, as well as an extremely economically burdened and politically turbulent, country. Forest products, coffee, and fruit formed its basic economy until the advent of oil and gas exploration and development in the late 1960s and early 1970s. These relatively new products, while providing a degree of transitional earnings and foreign exchange, also generated an unevenness in the Ecuadorian government's economic policies and wide swings in political attitudes. Boundary disputes with Peru (which continue today) did little to enhance the overall picture. As it was for most Latin countries, the major part of the 1980s was for Ecuador a span of difficult politics and lost economic opportunities.

When President Rodrigo Borja Cevallos commenced his term of office in August 1988, the country found itself with an inflation rate of over 100 percent, a highly inefficient and repressive tax regime, two widely varying exchange rates, and a high external commercial bank debt no longer being serviced. In addition, the frequent and severe cycles of economic and political events and a generally depressed economy contributed to the protectionist-driven situation in the labor market.

Ecuador is a particularly fortunate country in its natural resources, with excellent agricultural areas on both sides of the Andean cordillera that runs north and south through the country, oil and gas in the east, productive fishing grounds in the Pacific, and a climate producing unique and extensive forest products. Only about 10 million people inhabit its 100,000 square miles, with most of the work force competing for the relatively few industrial and manufacturing jobs in the oil, fishing, and other private-sector businesses. Unemployment or underemployment probably affects over 50 percent of the working population. The booms and busts in the oil industry, which dominates export earnings, have pro-

duced a generally stagnant mind-set. Shifting governmental and economic plans have been the rule.

What has been done, and what can be done, for this
small country to improve its lot? The Borja administration has accomplished some positive results, but the signals are still somewhat mixed and there is a great deal
yet to do.

A significant boost to Ecuador, and to all other debt-
burdened Latin countries, was the announcement in
June 1990 by President George Bush of the "Enterprise
for the Americas" plan, a significant program for the
countries needing to improve their economic situation
through nontraditional means. Its basic concepts are to
establish, over time, a free trade area throughout the
hemisphere and to have more investment attracted to
the Latin countries, presumably by the individual countries' making the reforms and taking the necessary internal steps to encourage this influx. A further element
of the plan would be the forgiveness by the United States
of the government-to-government debts of these countries if they achieve structural reforms and demonstrate
economic progress. A most important point is that, unlike traditional programs, this one promotes self-help
instead of giving aid. Parenthetically, the U.S. State and
Commerce Departments view this program as a way for
the United States to seek investment opportunities from
Latin American sources similar to those that developed
countries in Europe seek from the "new" East European
countries—another indication of the competition for
capital.

Trade and investment, keystones to the Enterprise
initiative, received major recognition when Ecuador
issued an Executive Decree in June 1991 to implement

the Cartagena Agreement Commission's Decision No. 291. This Decision had called for member countries to institute a common (and more liberal) regime for the treatment of both foreign investments and technology transfers.

Although this very recent Ecuadorian action generally increases investment opportunities for foreign investors, significant areas in Ecuador remain in which foreigners can hold only a minority interest (among them insurance, commercial banks, radio and press communications, and fishing). Under the Decree, profit remission is essentially without limitation, after taxes and worker participations are withheld, and technology transfers are generally allowed without prior permission and with only a registration process required. This foreign investment program is a substantial step forward, as was the tax reform Ecuador evolved early in 1990 to broaden the tax base, reduce top tax rates, and generally modernize the overall taxing process.

Some preliminary considerations have been given to privatizing state companies, with a focus on the airline and telephone enterprises—another helpful step. Additionally, *maquila* laws have been adopted, allowing in-bond status and tax benefits for imported products that are to be enhanced by local labor and reexported. Also, a comprehensive tariff reform program, drastically reducing import duties, is now in place. These changes all have been effected to open the economy and act as a brake on inflation.

It is hoped that a new mining law will attract foreign exploration and development in a potentially rich economic sector that until now has largely been dormant. Also being debated in the press and in Ecuador's Congress are labor law reforms that do away with many archaic, labor-protective legal provisions that have done much to discourage foreign investment.

Ecuador seems to be positioned for progress, but inconsistent actions have been taken that raise concerns that somewhat dim the investment picture. Although Ecuador appears receptive to petroleum exploration and development, since the Borja administration assumed office, the government has taken over a number of substantial oil facilities—not a very positive development to encourage investors. The impending presidential elections in 1992 may also be serving to impede meaningful efforts or initiatives in the economic and political areas.

What seems to need addressing, and sooner rather than later, is the formation of a consensus, much the same as in Mexico's experience with the *Pacto* in 1987. The Ecuadorian government has taken a number of steps to set the groundwork, but a deep commitment is needed by both the business and the labor factions to implement the trade and investment programs now available, as well as to provide further incentives. Labor must address the consequences of continuing to support protective and artificial devices that constitute barriers to investment. The private sector may have to show, by enlightened management and business policies, that the profit motive and private initiative can be a preferred route to creating a better living standard for the public in general.

In the meanwhile, renegotiation of the debt, which still is a major concern, and maintenance of a reduced inflation level of about 50 percent may have to await more positive moves by the government toward privatization and fiscal reforms, as well as the application of programs already in place.

Ecuador, along with many other countries again discovering that democratization encourages an eventual free market economy, has the distinct possibility of demonstrating that the basically moral features of such systems can produce results that, though currently appearing expedient, have a long-term beneficial and universal effect. The country is effectively positioned to move into the mainstream of economic recovery in Latin America if it accurately perceives, and responds meaningfully to, the signals sent up by the world's economy.

## C. Peru

Peru is another Andean country coping with difficult elements of its economic and political past and, to a major extent, its unsettled present. The seat of Spanish rule in the New World for centuries, as well as the main center of the Inca and predecessor civilizations, Peru is rich in both history and natural resources. It also has as three of its neighbors Chile, Bolivia, and Ecuador—a contentious border position for over a century, and one not yet totally resolved.

At the present time, Peru, for all its long history of mining and industrial-agricultural enterprise, is among the poorest and most strife-torn countries of the Latin world. Drugs and terrorism are evil realities in almost every aspect of the socioeconomic and political life of this country of about 22 million people. There is a tremendous lack of (and desire for) life's basic elements—nutrition, housing, health care, and security, to name a few. The stunning economic success of Chile, Peru's historical rival, in its long road back from the political and social travails existing two decades ago to its present highly successful economic position with its democratic underpinning has not gone unnoticed in Peru.

In October 1968, a military junta displaced Peru's constitutionally elected president, Fernando Belaunde Terry, whose regime had promise but lacked broad support. General Juan Velasco was installed as president of the country, and all major cabinet posts were filled by armed service officers.

Although foreign investment in Peru had been historically active and a very substantial contributor to the economy, it also had become highly politicized and was the subject of intense debate and obloquy in a number of elections; one or the other political group would claim that the incumbents had given unduly favorable treatment to foreign companies, especially in mining and oil, and that these concessions represented an inappropriate and unjust diversion of the national patrimony. Along with appeals to nationalism and pressure to take a highly populist domestic direction to solve inflation and unemployment, these claims constituted one rationale explaining the seizure of power by the military.

The Velasco government's first target was the International Petroleum Company (IPC), Peru's largest petroleum producer and an investment around which contention and nationalistic rhetoric had swirled for years. Within days of the military's accession to power, IPC's property was expropriated. Then followed a series of government occupations of major industry components and the establishment of state entities to develop, manage, and commercialize these sectors. As a matter of government policy, the role of foreign investors was thereafter to be severely limited. Many major foreign companies were expropriated over the ensuing years, with the primary focus being on mining and other natural resource areas. The establishment of "communities" in the mining and industry sectors was a new and populist government program that effectively turned over portions of the companies engaged in these sectors to their employees and constituted another substantial investment disincentive.

The severely negative attitude toward private enterprise, and especially toward foreign investment, was finally brought to a halt when the Francisco Morales Bermúdez presidency commenced in August 1975. Further positive events followed, including the adoption of a new constitution and in 1980 the free and constitutional election of former president Belaunde. Unfortunately, Belaunde's second term of office was not a success and offered little if any incentive or opportunity for Peru to take meaningful steps to reverse its course. The country, along with most of the rest of the continent, drifted into crisis management and a parochial approach to underlying problem areas.

Alan Garcia, the American Popular Revolutionary Alliance (APRA) candidate and an active leftist, served as president from 1985 to 1990 and proceeded during that period to institute a new series of increasingly ineffective and confusing measures that devastated the nation's economy. Coupled with the extreme (and warranted) preoccupation with the drug traffic, terrorist (Sendero Luminoso) activities, and further expropriations, the García term of office set back investment opportunity in Peru for another substantial period.

Failed theories and institutions, an extremely high debt, rapid inflation, a deteriorated infrastructure, and an international credibility gap produced a setting in 1990 that demanded a totally new approach. The Peruvian citizenry, suffering possibly the lowest per capita income in Latin America, confused by chaotic government actions, and apprehensive of the oligarchic and foreign-influenced style it perceived in the favored presidential candidate Mario Vargas Llosa, elected Alberto Fujimori as president. Fujimori, then a political unknown, effectively identified himself as a plebeian rather than a patrician and advocated a Peruvian approach keyed to stabilizing the dazzling rate of inflation and to building the country's economic credibility. Despite the lack of a specific program, he instilled confidence with the promise that he would address the daunting and related duo of terrorism and drugs in a practical way. Ironically, after election, his programs came very close to adopting the market-opening policies of his former opponent Vargas Llosa, including a heavy emphasis on individual rights and economic freedom.

Much has been accomplished in a short time by President Fujimori to lay a proper groundwork for Peru's economic recovery. Domestic stabilization measures were instituted in the summer of 1990, and many new actions were either taken or announced to advance the economic picture. Important to investors was the substantial decontrol in April 1991 of foreign exchange transactions. This assisted export industries by permitting the transfer abroad of hard currencies and thereby allowing foreign investors to have (and to expect) flexible remission of profits. Many other substantial reforms were made, including the virtual elimination of Minpeco (the government marketing arm for metals and concentrates); these reforms directly or indirectly assisted present investors in Peru or tended to attract new ones to the area. Very recently, legislation allowing foreigners a role in exploration and participation in oil refining and distribution has reduced the occupation of the petroleum sector by the government's entity (Petroperu)—this in a country that has historically considered oil as part of its patrimony!

These are all positive signs that permitted the "Paris Club" of major creditor nations to reschedule the bulk of Peru's foreign debt (over $6 billion) to allow repayment over a twenty-year period. In September 1991 the Inter-American Development Bank, following Peru's payment of balances then due, approved a twenty-year loan to Peru for $425 million—a really substantial boost for the nation's financial credibility.

Peru is a beset country with a daunting array of very serious problems, some man-made, others of natural origin. But it has recently taken bold and dramatic steps in attempts to break away from decades of stagnation and decline. A large part of what it has done relates to economic programs designed to bring it back among the investment-attracting areas of the world and to a free trade economy that its rulers appear firmly to believe will assist in the solution of its internal and external problems.

After two decades or more of anti-private-enterprise rhetoric and attitudes—including expropriatory acts and government preemption of major economic segments—how could Peru now come to accept free trade, the concept of privatization, and a range of other anti-statist and pro-investment concepts? One answer is that the government had been persuaded that the inability to access debt markets and the lack of local investment capability due to currency flight required a drastic agenda (a "shock") to attract foreign capital. Another rationale could be that, for a generation or more, the government had been pursuing two entirely different objectives, one vocal and the other actual. To stand before the world (especially the Peruvian electorate) with every indication of pursuing hard-line socialist goals for the national good was one thing and had domestic appeal; the implementation or actual activity that was carried on by the government with regard to the private sector, once those in power perceived that to assist that sector was an economic imperative, was quite another matter, however. The government often put ideology aside when the need for practicality became apparent.

I hope you will allow me a few anecdotal remarks here about a situation relating to Peru that I lived with for twenty years. Peru's largest copper mining company, which was foreign owned and directed, was an enterprise that could be deemed exemplary of the ability to survive during extremely negative economic and political climates. In fact, the story of its survival and growth during extremely hard times seems to take on an almost epic quality. Beginning in the mid-1950s, this entity endured every twist and turn of the period and encountered one adversity after another, any one of which might have sent others to seek friendlier shores. From 1969 to 1976 it actually attracted over half a billion dollars in financing to Peru to bring a second huge copper mine into production. How did the company not only survive but expand? The explanation seems to be that having the company in place was good for Peru, announced statist government policy aside. It provided jobs and security to tens of thousands of Peruvians, as well as an industrial labor ambiance with superior benefits and a broad range of social services. It also supplied the domestic economy with high tax revenue and with a large market for local products. An estimate of this enterprise's contribution to the Peruvian economy indicates a sum over the 1960 (first production) to 1990 period of more than $5 billion, not to mention a production for world consumption of about 12 billion pounds of copper.

Perhaps one answer to the question of how this entity survived lay in its continuing to invest, during extremely difficult times, in programs driven by long-range perspectives, whereas other entities may have been perceived as short-term exploiters or as uncommitted to Peru. Another rationale might be that being a well-run enterprise that takes great care to be a good and productive guest in a foreign country can, absent a completely irrational act, be of substantial benefit to its owners and to its host and, as a consequence, can weather many storms. It is hoped that these actions and forward-looking policies may serve as models for new investors in Peru.

It is good to recognize that Peru's economic infrastructure seems to be substantially in place, but sadly the battles against terrorism and the drug trade have yet to be won. Whether substantial foreign investments will be forthcoming until these problems are eliminated is still an open question.

## Conclusion

Although this lecture has focused on Latin America, it means to relate to all of the newly democratized and free trade countries. Free market systems and policies can exist and thrive only where democratic political under-pinnings are in place. Statist economies are no longer considered viable and are gradually, and in some cases abruptly, disappearing.

With free economies and enhanced trade among na-tions, selective investment is a logical way for optimum use of resources—mines and forests are where you find them, as are industrially trained and sophisticated work forces. Investments from the countries needing products and commodities certainly can enhance the economies where these products are found.

If a host country can keep its political views on invest-ment in the proper context and can properly regard in-vestment as beneficial to the nation and not exploitive, it wil find its economy greatly assisted. The successful in-vestor, on the other hand, is one who makes the invest-ment with logical assumptions of profit possibilities, is sincerely dedicated to being a good and law-abiding guest, and operates in a fashion that continues to recog-nize and accommodate to national interests.

This is a far from perfect world, but dramatic positive signs are now evident. We can hope the outcome will be one of broad and lasting improvement, and all of us should do our best, in our personal lives as well as in our public endeavors, to make a meaningful contribution to that trend.

# ETHICS, MORALITY, LEGALITY IN CORPORATE RELATIONS: SOMETIMES IT'S NOT EASY

by

Jon V. Heider

# Jon V. Heider

*Jon V. Heider is Senior Vice President and General Counsel of The B.F. Goodrich Company, with which he has been associated since 1984. Previously, he worked with the Philadelphia, Pennsylvania, law firm Morgan, Lewis and Bockius and later with Air Products and Chemicals, Inc., where he served as General Counsel and subsequently as Vice President–Corporate Development.*

*Mr. Heider obtained his undergraduate education at the University of Wisconsin and earned the J.D. at Harvard Law School. He has also completed the Advanced Management Program at Harvard Business School. He served for two years as a Lieutenant in the United States Naval Reserve, assigned to the National Security Agency in Washington, D.C.*

*Among other civic responsibilities, Mr. Heider serves as Trustee for the Summa Health System, Inc., the Saint Thomas Medical Center, and the Akron Hospital Foundation. He is a member of the University of Wisconsin Foundation and is on the Advisory Board of the School of Law at the University of Akron.*

# ETHICS, MORALITY, LEGALITY IN CORPORATE RELATIONS: SOMETIMES IT'S NOT EASY

by

Jon V. Heider

"We learned anew some curious facts.
First, everybody is an expert on ethics.
Second, nobody knows what ethics really is.
And finally, times change."

> Jefferson Grigsby, "Synoptics: Now for the Hard Part," *Financial World*, June 27, 1989, p. 20.

## Introduction

When I was invited to discuss the subject of ethics in corporate relations, I was greatly flattered. I have, however, found the topic to be a difficult one. I do not want to appear to be preaching a sermon to the choir or or be defensive of corporations. Moreover, I am not certain that I can adequately define ethics. However, to borrow a line from a noted jurist on a related subject, "I know it when I see it." Perhaps I might better say that "I knew it when I saw it." Times are changing, standards of ethics and legality in corporate relations have become complex and vague—and errors are increasingly costly.

Although everybody may be an expert on ethics, I am not a philosopher, a scholar, or an ethicist. I am an attorney who has spent a considerable part of his career employed by a profit-making business corporation. Public distrust of business corporations is at a high watermark, and I expect that throughout the history of modern man utopia has been defined as a place that is devoid of lawyers. At the outset, therefore, my qualifications to speak on ethics may be open to challenge simply by reference to these credentials.

Nevertheless, ethics, morality, and legality in corporate relations are extremely important topics. The headlines of the past few years have reinforced this conclusion with alarming frequency. Reports of illegality and corruption in some corporations and political and public reactions against business corporations in general should have heightened the sensitivities of corporate managers to the fact that they must devote additional resources to preventing and detecting improper conduct. Corporate managers should ask whether their companies can and should do more, not because they believe their companies may be unethical, but because their companies may be complacent, and complacency can be costly.

A business corporation is not simply an institution for profit. It is a community of people. These people enter the corporation with the ethical and moral values they have learned from their parents, teachers, and many years of past experiences. Those values plus personal ambitions, or in some cases lack of values or lack of ambitions, steer the conduct of these people while they are in their corporate community. Corporations do not themselves act ethically or unethically, legally or illegally. People do.

Ethics in corporate relations are the rules that ought to govern fairly the organizational and transactional behavior of this community. The norms of society are not sufficient to ensure compliance with these rules. It is up to the leaders of corporations to set and maintain standards and to elicit ethical behavior. These rules are, however, highly complex and frequently vague—and they are changing. It may be difficult for an organization to respond to change. An organization with thousands of employees, competing demands for resources, and operations at numerous locations across the country, or throughout the world for that matter, may be inherently slow to adapt. As a consequence, training, awareness, and standards of performance may not be uniform throughout the organization, despite the good intentions of its leaders.

Moreover, morality cannot be founded solely on authority. A large corporation cannot control the actions of each employee, but if its moral standards are broken by any one of them, the corporation may be branded as unethical, immoral, or criminal. Consequently, morality and legality are not standards that need to be expressed only in corporate policy statements written by lawyers and left in a desk drawer or file cabinet. They must be actively promoted and continuously managed as diligently as a corporate manager would manage cash, raw material inventories, and quality controls on the production line.

## Basic Premises About Corporate Ethics, Morality, and Legality

I would like to state some basic premises about ethics, morality, and legality in corporate relations that, based on my experiences and observations, I believe are true. They probably cannot be proved, and I expect that they are, at least in part, contrary to the views of critics of corporate behavior.

The Wall Street scandals that have shocked the nation and blackened the reputation of business were born of greed, and some involved amounts of money beyond the wildest imagination of the vast majority of Americans. My basic premise, however, is that the corruption of ethics that has seemed so prevalent in the past few years is not truly representative of corporate America. I believe that virtually all chief executives of U.S. corporations and the managers who report to them want their organizations to operate ethically and legally.

Several years ago, my employer, The B.F. Goodrich Company, was the leading producer in the world of polyvinyl chloride, or PVC, a commodity plastic with a U.S. demand measured in billions of pounds per year. Twenty-two companies produced PVC in the United States at that time, and several more produced it abroad. Goodrich's sales of this commodity accounted for more than one-third of its gross revenues.

A medical consultant in a community near one of the company's PVC plants noted an abnormal incidence of angiosarcoma, or liver cancer, among employees and retirees. This report was given to both the Chairman and the President of the company. At that time, neither PVC nor vinyl chloride monomer, the material from which PVC is made, had been clearly linked to cancer. A handful of specialty chemicals was on the list of toxic materials of the Environmental Protection Agency (EPA) and was the subject of special safeguards, but no commodity chemical had been identified as producing chronic injury to employees.

A special weekend meeting of the Board of Directors was held to consider the report of the medical consultant. On Monday the company advised the National Institutes of Health that it had evidence that vinyl chloride monomer, the chemical that, as I mentioned above, produced over a third of the company's revenues, may have caused liver cancer among some workers who had been exposed to it. The company was not aware of any investigators or employees who were about to make this pronouncement ahead of Goodrich.

The costs to Goodrich from this disclosure obviously would be profound, and the criticisms of the company from others in the industry were severe. Goodrich nevertheless had done the right thing. The directive came from the top, and I offer it as an example supporting my basic premise that chief executives want their organizations to act responsibly at all times.

My second premise is that ethics and legality must start at the top. A reinforcement of ethical standards by the seniormost executives will not assure ethical compliance throughout the organization, but complacency at the top may encourage unethical and perhaps illegal conduct within the organization. The chairman and the president represent the conscience of the corporation, and only they can establish the basic moral tone of the enterprise.

A chairman of one major U.S. company once confided to me his personal anguish over each serious injury or death of an employee who had been involved in an accident in the line of work. Du Pont at the time had proselytized its excellent safety program, and this chairman became a devout disciple of it. Consequently, safety was elevated from a poster on a plant wall to a topic that was actively managed. The safety report was the first subject discussed at each weekly meeting of the senior officers of the company. The safety department was invigorated with a change of personnel. Each serious injury was reported to the chairman, and each division president was expected to know why it had happened and what would be done to prevent its recurrence. The chairman showed that he cared, and within a short time every manager cared as well.

A third premise is that ethical behavior in the long run is good for business, even though temporary excursions may seem expedient and offer a short-term advantage. If the standard is to conduct the affairs of the corporation in an ethical manner, decisionmaking is infinitely easier and more consistent in quality. Similarly, excursions based on expedience should be less frequent.

I can offer a simple example to support this premise. Alert companies are beginning to realize that morality is not only a good feeling; it is necessary to preserve their businesses in the future. The demographic changes in the nation make it obvious that in approximately a decade a corporation's skilled work force, its managers, and senior executives must include more minorities and more females if the corporation wants to employ the best and the brightest. Astute companies will transform nondiscrimination policy statements from legal requirements to strategic imperatives. Nondiscrimination will be good for business.

My fourth premise is that although a corporation's policy is to act ethically and legally at all times, the chief executive of a large corporation cannot assure that result. Human frailty can make full compliance with that policy an impossibility. As I will discuss, however, the chief executive and those under him may be held responsible for any result that occurs within the company.

Changes in the law have created new, complex, and vague standards of criminality, and these changes have lowered the requirements for criminal conviction of corporations and their employees. In addition, the penalties for failure to comply with ethical and legal standards are rapidly increasing. *Business Week* has suggested there is a sudden fervor for ethics in corporate relations. (See "What's Behind Business' Sudden Fervor For Ethics," *Business Week*, September 23, 1991, p. 65.) My last premise is that a criminalization trend is occurring and that a fervor for ethics is justified.

## The Corporation—Unique Issues of Control and Responsibility

I would like to address some of the reasons why ethics, morality, and legality are often not easy standards to meet, and to mention some of the practices organizations implement to try to reduce improper and unlawful conduct and to encourage proper conduct.

### A. *Imputed Liability*

A corporation is an artificial person that is created by the laws of a state. It is an incorporeal body that may continue to exist in perpetuity and that has the legal capacity to sell ownership interests, own physical assets, purchase materials, manufacture and sell products, advertise, borrow money, and do the hundreds of other things necessary to administer the enterprise and to engage in business. It can, however, only conduct its many activities through people. Essentially three categories of persons compose the corporation: the shareholders who own it, the directors who are elected by the shareholders to oversee the corporation's affairs, and the officers and employees who conduct the day-to-day activities of the corporation.

A corporation has no soul and cannot of itself select between right and wrong. The corporate entity, however, is subject to the rules of the communities in which it operates and is deemed responsible when its employees and agents act on its behalf or within the scope of their actual or apparent authority. The result is that liability for an employee's error may be imputed to the corporation. Even though an employee acted contrary to a corporate policy for his or her own personal advantage or out of laziness or negligence, the corporation is responsible. The individual wrongdoer may also be liable, but the corporate employer is a more attractive target for prosecutors, private plaintiffs, and newspapers. The doctrine of imputed liability is applied in civil, administrative, and criminal law. The corporate employer can be found liable for civil damages, held criminally liable, and have administrative sanctions applied against it, all for the same violation by an employee or agent.

The doctrine of imputed liability is well established in the law and seems fair in personal injury and property damage actions. We accept that a corporate employer should pay for damages caused by an employee or agent acting in the course of his or her duties on behalf of the corporation. Criminal culpability, however, is not the moral equivalent of civil liability. Nevertheless, the doctrine of imputed criminal liability and harsh sanctions also seem fair when they are imposed on the corporation because of the unlawful acts of its most senior officers. If the chairman of a corporation, the very person who represents the conscience of the corporation, is criminally culpable, the values of the corporate entity as a whole seem to have been corrupted. If a criminal offense is committed within the corporation by lower-level managers or employees who are not policy makers, however, the actions may not at all reflect on the entity as a whole. The corporation may nonetheless be liable, but its culpability as an entity, in a moral as opposed to an economic sense, would seem to be less. In fairness, the sanctions imposed on it should be less as well.

## B. Causes of Unethical Conduct

The causes of unethical and unlawful conduct within a corporation are several. Competitive pressure is one that is cited most. Competitive pressure means beating the other company in the marketplace, but it sometimes also means outperforming a colleague or rival within the corporation. It would be an error, however, to conclude that competitive pressure is wrong and should be condemned. Competition is a positive force in industry and promotes new products, production efficiencies, and lower prices. The spirit of competition among business corporations is as important to a good economy as competition between political parties is to good government. The pressures of competition, however, can sometimes lead employees to compromise their personal integrity either to satisfy what they mistakenly believe are company goals or to accomplish their personal goals.

If competitors pay about the same price for their raw materials and if their processing and distribution costs are about the same, how does one of those competitors gain an advantage over its rivals? One company tried to reduce its costs of producing and marketing a name brand, well-known fruit juice by changing the drink to a concoction of mostly sugar and water but labeling it fruit juice. A corporate president and vice president were convicted, and the corporation suffered a substantial drop in its market share. Actions of this type cross over the line that separates vigorous but honest competition from the types of actions our society has deemed unacceptable.

Crises caused by factors inside or outside the corporation's control can also lead to unethical or unlawful conduct. The sudden prospect of incurring unexpected, exceptional costs as a result of design errors or the realization that significant amounts of money should be refunded to one or more customers as the result of overcharges or the risk of losing a contract because of production delays may severely test the integrity of a corporate manager. If ethical conduct is recognized as a fundamental value of the corporation, however, the manager's decision is infinitely easier. He or she can take comfort in the knowledge that the ethical choice will not be criticized by senior management. On the other hand, if the company's standards are doubted or have not been reinforced, the manager may more easily elect expediency.

Our system of financial rewards based on attainment of short-term financial goals also can contribute to expediency and challenge standards of ethics and morality. Corporations applaud the aggressive businessperson and encourage the taking of commercial risks. Shareholders expect and reward short-term results, and corporate managers may be tempted to take shortcuts to earn those rewards.

Equally disruptive and perhaps more pervasive is disinterest that is spawned by poor morale. Internal conflict can demoralize large groups of employees, not so much in terms of encouraging unethical or unlawful conduct but more in terms of creating indifference or frustration. It may result in substantial harm both to the company and to the public. Poor aircraft maintenance, for example, is morally reprehensible, can endanger large numbers of people, and undoubtedly could, in some instances, be traceable to poor morale and indifference at some level within the organization.

Another cause of substandard conduct is lack of knowledge or understanding of the rules to be followed. Ethical values may not be uniformly communicated or understood throughout the organization. Decentralization and multiple locations make communication more difficult. An ethical tone properly set at the top may not reach all of the employees. A recent sampling of attitudes within my own company showed that employees at or near corporate headquarters have a considerably better knowledge of corporate values than those at plant locations. Similarly, salaried employees have a better understanding of those values than do hourly employees.

A final cause of unethical or unlawful conduct in the business world, and one that should not be underestimated, is expediency. Millions of dollars of damages have been caused by individuals who will take the easiest and quickest route to their goals. In any community there will be persons who have low standards for integrity. There will also be managers whose personal ambitions are more important than their personal ethics. The excursions of a rogue employee acting out of laziness, indifference, or a desire for personal gain are not easily identified. His or her errant behavior is frequently not preventable and may not be easily detected. However, the frequency of such behavior may be effectively reduced through graphic reminders of the consequences. A dozen years ago a videotape called *The Price* was produced, depicting the personal consequences to an employee for violating federal antitrust laws. Losses of job, reputation, family, and status in the community were portrayed. That video and others produced subsequently are powerful tools to educate employees and remind them of the personal costs of antitrust violations.

## Corporate Policies and Practices for Corporate Ethics and Legality

Although business corporations exist to earn profits, it would be a myth to conclude that a contradiction exists between profits and ethics. There is a difference between goals of the game and the rules by which it is played. Few if any chief executives of large corporations would doubt that among a corporation's responsibilities is the setting of standards to promote ethical and legal behavior and the management of comprehensive programs to reinforce and assure compliance with those standards.

Written corporate policies are typical responses to the ethical and legal concerns of an organization. Some of those policies, however, are drafted by lawyers who are hired to protect the corporation rather than to influence and manage conduct. Although written policies are important documents, they do not by themselves create a climate or culture. They must be enforced in the day-to-day activities of the organization.

Since the corporate executive office cannot monitor every decision made or police every act performed on the corporation's behalf, the best ethics tool a corporation can utilize is ongoing education and awareness. To develop an ethical culture, a corporation must legitimate discussion about ethics, morality, and legality as part of the decisionmaking process. Corporations typically attempt to address this by giving a code of conduct to employees or by distributing copies of ethics, conflict of interest, and antitrust policies to employees annually and asking for a signed acknowledgment that the employees have read and understood these documents. Increasingly, corporations manage and reinforce their ethical standards through ethics training programs, ethics committees, ombudsmen, and a variety of other means.

Additional tools include an anonymous avenue for reporting suspected ethical and legal abuses. Several companies have established a hotline that allows an employee to report any suspected improper conduct by calling an 800 number. Calls are taken by or are reported to a senior executive or ombudsman and investigated. Typically callers are given an identification number and asked to call again for feedback. This program is not only morally sound, it makes economic sense. It gives management the opportunity to investigate charges of abuse and make corrections where appropriate and also can reassure a dissatisfied employee before he becomes a whistle-blower and elevates the problem to a new level.

Auditors and audit committees are popular and effective means by which corporate conduct is controlled. Corporations typically devote considerable resources to detecting financial abuse by employing a staff of auditors who are independent of the finance department and report directly to an audit committee of the board of directors. In my company that audit committee is composed entirely of outside directors and has oversight responsibility for ethics and legal compliance as well as financial reporting.

Equally important with any other program to prevent and detect unlawful conduct is the relatively new concept of the "environmental audit." There is no common design for environmental audit activities. A variety of methods is used. It is undoubtedly more important to begin some type of program and refine it through experience than to be inert because of the complexity of the task. The environmental audit in my company covers health, safety, and environmental matters. An independent audit staff that reports to an independent committee of the board conducts it.

Compliance standards adopted by members of an industry can be extremely important to ethical and legal awareness and compliance. Guiding Principles for Responsible Care have recently been subscribed to by members of the chemical industry in the United States, a separate but similar standard has been accepted by chemical companies in Canada, and the program is being adopted by companies in Europe as well. Those who subscribe undertake a commitment to operate their facilities safely and in compliance with all environmental laws and regulations. Similarly, defense contractors have subscribed to Defense Industry Initiatives that are designed to prevent abuse in federal procurement practices. Both sets of Initiatives go beyond policy statements and set out expectations for the active management of their compliance standards. Executives of companies who have subscribed to these Initiatives share ideas for their effective enforcement.

Although many tools encourage ethical and lawful behavior, there is no single design for an effective ethics and legal compliance program. The success of such a program will, of course, be the direct result of its comprehensiveness and the resources that are put into it. A strong commitment to safety will reduce industrial accidents. Education and oversight will reduce faulty government procurement practices. Hotlines will allow abuses to be reported anonymously. Resources are not limitless, however, and must be committed within reason. Unfortunately, resource commitments will appear to have been insufficient and unreasonable if violations occur, and there is no practical way a corporation can assure totally blameless conduct by its employees and agents.

Errors will occur and the trend to criminalization is changing the moral value society attributes to those mistakes and is making them more costly.

## The Trend Toward Criminalization

In 1990, at a conference in Washington, D.C., Professor John C. Coffee, Jr., of Columbia University Law School, put forward a thesis that is no doubt correct but disturbing. Professor Coffee observed that the line between civil law and criminal law has been blurred. What had once been a tort or a regulatory violation has been made a crime. He postulated that this trend toward criminalization not only will result in injustice but will ultimately weaken criminal law as an instrument of social control.

The criminalization trend will impose new liabilities on corporations that had heretofore not regarded their conduct as illegal. This development in the law risks degrading criminal sanctions to one of the costs-of-doing-business, while at the same time increasing their number to the point where, in the aggregate, they operate as a corporate death sentence.

## A. *The Clean Air Act Amendment*

The criminalization trend is evident in the Clean Air Act Amendment of 1990 (42 U.S.C. § 7401-7642), where Congress both created new crimes and greatly expanded the number of crimes that can be treated as a felony. Moreover, the new criminal offenses are based on tort standards that criminalize conduct that endangers others. Criminal liability is imposed on one who negligently or knowingly releases a hazardous air pollutant or extremely hazardous substance into the air and thereby places another person's health at risk.

The Clean Air Act and its 1990 Amendment also create strict liability standards by criminalizing violations of permits and violations of reporting and record-keeping requirements and by making it a criminal offense to fail to pay fees. Under the old law, violating emission standards could result in a civil penalty of $25,000 per day for each day of the violation. Under the Clean Air Act as amended, the same violation could result in a criminal fine of $250,000 a day against the corporation, a similar fine against the responsible individual, and incarceration of the responsible individuals, including a corporate officer who was not aware of the violation and did not participate in it but who was a "responsible corporate officer."

Traditionally, the law has required intent, or *mens rea*, as a necessary element for criminal conviction. "Negligently placing another person in imminent danger of death or serious bodily injury" is a fluid and vague concept, and it does not require intent to commit the crime as a necessary element for conviction. It, instead, uses the tort standard of negligence for determining criminal liability and requires a judge or a jury to decide between conflicting expert testimony whether another person was in fact in imminent danger of death or serious injury. Presumably, if the jury determines that negligence provided a near miss, even though no injury occurred, the individual defendant and corporation may be convicted and suffer the social and legal sanctions that are imposed as a consequence.

## B. Responsible Corporate Officer Doctrine

An additional development that corporate managers must become aware of is the "responsible corporate officer doctrine." A manager might assume that the obvious and only legal bases upon which he or she can be found guilty are personally committing or abetting a criminal act and participating in a conspiracy to commit a criminal act. Under the responsible corporate officer doctrine, however, a corporate officer can be guilty of a crime if he bore a "responsible relationship" to the violation, even if he had no knowledge of the criminal actions or was not aware of the problem that caused the event. In *U.S. v. Park* (421 U.S. 658 [1975]), the chief executive officer of a large supermarket chain with approximately 36,000 employees, 874 retail outlets, and sixteen warehouses was convicted of a violation of the

Food and Drug Act for unclean conditions at one of the corporation's warehouses, notwithstanding that he had inquired and had been told that the problem had been resolved. Knowledge of the violation was not required for conviction. It was enough that by virtue of the relationship he bore to the corporation, he had the power to prevent the act complained of.

Concepts corresponding to corporate officer responsibility have not been imposed in other relationships. A Cabinet officer or a member of Congress, for example, is not criminally liable for the conduct of a subordinate in his department or office. Parents are not criminally liable for the conduct of their children. Corporate officers, however, may be singled out for a higher and perhaps impossible standard.

## C. Increase in Criminal Statutes

A noted criminal defense lawyer recently told the audience at a conference that approximately 340,000 separate federal crimes now exist. This number is, of course, staggering. The lawyer did not attempt to count the laws one by one. Rather the methodology used to support this statement was an estimate of the number of federal regulations in effect and a conclusion that violations of federal regulations are today criminal. Whether the estimate of 340,000 federal crimes is reasonably accurate or not, it is inescapable that Congress produces more criminal statutes each session. Moreover, many of these criminal statutes are vague. Their number, vagueness, and complexity make it impossible for an ordinary citizen, a corporate employee, or even a federal prosecutor to know clearly how to separate lawful from unlawful conduct. This criminalization trend places enforcement pressures on prosecutors. At the same time, the vagueness of the statutes gives those prosecutors powerful advantages. No other nation in the world has such a vast array of criminal statutes and such a multitude of sanctions for violating them. Professor Coffee's comment that the criminalization trend will not only result in injustice but ultimately weaken criminal law as an instrument of social control seems a reasonable prophecy.

## D. *Criminalization at the State Level*

The criminalization trend is also occurring at the state level. On the first day of January 1991, the Corporate Crimnal Liability Act became effective in California (Section 387 of the California Penal Code). It would impose criminal sanctions on a corporation's failure to report a "serious concealed danger." An omission or failure to report could lead to the imposition of fines up to $1 million for the corporation and up to $25,000 for the culpable corporate manager plus incarceration for up to three years.

The California law requires that any appropriate corporate manager with "actual knowledge of a seriously concealed danger" report such danger to the Division of Occupational Safety and Health in the Department of Industrial Relations. If the danger is a workplace hazard, affected employees must be warned in writing within the same period of time.

One might at first glance view the California Act favorably. The Act, however, would permit criminal conviction of both a manager and the corporation merely on a showing that the manager had information that could have convinced a reasonable person who was in the manager's circumstance that the serious concealed danger existed. This showing, of course, may be with the benefit of 20/20 hindsight. The statute is ambiguous and needlessly duplicates to a substantial degree reporting requirements to a federal agency. Notably, California sometimes is seen as a trendsetter for the nation.

The California Act could be construed to put a manufacturer at risk for failure to notify the California authorities within fifteen days after receipt of the first lawsuit alleging that a product has a serious design defect. If the manufacturer chooses to defend itself in a civil action and loses, it conceivably could then face a criminal prosecution by the California authorities for not reporting within the prescribed period. If, however, it notifies the authorities of a serious design defect, it could be construed as having made an admission in the civil action.

Consider also the anomaly of a California jury concluding in a civil suit that the manufactured item did have a design defect and a California prosecutor seeking an indictment against the company and the manager for failure to report as required by the Corporate Criminal Liability Act, while in a similar civil case in another jurisdiction the jury held that the design was not defective.

## E. Qui Tam *Relators*

In the 1980s there was widespread publicity about alleged fraud in defense contracting. The American public believed that corporate illegality was a major cause of waste in the defense industry. The political response was the False Claims Reform Act of 1986 (31 U.S.C. § 3729, et seq.).

A primary purpose of this Act is to encourage citizens, called *qui tam* relators, to act as "private Attorneys General" and bring civil lawsuits on behalf of the United States alleging frauds upon the government. Congress acknowledged that this scheme of citizen law enforcement resulted from a shortage of government resources and that because each employee of a government contractor is a potential informant, the prudent corporation would police itself more carefully.

Civil penalties were increased to $10,000 plus treble damages for each false claim, the statute of limitations was expanded, and the definition of "knowingly" submitting a false claim was expanded to include (1) actual knowledge; (2) deliberate ignorance; and (3) reckless disregard. The amount of a *qui tam* relator's recovery was also increased. *Qui tam* civil actions do not bar criminal actions by federal prosecutors for the same abuse and they, therefore, operate effectively as both criminal and civil whistle-blowing.

The False Claims Act amendments provide strong incentives to those corporations that submit class claims to the federal government to implement and manage compliance efforts to prevent and detect abuse. Those incentives are not limited to members of the defense industry. Suppliers of vaccines to a federal agency and health care providers seeking Medicare reimbursement, for example, are subject to *qui tam* proceedings. Submitting false loan applications to a federally insured lending institution also could be covered.

Treble damages can be enormously costly, civil suits are expensive to litigate, criminal actions may be instituted as well, and suspension and disbarment are possible and extremely serious collateral sanctions. Compliance programs to prevent and detect fraud on the federal government are not only morally correct, they are prudent investments.

## F. Increase in Fines

Major increases in penalties for federal crimes were enacted in 1984 and again in 1987. On those occasions Congress increased the fine structure for both individual and corporate defendants. The maximum fine for a corporation for a felony was increased from $5,000 to $500,000. The sentencing judge, however, was also authorized to impose a fine determined from a new alternative fine provision that provides that

> "if any person derives a pecuniary gain from the offense or if the offense results in pecuniary loss to a person other than the defendant, the defendant may be fined not more than the greater of twice the gross gain or twice the gross loss, unless imposition of a fine under the subsection would unduly complicate or prolong the sentencing process." (18 U.S.C. § 3571[d].)

The twice the gain, twice the loss alternative adds the potential for a substantial increase in the penalty for a criminal violation.

In 1990, Congress also amended the Sherman Act to increase the maximum fines that may be imposed on a corporation from $1 million to $10 million and on an individual from $100,000 to $350,000 for a criminal violation of the antitrust laws. Congress did not limit the fines to these statutory amounts. The alternative fine of twice the gain or twice the loss may instead be imposed for a criminal antitrust offense. It is logical to assume that federal prosecutors will seek the alternative if it would produce a fine greater than $10 million.

Clearly, the criminal penalty for unlawful conduct has substantially increased.

## U.S. Sentencing Commission

Congress has both increased the criminal penalties the corporate entity will face for the transgressions imputed to it and removed to a substantial degree the discretion of the sentencing judge to fashion a penalty based on the judge's assessment of the true culpability of the corporation; furthermore, it has limited the judge's ability to take into account the collateral consequences that the corporation will suffer.

Congress had expressed concern about the disparity of sentences given to individual offenders of federal criminal law. In 1984, it passed the Sentencing Reform Act, which created the U.S. Sentencing Commission (28 U.S.C. § 991, et seq.). A seven-member Commission was established to study sentencing practices, develop a foundation for uniformity in sentencing, and recommend to Congress guidelines for the sentencing of individual offenders. The Commission was established as a full-time organization, with power to recommend a basic set of guidelines and thereafter to propose amendments to them. The Commission was directed to submit its proposals to Congress no later than the end of April in each year. Pursuant to the scheme Congress had established, those proposals automatically become law six months after submission unless amended or rejected by Congress.

In 1987, the Commission proposed comprehensive guidelines for the sentencing of individuals. With the single exception of fines on individuals and corporations for antitrust offenses, these guidelines apply only to natural persons who have been convicted of violating federal law. Those 1987 individual guidelines removed the discretion of a sentencing judge to place the individual defendant on probation or suspended sentence, and they mandate imprisonment for individuals convicted of certain offenses, including first-time offenders. The individual guidelines require that a judge treat uniformly a person who steals to feed his family and a person who steals to support a drug habit.

Consistent with the statutory scheme, the guidelines for individuals recommended by the Commission to Congress in 1987 were not amended or rejected. Six months after submission they automatically became law.

In 1988, the Commission began to address guidelines for the sentencing of organizations. Interestingly, the Sentencing Reform Act of 1984 does not require the Commission to propose mandatory guidelines for sentencing organizations. Congress was concerned with the disparity of sentencing of individuals, not with the sentencing of corporations. Moreover, the concept of uniformity in sentencing corporations is basically flawed. A corporation can act only through its employees and agents. There is a vast difference in the culpability of an organization that is convicted of criminal fraud because of the actions of the seniormost executive officer and one that is convicted because of the conduct of a field sales manager who has acted against the policy of a company that has tried to be a good citizen. Differing facts can indicate differing degrees of culpability for the same criminal offense. It is essentially unfair to remove or limit the discretion of the court to fashion an appropriate sentence under these circumstances. The Commission also had relatively little statistical data concerning the sentencing of organizations. Only approximately one percent of the federal prosecutions in the Commission's data base concerned corporations and there had not been sufficient time to assess the deterrent effect of the substantial increases in fines in 1984 and 1987.

The Commission, with the urging of the Department of Justice, was nevertheless intent on issuing guidelines for organizational sanctions, and Chapter Eight—Sentencing of Organizations (56 Fed. Reg. 22,786 [May 16, 1991]) was submitted to Congress at the end of April 1991. Predictably, Congress did not reject or amend the recommendations. In fact, neither the House nor the Senate held hearings on them or made any public inquiry into their reasonableness. They automatically became law on November 1, 1991.

## A. Guideline Sanctions

The organizational guidelines provide for three separate sanctions to be imposed on corporations convicted of a federal crime: restitution, fines, and probation. The provisions concerning restitution and probation are mandatory for all federal offenses. The fines section is mandatory for certain crimes and operates as a policy statement for those federal offenses that are not specifically designated. At the moment, for example, environmental offenses and food and drug violations are among the offenses not within the mandatory fines provisions. However, the chairman of the Commission has announced that the Commission will now address environmental fines with a view to submitting recommendations to Congress by the end of April 1992.

The organizational guidelines make restitution mandatory for all federal offenses, notwithstanding that the relevant statute does not include restitution as a sanction to be imposed. Consequently, it appears that the Commission has gone beyond the warrant given it by Congress to provide uniformity in penalties and established new ones.

The fines provisions incorporate a so-called carrot and stick approach. The stick is the penalty of a maximum fine. The carrot is a reduced fine for those organizations that the Commission views as having a low culpability score.

The fine is determined by a complex, mechanical formula. In a very simplistic example, if the guidelines assign a starting point of $25,000 because of the relatively low severity of the crime but the gain to the corporate defendant or loss to the victim from the offense was $500,000, the court must start with a base level fine of $500,000, even though the corporate defendant will make full restitution of this amount. The guidelines then require the sentencing judge to consider a fine range of $500,000 to $1 million, absent any consideration of the aggravators and mitigators established by the guidelines. Aggravators could increase that fine to a range of $1 million and $2 million and mitigators could reduce it to a range of $25,000 to $100,000.

Note that the maximum fine may be four times the gain or loss. Although the increases in allowable fines that Congress adopted in 1984 and in 1987 created an *alternate, discretionary* fine of *two* times the gain or loss, the fine provisions of the guidelines can operate to *require* a sentencing judge to compute a penalty that is up to *four* times the gain or loss. The judge is then directed to reduce the fine to the statutory maximum that may be imposed on the defendant. Again, the Commission has gone beyond establishing uniformity in sentencing and accounting for aggravators and mitigators within the fine structure provided by Congress and has skewed the mandatory penalties upward.

## B. *The Carrot and the Stick*

Aggravators and mitigators will be a battleground of the sentencing process.

Indifference and complacency by high-level policy-making executives may operate as aggravators and raise the fine to the maximum if the executives did not investigate the *possible* occurrence of unlawful conduct despite knowledge that would have led a reasonable person to investigate. Presumably, the corporation has the burden to prove that it did in fact so investigate in order to avoid an increase in its penalty for aggravation, which may require it to waive the attorney-client privilege and in effect deliver its investigative results to the prosecutors and thereafter to private plaintiffs.

A second aggravator deals with prior history of criminal conduct. The criminalization trend, however, may make it impossible for a large corporation to have avoided a similar criminal conviction or civil or administrative adjudication within the relevant time period.

The Commission offers only two mitigators to lower a corporation's culpability score. The first is the prior establishment of an effective program to prevent and detect violations of law. This is commonly called a compliance program. The second is self-reporting to appropriate authorities within a reasonable time after discovery of the offense, plus cooperation in the investigation and acceptance of responsibility.

## C. Compliance Programs

The guidelines describe seven minimum steps a corporation must take to have an effective program to prevent and detect violations of law. Mitigation, however, is not likely to result if these steps have been met because, *inter alia*, the Commission has inserted a rebuttable presumption that the compliance program was not effective if a person with "substantial authority" participated in the offense. The definition of a person having substantial authority is written broadly. It includes, for example, a field salesman or agent who can sign a contract or set a price or any employee who can exercise discretion on behalf of the corporation. At hearings before the Commission it was stated that 70 percent of the offenses for which corporations are convicted are committed by employees or agents who come within that definition. Compliance mitigation also does not apply if a person responsible for the administration or enforcement of its compliance program failed to detect the unlawful conduct.

It is certainly the duty of corporate executives to investigate possible criminal violations, to stop any unlawful conduct that is discovered, and to prevent such conduct from recurring. Several statutes, particularly those dealing with health, safety, and environmental matters, impose a duty to report. Apart from statutory requirements, company lawyers often recommend voluntarily reporting unlawful conduct. Nevertheless, reporting a possible violation in all instances may pose special hazards for the corporation.

Assume that a salesperson in a field office commits an antitrust violation. If the corporation reports the violation to federal authorities, it, of course, opens itself to criminal prosecution and substantial fines for the acts of a rogue employee. In addition, the corporation must expect to defend itself from treble damage civil suits by plaintiffs claiming to be direct purchasers from the corporation and damaged by the salesperson's unlawful conduct. Also, several states allow second-tier, indirect purchasers to bring treble damage actions against the corporation as well for the same offense, based on state laws. If found liable, the corporation will have to pay threefold damages to the successful plaintiffs in each action, perhaps based on the joint and several liability of other coconspirators, the plaintiffs' attorneys' fees, interest, and, of course, its own attorneys' fees.

In another, less hypothetical instance, the president and owner of a company selling fuel oil to the government at Fort Knox suspected that some of his employees delivered less than the quantities invoiced and that they sold the remainder for their own profit, thereby defrauding both their employer and the government. The president of the company reported his suspicions to the FBI and asked it to investigate. Despite this voluntary disclosure and assistance, the company's willingness to make good on the government's loss, and the failure of the government to comply with its own procedures to monitor and measure the offloading of the fuel oil, the company was indicted for violating the False Claims Act and suspended from further government contracts. (See 55 Federal Contracts Reports 71 [January 21, 1991].)

In some cases, therefore, corporations may be understandably reluctant to report and unleash a chain of punishments that may be unfair and disproportional to the offense.

## D. Disclosure, Cooperation, Confession

The second mitigator allowed by the guidelines is based totally on postoffense conduct, that is, reporting the offense, cooperating fully in the investigation, and accepting responsibility. The corporate defendant will generally be required to plead guilty in order to qualify for any postoffense credit. The credit will be increased if the corporation also cooperated in the investigation. It will be increased further if the corporation reported the offense to appropriate authorities in a timely manner. Those corporations having an effective compliance program but that discover unlawful conduct by an employee will again be faced with a dilemma with respect to mitigation. If they disclose the employee's unlawful conduct to the prosecutor, they may waive the corporation's attorney-client privilege with respect to the investigation they had a duty to undertake. Further, by their disclosure they may have waived the privilege with respect to civil suits that may follow and they may have made defense of those civil suits impossible. Conviction can also lead to other consequences, such as debarment and derivative suits, and affect the ability of individuals charged with the same offense to defend themselves.

## Should a Compliance Program Meet Guideline Standards?

If the likelihood of receiving mitigation credit is slim, why should a corporation commit its resources to a compliance program that conforms to guideline standards?

A simple and obviously true answer is that programs that promote ethical and legal conduct by employees and agents are part of good management. They are good business. The guidelines add a requirement of formality to compliance programs. They state that a program should be reasonably designed, implemented, and enforced so that it generally will be effective in preventing and detecting criminal conduct. Failure to prevent or detect an offense does not by itself mean that the program was not effective. The hallmark of an effective program is due diligence. Moreover, apart from the guidelines, the criminalization trend, significant increases in penalties for unlawful conduct, and hostile public attitudes toward corporations should indicate to corporate executives that a formal and comprehensive compliance program is a prudent investment.

The guidelines list seven steps for an effective compliance program. These steps are described as being the minimum standards acceptable. Certain of them would seem to have the potential for being unfair. A corporation is told, for example, that it must discipline, as appropriate, individuals responsible for failure to detect an offense. Corporate employees are not trained investigators, and unlawful conduct is often concealed. Discipline "as appropriate" is a vague standard. A corporation may have to exercise substantial wisdom to apply it fairly.

Additionally, an effective program to prevent and detect violations of law requires the organization to have used due care not to delegate substantial discretionary authority to individuals whom the organization knew, or should have known through the exercise of due diligence, had a propensity to engage in illegal activities. This standard may on its face seem reasonable, but the guidelines have the potential for unfortunate and unfair consequences. Should a corporation deny promotion to an apparently worthy employee who has a criminal record as a teenager, and should a corporation discharge an executive who has been indicted or convicted under the corporate officer responsibility doctrine? Not only could this standard be applied unfairly by the corporation, it could also be applied fairly by the corporation but nevertheless subject it to the risk of civil charges for discrimination.

A corporation may be at substantial risk if it ignores the Commission's mandate to implement a compliance program that meets guideline standards. Commentators have observed that the directors and senior officers of a corporation may be exposed to shareholder derivative actions if the corporation should be found guilty of a federal offense and cannot show that it has an effective program to prevent and detect violations of the law. Additionally, the court is required by the guidelines to place a corporation having 50 or more employees on probation if at the time of sentencing it does not have an effective compliance program, and to supervise the implementation and management of such a program. A corporation, therefore, may face its first federal conviction without a compliance program, but the court will impose one thereafter. Also, a sentencing judge may depart from a mandated fine and increase it if the offense occurred after the imposition of a compliance program by a court following a prior conviction.

## Collateral Consequences

The criminal sanctions a federal judge imposes on a convicted corporation are only a portion of the adverse consequences a corporation may face for unlawful conduct. The corporation may also confront administrative sanctions, civil liabilities, substantial legal costs, diminishment of its public image, loss of reputation among financial analysts and investors, and internal conflict. The variety and severity of the collateral consequences of conviction have grown exponentially in recent years. The size of the liability iceberg below the waterline can be illustrated with the example of a corporation convicted of defrauding the Defense Department. Several noncriminal consequences may follow:

- The corporation may be suspended or completely disbarred from governmental contracting.
- False Claims Act penalties, including treble damages and fines of up to $10,000 per claim, may be levied.
- The corporation may face other administrative sanctions, such as probation or removal of corporate officers or managers.
- Private civil suits may compound the punishment, often with punitive or multiple damages.
- Derivative actions may be instituted against directors and officers.
- The corporation's reputation may be blackened and it may suffer a loss of goodwill in its marketplace and among investors.

In these circumstances, the boundary between criminal, administrative, and civil law can become hazy and arbitrary. The collateral consequences may be regarded as separate and discrete sanctions and not given fair consideration when attempting to calibrate the proper level of punishment for convicted corporations. (See *Final Report, Collateral Consequences of Convictions of Organizations*, American Bar Association [February 1991].)

In the 1970s, America began to experience a litigation explosion. (See Walter K. Olson, *The Litigation Explosion: What Happened When America Unleashed the Lawsuit*, Truman Talley Books—Dutton, 1991.) The focus of this paper has not been the civil penalties for improper conduct, but they cannot be ignored. Corporate counsel must regard a violation of federal regulations or criminal law and a potential for a civil suit as well as defend the regulatory violation or criminal action with a view that one or more civil suits will follow. Corporations are viewed as having deep pockets, and new theories of liability reach into them for both compensatory and punitive damages. Corporations, therefore, must rely heavily on attorneys. A good part of the corporation lawyer's responsibility should be to decrease the overall risk of lawsuits as well as to keep the corporation in the best position possible in the event litigation is inevitable.

It is also important to consider who actually pays for the consequences of unethical or unlawful conduct. In the case of corporations, the penalties may not be paid by the individual wrongdoer. Since the corporation is liable for the unlawful conduct of its employees and agents, and monetary penalties are paid from company coffers, the economic penalty will fall largely on the owners of the corporation. To the extent that the owners are the managers, there will be little sympathy for their loss. Owners may not be the partner-managers, however, but may instead be public and private pension funds, foundations, trusts, small investors, and employees. The real effect of the economic loss will hit them. In addition, if the corporation is injured significantly, employees may also suffer, through job loss or lack of opportunity for advancement. If fines and penalties are a cost of doing business, the consumer pays as well.

## Conclusions

The consequences for the breach of an ethical or legal obligation are potentially numerous. If, as I have heard suggested but have never observed, it is true that a corporation compares the rewards expected from its illegal conduct against the risk and penalties of being caught, this risk analysis can be practiced only by a manager who is naive, reckless, or criminally inclined.

### A. On the One Hand

The message should be obvious to corporate managers. Legislatures are demanding higher standards of conduct from corporations. This is the clear trend. It is unlikely to be reversed, and there are no indications it is abating. Corporations have strong incentives to adopt and manage formal and comprehensive programs to prevent and detect unethical and unlawful conduct. It is no longer only morally desirable but strategically necessary for corporations to build ethical standards into the climate and culture of the organization.

Leadership at the top is the single most important factor in creating and maintaining that climate and culture.

Leadership, however, does not have the capability to create ethics, morality, and legality by fiat, and the tools to assure ethical and legal compliance are as fallible as man himself. Leadership, however, can create the climate and culture, even though it cannot assure a perfect result.

The ethics of a corporation should begin with an articulation of the fundamental values of the organization. Those values should go beyond policy statements asserting that the corporation will abide by the laws applicable to it. They should include declarations of moral values, such as respect for individuals; recognition of responsibility to the several constituencies that the corporation serves, including shareholders, employees, suppliers, and customers; acknowledgment of responsibility to communities affected by the corporation's actions; adherence to quality and reliability standards for products and services the corporation provides; and expectations of fairness by employees when acting on the corporation's behalf. Open discussion of the organization's fundamental values and training with respect to job requirements are among a manager's means to reinforce standards for an ethical climate and culture.

Corporations must also implement and manage reasonable programs to detect unlawful conduct and to reduce the likelihood that it will recur. The broad concepts in the guidelines, the Defense Industry Initiatives, the Guiding Principles for Responsible Care, and similar programs formalize what should be obvious.

## B. And on the Other Hand

If ethics and morality are applied within the corporation, is the corporation assured that it will be judged fairly by society, prosecutors, and the courts?

The penalties for the errors of executives, managers, and employees have become increasingly costly. The criminalization trend has resulted in a substantial increase in the number of potential crimes at the federal level, and the trend may be repeated at the state level as well. Criminal statutes have become vague and thereby give a powerful advantage to prosecutors, and courts are directed to apply tort standards for criminal convictions. Strict liability has been substituted for culpability. Given the enormously complex and ever-changing criminal standards, particularly in the environmental area, can any large corporation ever be in total compliance? Criminal indictments, particularly of a large corporation, seem likely.

The corporation may be required to pay substantial penalties for the unlawful conduct of an employee, notwithstanding that the employee acted willfully, in violation of company policy, and concealed the crime. In other instances, unlawful conduct may not be intentional or obvious to the employee, but both the employee and the corporation may be criminally liable.

Congress has increased the penalties for organizations convicted of a federal offense, and the U.S. Sentencing Commission has racheted the application of these penalties higher. Prosecutors are attempting to extend the application of criminal laws to managers and executives whom they contend should have known of the conduct.

The procedures used to impose sanctions on corporations are changing, and it is unlikely that the corporate lawyer will at first understand them. In the past, conduct that was a civil violation led to the raiding of corporate files under discovery methods provided by the rules of civil procedure. If the same conduct is made criminal, federal marshals armed with search warrants can simply carry away file cabinets of documents. Those who might protest such treatment may be threatened with charges of obstruction of justice. In such instances the attorney-client privilege can be made meaningless. The desirable objectives of promoting internal investigations, reporting environmental audits, and conducting other self-assessments will be frustrated if corporate attorneys and business executives are made fearful of the seizure of their written reports and responses.

What are the objectives of the sanctions imposed on corporations for unlawful conduct? The guidelines say that they are just punishment, adequate deterrence, and incentives to maintain internal mechanisms for preventing, detecting, and reporting. In what seems to be a religious fervor to criminalize and to punish, however, Congress, prosecutors, administrators, and courts now impose numerous and costly sanctions on corporations, separately designed and administered without any apparent regard for the cumulative effect as a whole. Is the entire array of criminal, civil, and administrative penalties that may be imposed on a corporation fair and in proportion to the offense? How many penalties are required to satisfy the goals of retribution and deterrence and to get the attention of a board of directors? How much of today's criminalization process has been a political response to this religious fervor?

Notwithstanding the different labels attached to criminal, civil, and administrative proceedings, in each the tribunal has the authority to impose penalties that are not compensatory or remedial but punitive. Criminal sanctions, therefore, may be imposed more than once on a corporation for the same offense. The United States

Supreme Court addressed a similar problem in *U.S. v. Halper.* (490 U.S. 435 [1989].) There the court said that a civil as well as a criminal sanction constitutes punishment when the sanction serves the goals of punishment. The court recognized that punitive damages in civil cases serve the punitive goals of retribution and deterrence. It would seem to follow then that if a corporation has been convicted and fined in a criminal proceeding, societal goals have been served and it is fair to question whether the corporation should also be subjected to punitive damages in a civil proceeding for the same conduct. Conversely, if punitive damages have been imposed on the corporation in a civil proceeding, the aims of criminal justice should thereby have been satisfied, and it seems arguable that the corporation should not then be subjected to criminal fines for the same conduct. These, of course, are not easy questions to answer and, depending on one's view, may also raise the question whether, as a matter of public policy, a private party rather than the state should be entitled to receive punitive awards for conduct that the state can punish under its criminal laws.

We can find today an anomaly and perhaps a perversion in the criminal justice system where conduct can be ethical and moral but at the same time criminal. Consider the failure of a plant manager to report a chemical spill occurring on company property at midnight to environmental authorities within the prescribed period because he was busy handling the cleanup. The plant manager may face a criminal indictment and the employer may thereby be pressured to agree to a large administrative settlement to avoid criminal prosecution of its employees. Have our criminal laws been perverted into revenue measures? Do the guidelines for organizational sanctions treat corporate defendants fairly or, like *qui tam* proceedings, are they intended to increase productivity, in this instance by adding to the abilities of prosecutors to coerce quicker resolutions of indictments?

What conduct should fairly be regarded as criminal and what penalties should fairly be imposed for a violation of criminal and civil standards are enormously complex issues. Corporate America has a duty to see that its employees act responsibly, and appropriate penalties should be administered for errors. In fairness, however, such penalties should not be piled on as a result of separately enacted, uncoordinated schemes for addressing civil, administrative, and criminal offenses and liabilities. Moreover, because the economic penalties can be borne by innocent stockholders, and the aggregate effect of the sanctions can affect competitiveness, a balance should be struck in the national interest. As it stands today, however, no one seems to be looking out for the whole. The overview has been sacrificed, and the result is a criminal law system that, like its civil law counterpart, is running out of control.